ECONOMICS OF URBAN HIGHWAY CONGESTION AND PRICING

Transportation Research, Economics and Policy

VOLUME 9

The titles published in this series are listed at the end of this volume.

ECONOMICS OF URBAN HIGHWAY CONGESTION AND PRICING

by

John F. McDonald
University of Illinois at Chicago

Edmond L. d'Ouville
Indiana University Northwest

and

Louie Nan Liu
Louis Berger and Associates

KLUWER ACADEMIC PUBLISHERS
BOSTON / DORDRECHT / LONDON

Distributors for North, Central and South America:
Kluwer Academic Publishers
101 Philip Drive
Assinippi Park
Norwell, Massachusetts 02061 USA
Telephone (781) 871-6600
Fax (781) 871-6528
E-Mail <kluwer@wkap.com>

Distributors for all other countries:
Kluwer Academic Publishers Group
Distribution Centre
Post Office Box 322
3300 AH Dordrecht, THE NETHERLANDS
Telephone 31 78 6392 392
Fax 31 78 6546 474
E-Mail <services@wkap.nl>

Electronic Services <http://www.wkap.nl>

Library of Congress Cataloging-in-Publication Data

McDonald, John F., 1943-
Economics of urban highway congestion and pricing / by John F. McDonald, Edmond L. d'Ouville, and Louie Nan Liu.
p. cm. -- (Transportation research, economics and policy ; v. 9)
"Much of the research reported in the book was done originally as the doctoral dissertations of Edmond d'Ouville and Louie Nan Liu that were completed at the University of Illinois at Chicago"--Pref.
Includes bibliographical references and indexes.
ISBN 0-7923-8631-0
1. Congestion pricing. 2. Roads--Finance. 3. Transportation. 4. Transportation and state. I. d'Ouville, Edmond L. II. Liu, Louie Nan. III. Title. IV. Series.
HE336.C66M38 1999
388.1'1--dc21 99-44505
CIP

CONTENTS

LIST OF FIGURES

LIST OF TABLES

PREFACE

This book came about because we realized that, over the years, we had been pursuing a resonably coherent research program on urban traffic congestion that concentrated on the supply side of the problem, but also included some investigation of the demand for urban tollways and the value of commuting time. Interest in the topic has been heightened by the increase in traffic congestion in many urban areas around the world and the resultant search for policies to address the problem.

As we explain in the Introduction, our approach in many ways embodies the traditional methods employed by economists. However, our work differs from that of several prominent transportation economists who have adopted the newer "bottleneck" model as the main device for explaining urban traffic congestion. We have important disagreements with this group of scholars, as we explain throughout the book.

Much of the research reported in the book was done originally as the doctoral dissertations of Edmond d'Ouville and Louie Nan Liu that were completed at the University of Illinois at Chicago. This book can therefore be thought of as the compilation of the work of the "UIC School" of urban traffic congestion.

John F. McDonald
Edmond L. d'Ouville,
Louie Nan Liu

ACKNOWLEDGMENTS

The authors gratefully acknowledge the assistance provided by Kenneth Small, the editor of this book series. He provided us with helpful comments and the latest versions of his own related work. Our profession is fortunate to have Ken Small as one of its leaders. Ranak Jasani of Kluwer Academic Publishers handled the review process and the contract matters with efficiency. We also thank two anonymous reviewers for their helpful and encouraging comments.

We acknowledge permission to reprint our previously published material that was provided by Academic Press, Elsevier Science B. V., and Pergamon Press. Chapter 2 is based on an article that appeared in Regional Science and Urban Economics in 1988, and Chapters 4 and 5 are taken from an article from Transporation Research B in 1983. Chapter 7 is a reprint of an article that appeared in Transportation in 1995, and Chapters 8 and 9 are based on an article from Transportation Research B that appeared in 1999. A portion of Chapter 10 appeared as an article in the Journal of Urban Economics in 1998. Chapter 14 appeared as an article in Transportation Research B in 1989, and Chapter 16 is a reprint of an article in the Journal of Urban Economics from 1991.

INTRODUCTION

This book collects in one place the research that we have done over the years on the economics of urban highway congestion and pricing. The book includes theoretical contributions, empirical studies, and some simulation experiments that all pertain to the general topic. The bulk of the work that is reported (and updated) in this book actually was completed over a period of ten years, and research on one topic was actually begun by the first author over 25 years ago. We have decided to produce this work in book form because the various pieces of the research now add up to a reasonably coherent and comprehensive set of original studies.

The book is organized into four sections as follows:

- Highway traffic flow,
- Commuter choice of tollways versus freeways,
- Congestion pricing in the short run, and
- Road capacity and pricing in the long run.

The basic themes of these sections are discussed here.

The first section on highway traffic flow examines the chief models and empirical studies of vehicular flow on urban highways. The two main alternative models of traffic flow are the continuous-flow model and the bottleneck model. The continuous-flow model is based on the idea that the traffic flow and speed on an urban highway varies with the density of vehicles on that highway. Vehicle density of sufficient magnitude creates traffic congestion that gets progressively worse as density increases. The bottleneck model supposes that urban highway systems contain bottlenecks through which only a limited number of vehicles may pass per unit of time. If the demand for travel through the bottleneck is sufficiently high, then a queue will develop behind the site of the bottleneck.

These two models have been discussed extensively in the urban transportation economics textbook by Small (1992), so there is no need to repeat his presentation. Instead, after a short introductory chapter on the topic, we concentrate on the continuous-flow model of highway traffic flow that we shall use in the remainder of the book. This discussion includes our point of view that the continuous-flow model is useful partly because it is closely analogous to the conventional production function that is used generally in economics. We also include new empirical studies of highway traffic flow that are based on the continuous-flow model. Our choice of the continuous-flow model for most of our work is not intended to imply that the bottleneck model is not also a useful approach to the economics of urban highway congestion. Indeed, the most realistic models of traffic flow in urban highway systems probably will need to include models of both types, and our empirical study of highway traffic flow in Chapter 3 combines the two approaches.

The second section of the book is a theoretical and empirical examination of the choice that commuters make between urban tollways and freeways. Theories of route choice and the value of reductions in commuting time are presented. These theories are tested using data on actual choices that were made by commuters in suburban Chicago between a tollway and substitute free highways and streets. The empirical estimates presented here are used in subsequent chapters.

The third section of the book is devoted to congestion pricing in the short run, the time period in which the urban highway facilities are taken as given. This section is the most important part of the book from the standpoint of public policy. In a recent survey article Small (1997) concludes that:

- Congestion pricing would promote good urban transportation,
- Congestion pricing is the only policy that will make a noticeable difference in peak congestion levels in the world's most congested cities,
- Congestion pricing would aid the urban economy,
- Congestion pricing is a respectable policy alternative, but
- Widespread adoption of congestion pricing is not likely in the foreseeable future.

Our goal is to contribute to the discussion of congestion pricing by specifying more precisely some of the circumstances under which congestion pricing is most beneficial. This section contains several of our recent contributions to the field. The basic model of traffic congestion on a single highway is familiar, and is introduced briefly. We then concentrate our attention on the situation in which there are two (or more) routes that can be used for the same trip (i.e., the same origin and destination). We begin with an examination of highway congestion and pricing with two routes in a single time period. The usual results for optimal congestion tolls are obtained if both routes can be subjected to tolls. However, the situation in which only one route is subject to a toll is more complex. A full exploration of the theory of the "second best" is provided for this case. The basic theorem can be stated briefly. If the two routes are substitutes, then the efficient "second-best" toll is less than the fully optimal toll that would be charged on that route if all routes can be subject to tolls. In contrast, if the two routes are complements, the efficient "second-best" toll is greater than the fully optimal toll that would be charged on that route.

This discussion is followed by a detailed examination of the case of two routes and two time periods; a peak period and an off-peak period. We wish to explore the extent to which the results of the previous model are sensitive to the assumption that there is only one time period, and we wish to make our models more realistic because the urban traveler does have some discretion over the choice of time of day for the trip. This model also creates another policy instrument, the toll in the off-peak period. An extensive set of simulation experiments is included in order to determine how the optimal tolls vary with the characteristics of demand and of the two routes that make up the highway system. This section of the book ends with an examination of the situation presented by California State Route 91, the only highway in the U. S. that currently is subject to peak-period congestion tolls. This particular facility has congestion tolls on two lanes (each way), but the other four lanes (each way) are not subject to tolls. We find that the lanes subject to tolls are substitutes for the other four lanes of the highway and complementary with other free highways that are downstream from the facility in question. Under these conditions the optimal second-best toll can be either greater or less than the toll that would be charged if all relevant highways could be subject to tolls.

The fourth section of the book considers road capacity and pricing in the long run. The topic is examined primarily from a theoretical standpoint, but several numerical examples are given and some practical rules of thumb are derived. We begin with a brief discussion of optimal road capacity with optimal congestion tolls. This topic is standard, and does not require detailed treatment here. Our first extension is to conduct a detailed exploration of the case of optimal road capacity with a suboptimal congestion toll. In particular, optimal road capacity in the absence of congestion tolls is compared to optimal road capacity with congestion tolls. This is another examination of the economics of "second-best" decisions, and sufficient conditions are found for optimal "second-best" capacity to be the larger. These conditions are that demand for traffic flow is inelastic and that it is relatively difficult to substitute drivers' time for road capacity in the production of traffic flow. This analysis is then extended to the case of two roads (that are imperfect substitutes), only one of which can be subject to a toll. As the ease with which the two roads can be substituted increases, a point is reached at which the optimal policy is not to build a road than cannot be subject to a toll.

The other chapters in this section of the book are additional studies of long-run investment decisions for road capacity. One chapter examines a model in which the demand for road use is numerically identical to the density of traffic (rather than the traffic flow). The next chapter examines the case of uncertain demand, wherein the optimal capacity and toll depend upon the amount and nature of the demand uncertainty. The final chapter in this section examines the capacity question in the bottleneck model than was mentioned briefly above.

The concluding chapter of the book gathers our main results in one place and makes recommendations both for current policy and for future research. Our policy recommendations include the following:

- The welfare benefits that can be obtained through congestion pricing in the short run depend heavily on the extent to which substitute and complementary routes are covered by tolls. Therefore, attention must be paid to the problem of traffic diversion and to the downstream use of roads that are not subject to tolls.

- If significant portions of the relevant urban highway and road system cannot be subjected to congestion tolls, then tolls must be modified substantially from the standard "textbook" toll. Indeed, there is a point at which the cost of imposing the tolls may exceed the benefit. Imposing a high congestion toll on a small fraction of an urban highway and road system can be worse than imposing no toll at all. On the other hand, imposing a high toll on a small fraction of the system can be the correct policy if complementary routes cannot be subjected to tolls.

- Rules for the construction of urban highway capacity need to be modified if future demand contains a sizable element of uncertainty. Under reasonable assumptions, the costs imposed by uncertain demand are not symmetric. Demand that exceeds expectations by a large amount will impose heavy congestion costs, and those costs exceed the costs that result from demand that falls short of expectations.

- Optimal road capacity in the absence of congestion tolls is sometimes larger (and sometimes smaller) than optimal capacity if congestion tolls can be charged. This result means that efficient use of resources in the long run also depends on the ability to levy congestion tolls. The inability to levy congestion tolls on all or a portion of the road system makes long-run capacity decisions far more complex.

- Urban commuters are sensitive to the amount of a highway toll and to the amount of time that can be saved by taking the tollway (compared to a free highway or road). Policy in both the short run and the long run must be based on realistic assumptions regarding commuter behavior.

We believe that these lessons are important because of the interest that policy makers around the world have in implementing congestion tolls in some form. A useful survey of current policy initiatives has been provided by Small and Gomez-Ibanez (1998). They categorize congestion pricing methods as follows:

- City center congestion pricing,
- Toll rings,
- Single facility congestion pricing, and
- Area-wide congestion pricing.

City center congestion pricing was first pioneered in Singapore in 1975, and their system for 23 years used a paper windshield sticker that permits a vehicle to enter the city center. An electronic "smart card" system was introduced in March 1998. Electronic systems for city center congestion pricing were studied in depth in Hong Kong and Cambridge, England, but not implemented. The Singapore scheme has changed over the years. At first a fee of \$1.50 to \$2.50 was imposed on cars carrying fewer than four persons that entered the restricted zone during the morning rush hour. In 1989 the fee was extended to all vehicles (except public transit), and the afternoon rush hour was also included. The time between the morning and afternoon rush hours was included in 1994. The fee for the permit to enter the restricted zone between 10:15 A.M. and 4:30 P.M. is lower than the price of the permit for the entire day (7:30 A.M. to 6:30 P.M.). The amount of traffic entering the restricted zone dropped by 44% after the scheme was put into operation in 1975. However, commuting times failed to drop for workers in the restricted zone who did not change modes. Traffic congestion was created in areas just outside the restricted zone. After reviewing the studies of the Singapore system, Small and Gomez-Ibanez (1998, p. 217) conclude that

> "Problems of spillover across spatial time boundaries may make this scheme too crude an approximation of marginal-cost pricing to provide the net economic benefits achievable in theory. On the other hand, the problem could be that the fee was set too high..."

We would suggest that the Singapore scheme is an example of an attempt at second-best optimization. Spillover across spatial and time boundaries is the very nature of the policy problem, and the toll that is charged should be set with these spillover problems taken into account. We find that, if spillover is the main problem, the optimal second-best toll consistently is only a fraction of the first-best toll. The problem with the Singapore system may well be that the fee was too high given the nature of the spillover problems.

Toll ring systems exist in three cities in Norway (Bergen, Oslo, and Trondheim). The system in Bergen was put into operation in 1986, and the other two cities followed in the early 1990s. These tolls are used primarily to raise revenue to pay for transportation facilities and do not vary appreciably by time of day. In addition, Stockholm has been planning to implement a toll ring system that does not vary by time day. The tolls are to be collected by a fully automated electronic system, but as of 1998 public opposition has delayed implementation indefinitely.

There are two individual facilities that are subject to congestion tolls. Autoroute A1, the expressway that connects Paris north to Lille, since 1992 has had a toll designed to spread the Sunday evening peak. Autoroute A1 is part of a system of tollways owned by the government but run by quasi-commercial tollroad operators. The A1 toll system is regarded as a success in that the timing of trips has been influenced in the desired manner. Since December, 1995 State Route 91 in Southern California has had a system of congestion tolls that are assessed via a transponder mounted on the dashboard of the auto. This project is the only true example in the world today of an urban highway with a congestion toll, and it is discussed in detail in Chapter 10. Also, since 1996 a high-occupancy lane on an expressway in San Diego has been available for use by low occupancy vehicles if a permit is purchased. This fee is, in effect, a peak-period toll because there is little or no incentive to buy a permit if one's use of the expressway does not occur in the peak periods. Public acceptance of both California projects has been good, probably because paying the toll can be seen as paying for access to additional road capacity. Similar projects have been or are being considered in several other locations in the U. S., including New York and Minneapolis. However, proposals for peak-period tolls on individual facilities were defeated by public opposition in Seattle and San Francisco.

Systems for area-wide congestion pricing have been under intensive study in Randstad region of the Netherlands and London. Various complex systems have been proposed for the Randstad, which is a large, polycentric urbanized area that includes Rotterdam, Amsterdam, The Hague and Utrecht. As of late 1996 the Ministry of Transport was planning to implement congestion charges in the year 2001, but it is not clear whether public support is sufficient. Also, over the past 30 years a series of extensive studies has been undertaken for London. However, at the conclusion of the latest series of studies in 1993, the Ministry of Transport stated that there would be no congestion pricing in London for at least the remainder of the decade of the 1990s.

While Small (1997) is almost certainly correct in concluding that widespread use of congestion tolls is unlikely in the foreseeable future, the continuing interest in this policy around the world is sufficient to stimulate further study. This book is our response.

References

Small, K., 1992, Urban Transportation Economics, Chur, Switzerland: Harwood Academic Publishers.

Small, K., 1997, Economics and urban transportation policy in the United States, Regional Science and Urban Economics, 27, 671-691.

Small, K. and J. Gomez-Ibanez, 1998, Road pricing for congestion management: The transition from theory to policy, in K. Button and E. Verhoef, eds., Road Pricing, Traffic Congestion and the Environment, Cheltenham, England: Edward Elgar.

PART I

HIGHWAY TRAFFIC FLOW

1 AN ENGINEERING MODEL OF TRAFFIC FLOW

A. INTRODUCTION

This book deals with urban highway congestion of a particular type, the congestion that arises on limited-access highways of reasonably large capacity. We presume highways that are not controlled to any significant extent by traffic lights (because there are no intersections that require them), and we assume that the highways do not have bottleneck problems (e.g., tunnels, bridges). Excellent models have been devised to study both of these types of problems. Textbooks in transportation engineering [such as Papacostas and Prevedouros (1993)] contain models of signalized intersections, and the text by Small (1992) covers bottleneck models. We concentrate on traffic flow for urban highways that are chosen by large numbers of urban commuters who typically make fairly long journeys to work.

The basic model that is presented in this chapter depends upon a car-following rule that drivers adopt in an attempt to maximize speed while maintaining a level of safety. The distance between vehicles is adjusted according to the speed of travel, and these adjustments determine the relationship between the three basic variables that describe the traffic conditions on the highway; mean speed, traffic flow (or volume), and vehicle concentration (density). Some of the presentation in this chapter roughly follows Papacostas and Prevedouros (1993).

B. VEHICULAR FOLLOWING AND INTERVAL SPACING

We consider the case of vehicles that follow each other on a limited-access highway. There are no external forces that require the vehicles to alter their motion. The only interference that a vehicle encounters is the other vehicles in the stream of traffic. Vehicles travel at speed S, and interval I is the distance from the front on one vehicle to the front of the one behind it. The basic idea is that interval I is sufficient for safe stopping should the lead vehicle find it necessary to stop. The driver of the following vehicle must perceive the situation, react to it, and decelerate safely.

Drivers are taught rules of thumb to follow in this regard. For example, drivers in the State of Illinois are instructed to use a "two-second" following rule. A driver should be following a leading vehicle by no less than the distance travelled in twoseconds. According to State of Illinois publication "Rules of the Road" (1995, p. 76), the two-second rule translates into these following distances:

Vehicle Speed		Following Distance
25 mph	36.67 ft/sec	73.33 feet
35 mph	51.33 ft/sec	102.67 feet
45 mph	66.00 ft/sec	132.00 feet
55 mph	80.67 ft/sec	161.33 feet

If the average vehicle is L feet in length, then the equation for the interval I recommended by the State of Illinois is

$$I = L + 2S,$$

where S is measured in feet per second.

Let us consider the following distance problem in more detail. Introduce notation as follows:

S = initial speed of vehicles (ft/sec),
L = length of vehicle (feet),
I = interval from front of vehicle tofront of next vehicle (feet),
r = reaction time for following vehicle (seconds),
d_l = deceleration rate for leading vehicle (ft/sec. squared),
d_f = deceleration rate for following vehicle,
x_0 = safety margin after stopping (feet), and
x = distance (feet).

If deceleration is constant, the braking distance for the leading vehicle is

$$x_l = S^2/2d_l. \tag{1}$$

This equation follows from the equation for speed;

$$S = dx/dt,$$

and the equation for acceleration (or deceleration);

$$a = dS/dt,$$

where a is the rate of acceleration (a negative number in the case of deceleration). From these two definitions

$$S/a = (dx/dt)/(dS/dt) = dx/dS.$$

The indefinite integral (ignoring the constant of integration) of dx/dS is

$$x = S^2/2a,$$

so the braking distance is the initial speed squared divided by twice the rate of deceleration. Similarly, the braking distance for the following vehicle is

$$x_f = Sr + S^2/2d_f.$$

Given initial spacing interval I, the length of the vehicles L, and the safety margin x_0,

$$x_f = I + x_l - L - x_0 \tag{2}$$

Substitution for x_f and x_l from above and solving for I yields

$$I = Sr + L + x_0 + (S^2/2d_f) - (S^2/2d_l). \tag{3}$$

This equation says that, given operating speed and other variables, one can compute the spacing necessary to permit the following vehicle to avoid collision. The application of equation (3) to an actual situation requires that one specify the deceleration characteristics of the leading and following vehicles.

Traffic engineers distinguish between normal deceleration and emergency deceleration. Papacostas and Prevedouros (1993, p.130) assume that emergency deceleration is three times as large as normal deceleration. Clearly the value of the spacing interval I depends upon the combination of deceleration assumptions used. If the leading vehicle is assumed to use emergency deceleration and the following vehicle uses normal deceleration, then the required spacing interval is large. The opposite set of deceleration assumptions generates a very small spacing interval (and following drivers who slam on the brakes frequently). On the other hand, if both vehicles are assumed to use the same deceleration rate, then the spacing interval is simply

$$I = Sr + L + x_0,$$

which can be rewritten as

$$I = (L + x_0) + rS, \tag{4}$$

which states that the spacing interval is a linear function of speed. Recall that the State of Illinois recommends such a linear equation for the spacing interval with r of 2 seconds. We now see that this kind of recommendation is based on the assumption that the leading and following vehicles have equal rates of deceleration (and on the assumption that $L + x_0 = 0$). Note also that the recommended spacing interval depends upon the recommended value of r, which is the reaction time in the model. A quicker reaction time implies a shorter spacing interval, so the highway can accommodate more vehicles at a given speed. This is the trade-off between safety and capacity.

C. DENSITY, SPEED, AND TRAFFIC VOLUME

Consider now the operation of the highway in the preceding section that is operating under a linear interval spacing rule. A photograph of the highway would show equally spaced vehicles in each lane. Define the density of traffic D as

$$D = 1/I.$$

The spacing interval is measured in distance per vehicle, so density is measured in vehicles per unit of distance. For example, if I is 100 feet per vehicle, then D is 52.8 vehicles per mile (5280/100) per lane.

An observer standing next to the highway would observe vehicles passing at uniform time intervals. This interval is known as the headway, and is measured in units of seconds per vehicle. The inverse of headway is the more familiar variable traffic volume (or traffic flow). For example, we know that the State of Illinois recommends a headway of two seconds per vehicle. This value of headway translates into traffic volume V as follows:

$$V = (60 \text{ sec/min})/(2 \text{ sec/vehicle})$$
$$= 30 \text{ vehicles per minute (i.e., 1800 per hour).}$$

If vehicles are traveling with spacing interval I and at speed S, the headway between them is $H = I/S$. For example, if the interval is 102.67 feet per vehicle and the speed is 51.33 feet per second (35 miles per hour), then the headway is 2 seconds per vehicle. The alternative equation for H is $H = 1/V$, and we have already seen that $I = 1/D$. Therefore:

$$H = 1/V = 1/DS, \text{ or}$$

$$V = DS. \tag{5}$$

This is the fundamental equation for traffic volume; traffic volume equals the traffic density times the rate of speed. The fundamental equation can also be written as

$$S = V/D,$$

which states that speed is traffic volume divided by density. Finally, traffic density can be written

$$D = V/S.$$

The observer of a highway needs only to measure two of the variables to infer the third. An economic interpretation of these equations is provided in the next chapter.

D. DENSITY, SPEED, AND TRAFFIC VOLUME RELATIONSHIPS

The fundamental equation for traffic volume says that

$$V = DS,$$

but this equation, by itself, does not tell us how traffic volume behaves. The behavior of drivers must be specified, as in Section B above. Recall that the linear equation for the spacing interval says that the interval increases with speed;

$$I = (L + x_0) + rS,$$

and recall that $D = 1/I$. Therefore,

$$S = (1/rD) - (L + x_0)/r, \qquad (6)$$

which states that speed is negatively related to traffic density.

The corresponding equation for traffic volume is

$$V = SD = (1/r) - (L + x_0)D/r. \qquad (7)$$

This equation says that traffic volume is simply a linear function of traffic density with a negative coefficient.

Numerous empirical studies of highway traffic volume, many of which are reviewed by Small (1992, pp. 61-69), have shown that the relationship between traffic density and volume is not so simple. One problem with equation (7) is the behavior of traffic volume at low densities. If traffic density is very low, then traffic moves at the speed limit (or higher), and the spacing interval is not a concern because it exceeds the amount required for traffic to move at the speed limit. Under such conditions an increase in traffic density translates directly into an increase in volume via the equation $V = S^*D$, where S^* is the speed limit. Traffic volume increases linearly with density up to the point at which the spacing interval reaches

$$I = (L + x_0) + rS^* = 1/D.$$

For example, assume that $S^*=55$ mph and $r=2$ seconds (.0005556 hours). Further assume that $L=20$ feet (average length of vehicles) and $x_0=15$ feet so that $L+x_0=.0066$ miles. These assumptions imply that $I=.0372$ and that $D=26.88$ vehicles per mile. At this density, traffic volume is 1485 vehicles per hour.

This modification of the model to account for low traffic densities implies that traffic volume is at its maximum of 1485 vehicles per hour when traffic density is 27 vehicles per mile and traffic is moving at the speed limit. Equation (7) says that any further increase in density (reduction in spacing interval) leads to a reduction in traffic volume. Using the above numerical values, the effect of an increase in density on traffic volume is

$$dV/dD = - (L + x_0)/r = -.0066/.0005556 = -11.93.$$

In other words, traffic volume declines by about 12 vehicles per hour as density increases by one vehicle per mile above 27 vehicles per mile. For example, a doubling of density to 54 vehicles per mile reduces traffic volume by 324 vehicles per hour from 1478 to 1154 vehicles per hour.

We know that this simple model of traffic is unrealistic. As we shall see in Chapter 3, traffic volume is at a maximum when speed is considerably below the speed limit. Driver behavior at speeds below the speed limit is more complex than that implied by the linear spacing interval equation. Nevertheless, the spacing interval model provides a powerful reason for the existence of a negative relationship between traffic density and traffic volume if traffic density exceeds some amount. Overall, then, we expect that traffic volume rises and then falls as traffic density increases.

In the next chapter we present an economic model of traffic volume which captures this expected relationship. The basic idea is that there are two inputs that enter into the production of urban travel, the (fixed) capital embodied in the highway, and the variable inputs embodied in the drivers and their vehicles. This insight permits us to use standard economic concepts of the production function, fixed and variable inputs, average and marginal products, and so forth. An empirical study based on this model is presented in Chapter 3.

References

Papacostas, C. and P. Prevedouros, 1993, "Transportation Engineering and Planning, 2nd ed. Englewood Cliffs, NJ: Prentice-Hall.

Small, K., 1992, Urban Transportation Economics, Chur, Switzerland: Harwood Academic Publishers.

2 HIGHWAY TRAFFIC FLOW AND THE 'UNECONOMIC' REGION OF PRODUCTION

A. INTRODUCTION

The purposes of this chapter are to develop an economic model of highway traffic flow, and to demonstrate the economic relevance of the 'uneconomic' region of production for this important concrete example. An empirical version of the model is presented in Chapter 3. The focus of this chapter is on the neighborhood in which the marginal product of the variable input in the short run falls to zero and becomes negative. This economically relevant uneconomic region of production is known in the textbooks as 'Stage 3' of the Law of Variable Proportions. The conventional argument, as presented by Borts and Mishan (1962), is that a firm would not produce in Stage 3. Indeed, they argue that it is not proper to construct a production function for a firm with a negative marginal product for a variable input. However, if we reformulate the fundamental diagram of highway traffic volume as a short-run production function, then we do observe production that takes place in Stage 3, and we can estimate a production function over this domain. The domain in question corresponds to the portion of the traffic density - volume function in Chapter 2 where traffic volume declines as traffic density increases. Recall that the spacing interval model in Chapter 2 provides a strong reason for the existence of this negative relationship.

Our model is one in which the output, traffic volume, is produced by a fixed highway (capital) input and a variable driver (labor) input. The relevance of Stage 3 arises because traffic volume is a classic example of a congestion externality in which there is no rational being present to prevent the addition of drivers (labor) beyond the point at which marginal product is zero. The purposes of this chapter are to present this reformulation of the standard model, and to examine the empirical literature from this perspective.

It should be noted that the normal notion of traffic congestion externality corresponds to 'Stage 2' of the law of variable proportions; the portion in which the average product of the variable input is declining and its marginal product is greater than zero. Stage 2 corresponds to the region of rising average cost, a region that is depicted in numerous textbooks. In this region the marginal cost of traffic volume exceeds the average variable cost by the amount of the congestion externality at that level of traffic. These matters are discussed in detail in Chapter 6.

B. ECONOMIC ANALYSIS OF HIGHWAY TRAFFIC VOLUME

In order to characterize what happens on urban highways as a production function, it is necessary first to identify the output of the highway. Quantity of highway travel Q is measured as a physical distance (i.e., total miles traveled). On a given highway is it normal to record traffic volume V, traffic density D, and average speed S. As we discussed in Chapter 1, traffic volume is measured in units of vehicles per unit of time, traffic density is measured in units of vehicles per unit of distance,and average speed is measured in units of distance per unit of time. In common usage V is referred to as volume or flow. However, actually it is speed which measures miles of travel produced per unit of time by an individual driver.

Consider a highway of fixed length and a time period T_0 of fixed duration. With no loss of generality choose the units of distance and time such that both are unity. Assume that the highway is in a steady state over this unit of time, so that V, D, and S are constant for purposes of this analysis. It is helpful to imagine that the highway is a circle of unit circumference. Traffic density D is the number of vehicles on the highway at each point in time, so the total quantity of travel produced and consumed during one period of analysis is given by

$$Q = DST_0 = V \tag{1}$$

(given $T_0 = 1$). Each vehicle on the circular highway of unit length will pass a given point on the circle S times per unit time; the total quantity of travel Q is thus DS = V, which is the total number of vehicles which pass a given point on the circle per unit time. This establishes the numerical identity between Q per unit time and V for this model. The assumption that the highway is a circle of unit circumference is only a pedagogical device and is not essential.

The key to converting this analysis into the conventional economics of production is to recognize that traffic density D is numerically identical to the variable input (i.e., labor and vehicle time). Speed is the inverse of average variable cost measured in units of time, and volume is the output of the highway. Thus

$$AVC = (1/S) = D/V, \tag{2}$$

where AVC = variable (time) cost per mile of travel, and

$$VC = (AVC)V = D, \tag{3}$$

where VC = total variable cost measured in units of time, which is identical to the variable input. Total variable input is thus identical to traffic density. For example, suppose that there are 50 vehicles (each with drivers) on the circular highway of one mile in circumference. Further assume that the steady-state speed is 30 miles per hour. In one hour these drivers and their vehicles produce 1500 miles of travel; output is a flow of 1500 units per hour. The average product of each driver and vehicleis 30 miles per hour, and the driver and vehicle input is 50 hours. All of these measurements are in the units conventionally used in the economics of production. An observer standing at a point along the highway would observe a traffic volume of 1500 vehicles in that hour. The variable costs can be converted to monetary units using values of driver and vehicle time, but this conversion is not necessary for the production function interpretation of the model

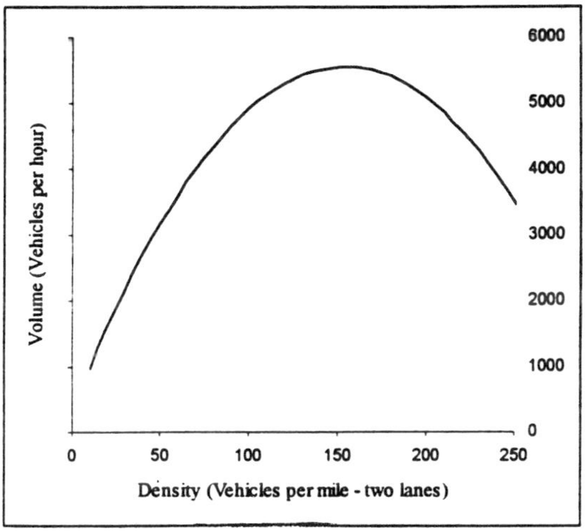

Figure 2-1
The Fundamental Diagram of Traffic

A familiar concept in highway engineering is called the Fundamental Diagram of Traffic, which relates traffic volume and traffic density for a given highway facility. As we discussed in Chapter 1, and as Figure 2-1 shows, traffic volume increases with traffic density up to the capacity of the highway, and declines with further increases in density. This empirical relationship has been confirmed by numerous empirical studies, including engineering studies reviewed by Carter, Merritt, and Robinson (1982) and recent economic studies such as Boardman and Lave (1977), Keeler and Small (1977), Inman (1979), and Fare, Grosskopf, and Yoon (1982). Many of the empirical studies are also reviewed by Small (1992). The classic empirical study in economics is Walters (1961).

Given the definition of variable cost, the Fundamental Diagram of Traffic can be reinterpreted as a short-run production function in which output is related to the variable input. As shown in Figure 2-2, the average and marginal product curves for the variable input can be derived from this short-run production function. The average product of the variable input is simply average speed; S = V/D. The marginal product of the variable input is zero at the density corresponding to capacity of the highway and is negative at higher densities.

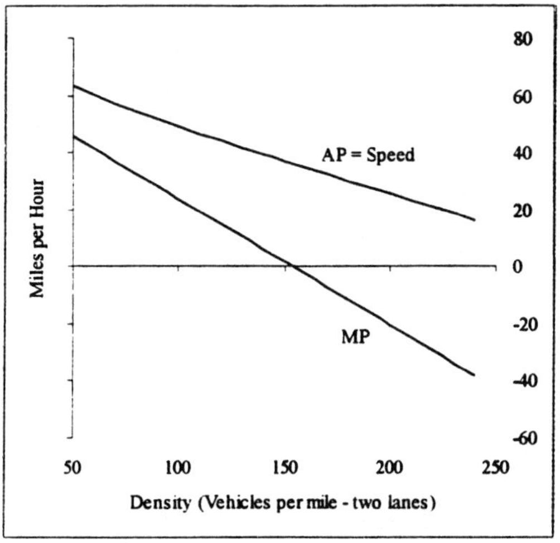

Figure 2-2
Average and Marginal Products of Traffic Density

C. EMPIRICAL EXAMPLES

The purpose of this section is to present a good empirical example from the literature in which the short-run production function discussed above has been estimated. The production function can be written

$$V = f(D,K^*) = V(D), \tag{4}$$

where K^* is the fixed capital input embodied in the highway. The short-run production function can be approximated by a Taylor series expansion of equation (4) around the density at which volume is maximized, D_0. Using the first three terms to obtain a quadratic approximation,

$$V(D) = V(D_0) + (D-D_0)V'(D_0) + 0.5(D-D_0)^2V''(D_0), \tag{5}$$

where V' and V'' are the first and second derivatives of V(D). Since $V'(D_0) = 0$, equation (5) can be written as

$$V(D) = [V_0+0.5D_0{}^2V_0''] - D_0V_0''D + 0.5V_0''D^2, \qquad (6)$$

or V is a quadratic function of D. The sign of V_0'' is negative,so the signs of the coefficients of D and D^2 are positive and negative, respectively.

Onc of the best econometric studies of the volume-density function was done by Boardman and Lave (1977). They actually estimated equation (6) as well as many other functional relationships between S, V, and D. But they did not consider their estimates specifically of equation (6) to be estimates of a short-run production function. The data used for the estimation of equation (6) were collected by Lerch (1970). Lerch observed speed for over 10,000 vehicles on the two southbound lanes of an expressway in the Washington, D.C. area on August 20, 1968 from 3:30 PM until 6:30 PM. The road was dry and visibility was good,and there were no entrances or exits near the observation points to affect flow. For each vehicle Lerch recorded the time a vehicle passed the observation point in thousandths of an hour, individual vehicle speed, and whether the vehicle traveled in the slower or the faster lane. Speed was calculated from the time taken to travel across bands placed 30 feet apart (15 for heavy traffic). Speed limits were 70 mph for cars and 65 mph for trucks. The volume measure used is vehicles in both lanes per 6 minutes and the average speed is miles per hour of vehicles in the faster lane only. Boardman and Lave (1977) provide a more extensive discussion of the data and these choices for volume and speed measures.

The econometric results obtained by Boardman and Lave (1977, p. 352) are that

$$V = 2882 + 2.173\ D - 0.05207\ D^2, \qquad (7)$$

where adjusted R^2 = 0.48 and all three regression coefficients are highly statistically significant. Given that

$$-\ (V_0''/2) = 0.005207 \text{ and}$$

$$D_0V_0'' - 2.173,$$

these results imply that D_0 = 209 vehicles per mile (two lanes), V at D_0 equals 5149 vehicles per hour (two lanes), and S at D_0 equals 24.7 mph. Boardman and Lave (1977) also estimated equation (6) including a set of dummy variables to control for the time of day. These results imply that D_0 = 219 vehicles per mile, V at D_0 equals 4829 vehicles per mile, and S at D_0 equals 22 mph. Other empirical results presented by Boardman and Lave using the same data base indicate that S at D_0 is about 30 mph.

We have replicated the Boardman-Lave study excluding the observations where speed is less than 18 mph. These observations were excluded because it appeared that they are not part of the same volume-density function and because the scatter diagram of data points indicates that speed at maximum volume is 30 to 40 mph. The results obtained are that

$$V = 329.07 + 68.43\ D - 0.221\ D^2. \tag{8}$$

These coefficient values imply that D_0 = 155 vehicles per mile (two lanes), V at D_0 equals 5638 vehicles per hour (two lanes), and S at D_0 equals 36.3 mph. Another empirical study by Keeler and Small (1977) of three expressways in the San Francisco area indicates that S at D_0 equals 30 to 47 mph. Clearly the empirical issues are not settled given this rather wide divergence of estimated speed at maximum traffic volume (22 mphto 47 mph).

D. A PRODUCTION FUNCTION FOR HIGHWAY TRAFFIC VOLUME

The purpose of this section is to formulate a production model for highway traffic volume that possesses standard measures of production functions. Our task is to formulate a production function with two inputs (capital and vehicle density) in which the marginal product of density can be negative at relatively large densities; i.e., the production function must have one 'ridge line.' We present such a function here for use in subsequent chapters in this book and so that future researchers can conduct empirical studies in which the capital input varies.

Generations of students have learned from Allen (1938) that there is a generalization of the Cobb-Douglas production function that exhibits linear homogeneity and two ridge lines;

$$x = (2Hab - Aa^2 - Bb^2)^{0.5}, \tag{9}$$

where x is output, a and b are inputs, and H, A, and B are constants. This function has one ridge line if B = 0, but this function does not provide enough flexibility to capture the curvature of the volume-density relationship. We have found that the following generalization of equation (9) possesses desirable properties;

$$V = k[g(hK)D^{g-1} - (g-1)D^g]^{1/g}, \tag{10}$$

where $g > 1$, K is the amount of capital embodied in the highway, and h and k are other parameters. This function is homogeneous of degree one, and it reduces to equation (9) with B = 0 if g =2, i.e.

$$V = k[2hKD - D^2]^{0.5} \tag{11}$$

The production function (10) has three basic properties. The density at which volume is a maximum is located where V'(D) =0, or D_0 = hK. The speed at D_0 is simply k because if D_0 = hK, equation (10) reduces to

$$V = hkK$$

and S = V/D. Finally, g-1 is a dimension-free measure of curvature of the rate of change of volume as one moves away from maximum volume. Our estimates of equation (10) using the Lerch data (1970) indicate that g = 2.9 (g-1 = 1.9), so the generalization of equation (9) is needed to capture the curvature of the volume-density function at maximum volume in this data set.

E. CONCLUSION

We have formulated the highway volume-density relationship as a standard short-run production function in which Stage 3 is economically relevant. Empirical estimates indicate that the marginal product of the variable input (vehicle density) is negative at speeds less than 22 to 47 mph, depending upon the highway studied and the empirical specification employed. We note that the condition of negative marginal product has been observed by virtually every study of urban highways for at least part of the time during the morning and/or evening rush hours. Also, we have proposed a linear homogeneous production function for two inputs with one ridge line so that variations in the capital input can be studied in the same framework. The next chapter contains our own empirical study of the short-run production function.

References

Allen, R., 1938, Mathematical Analysis for Economists, New York: St. Martin's Press.

Boardman, A. and L. Lave, 1977, Highway congestion and congestion tolls, Journal of Urban Economics 4, 340-359.

Borts, G. and E. Mishan, 1962, Exploring the 'uneconomic' region of the production function, Review of Economic Studies 29, 300-312.

Carter, W., D. Merritt, and C.Robinson, 1982, Highway capacity and levels of service, in W. Hamburger et al., eds., Transportation and Traffic Engineering Handbook, Englewood Cliffs, NJ: Prentice-Hall.

Fare, R., S. Grosskopf, and B. Yoon, 1982, A theoretical and empirical analysis of the highway speed-volume relationship, Journal of Urban Economics 12, 115-121.

Inman, R, 1979, A generalized congestion function for highway travel, Journal of Urban Economics 5, 21-34.

Keeler T., and K. Small, 1977, Optimal peak-load pricing, investment, and service levels on urban expressways, Journal of Political Economy 85, 1-25.

Lerch, G., 1970, A study of the speed-volume relationship on high speed highways, Unpublished Master's dissertation, The Catholic University of America, Washington, D. C.

Walters, A., 1961, The theory and measurement of private and social cost of highway congestion, Econometrica 29, 676-699.

3 AN EMPIRICAL MODEL OF HIGHWAY TRAFFIC FLOW

A. INTRODUCTION

The purpose of this chapter is to formulate and estimate an improved model of urban highway traffic volume using standard econometric techniques. Transportation economists (and other transportation researchers) have used two models of traffic that are considered to be alternative approaches to the study of urban highways; the continuous (steady-state) flow model and the bottleneck model. These two models are discussed briefly below. The point of this chapter is to show that the continuous flow and the bottleneck models can be combined into one econometric model of traffic volume on the Eisenhower Expressway in Chicago. The approach that is taken in this chapter can be applied generally to empirical studies of highway traffic flow provided that data on downstream traffic conditions are available.

B. MODELS OF TRAFFIC FLOW

One of the main preoccupations of transportation researchers is the formulation of models of traffic flow, and several alternative models exist in the literature. However, Small (1992, p. 61) points out that a fundamental distinction is between models that are static (i. e., steady state) and those that are dynamic (not steady state).

The static (steady-state) economic model of highway traffic flow is discussed in Chapters 1 and 2. In this model an analogy with standard production theory is used in which the output is traffic flow (all economic outputs are flows). The inputs are driver/vehicle time (variable input) and the services of the highway (capital), which are also flows. A more complex model would add operating expenses, but this is not needed to focus on congestion. Consider a one-lane circular highway (i. e., a one-lane racetrack) of unit circumference. Suppose that there are N vehicles on the highway, so traffic density is N. The output of the highway is traffic volume per unit of time V, or

$$V = N \times S, \qquad (1)$$

where S is the speed at which the vehicles travel. Speed S is the average product of the variable input N. The conventional theory of production says that, with the capital input (K) fixed, the average product of the variable input will start to decline at some level of N. Also, it is possible that the marginal product of the variable input will fall below zero; additional vehicles will result in a reduction in traffic volume. In essence the static economic model posits a production function V=f(N,K), and includes the possibility that this production function has one ridge line at which the marginal product of N falls to zero. In the transportation literature the region of the domain of the production function with marginal product of N less than zero is known as hypercongestion; this region is also Stage III of the Law of Variable Proportions. The normal notion of the congestion externality corresponds to the region in which the average product of N is falling, but its marginal product is positive; this is stage II of the Law of Variable Proportions.

Various dynamic models of traffic flow are presented by Ross (1988) and Small (1992). These models assume that the flow of traffic is, to a degree, interrupted by a bottleneck of some sort. The purpose of the model is to work out the implications of the bottleneck for traffic flow over time for locations both upstream and downstream from the bottleneck. A sizable literature now exists in economics [e. g., Arnott, dePalma and Lindsey (1990)] on traffic bottleneck models that permit endogenous scheduling of trips. The reader can consult Small (1992, pp. 85-94) for a lucid introduction to these models. In essence these models hypothesize that there is a maximum traffic flow that a given highway can carry, but that an <u>isolated</u> highway will not display declining traffic flow as traffic density (N) increases. As Small (1992, p. 69) puts it,

> "A speed-flow curve with a maximum flow cannot tell us what happens when demand exceeds that flow. Furthermore, although economists have made much of the apparent pure inefficiency of hypercongestion (since the same flow could be carried at a better level of service by moving to congested regions), there is no conclusive evidence that hypercongestion ever occurs in an isolated system. Rather, it appears to describe the flow of vehicles in a queue resulting from some downstream bottleneck, as shown elegantly (via traffic simulations) by Ross (1988, pp. 429-430)."

He goes on to suggest that it is more fruitful to model the bottleneck rather than the traffic flow in the queue upstream from the bottleneck.

The purpose of this paper is to formulate and estimate a model of highway traffic flow that uses ideas from both of these types of models. The variable to be explained is the traffic flow per hour on the Eisenhower Expressway in Chicago. Data on traffic flow for a shorter time period (e. g., six minutes) would be desirable, but such data are not available in the Chicago metropolitan area. Traffic conditions during the rush-hour period can change over periods that are much shorter than one hour. The data in used in this study have, in effect, been smoothed to hourly periods. Nevertheless, the performance of the highway over periods of an hour in length is of interest.

C. THE DATA

The Eisenhower Expressway runs a distance of 14 miles from downtown Chicago to the West. The highway has four lanes in each direction for the first seven miles, and three lanes thereafter. This study considers only the outbound side of the highway. At its western end the outbound side of the highway splits into two sections, each with two lanes. Each of these two sections then leads almost immediately into various options with more lanes. Traffic flow and density are monitored at six stations during the morning and afternoon rush periods. The monitoring stations are located about 2.5 miles apart. Traffic volume per hour is recorded along with occupancy, the percentage of the time that a detector is occupied by vehicles.

Occupancy corresponds to traffic density. Consider an hour in which occupancy is .20. In the steady state, this means that 1056 feet out of a mile are occupied by vehicles. If the average vehicle is 20 feet in length, an occupancy of .20 corresponds to a traffic density of 53 vehicles per mile. Vehicles come in all sizes (from 18-wheel trucks to small cars), and the occupancy variable includes each vehicle according to its actual length. Therefore, it is conventional in traffic data sets of this type to use occupancy as the measure of the "variable input," rather than first to make a conversion to traffic density.

The Illinois Department of Transportation provided the data on traffic volume and occupancy for the week of Monday, May 2 to Friday, May 6, 1994, a week in which there was no rain or other weather conditions that impeded traffic. Hourly data for 5 AM to 10 AM and 2PM to 7 PM were provided for the six monitoring stations, yielding a total of 60 observations on outbound volume and occupancy per day. Mean traffic volumes per hour and occupancy rates for the five morning and five afternoon hours (five week days) for the four-lane and three-lane stations were as follows:

	Traffic flow	Traffic flow per lane	Occupancy
Four lanes (eastern half)			
AM	5297	1324	11.0%
PM	5573	1393	32.1%
Three lanes (western half)			
AM	5165	1722	22.0%
PM	5272	1757	25.6%

Note that traffic volume was about the same on both the four-lane and the three-lane portions of the highway, and only slightly lower in the morning hours than in the afternoon hours. However, the occupancy rate on the four-lane portion of the highway was far smaller in the morning and greater in the afternoon. Also, traffic volume per lane was less on the four-lane portion of the highway. These summary statistics suggest either that there was hypercongestion on the four-lane portion of the highway in the afternoon, and/or that the apparent hypercongestion was in fact a queue of vehicles as they were being squeezed from four lanes to three. The empirical task is to test these hypotheses.

A preliminary examination of the data is displayed in Table 3-1, which shows cross tabulations of volume and occupancy separately for the three-lane and four-lane portions of the highway. The upper half of Table 3-1 contains the data that are used in the regressions reported below for the three-lane portion of the highway. Occupancy varies from 12.8% to 37.7%, and traffic volume varies from 4112 to 6186 vehicles per hour. At low occupancy levels (12.8% to 17.78%) volume has a mean of 5017 vehicles per hour. Mean volume for the next occupancy range (17.78% to 22.76%) rises to 5564, but falls successively to 5432, 4880 and 4616 for the other three occupancy ranges. The biggest drop in volume occurs when occupancy increases from the 22.76%-27.74% range to the 27.74%-32.72% range. Occupancy exceeds 27.74% for 51 of the 100 hours included in the table. The results for the four-lane portion of the highway are similar, except that the ranges for occupancy (5.4% to 47.6%) and volume (2911 to 7223) are wider than for the three-lane portion of the highway. The mean volume for the lowest occupancy range (5.4% to 13.84%) is 5153 vehicles per hour, and mean volume rises to 6361 for the next occupancy range (13.84% to 22.28%). But then mean volume drops as occupancy rises. Mean volume for the highest occupancy range (39.16% to 47.60%) is 4944 vehicles per hour, or only 1236 vehicles per lane per hour. Note that occupancy exceeds 30.72% for 48 of the 150 hour periods shown in the table.

D. EMPIRICAL RESULTS

Consider first the traffic volume on the portion of the highway with three lanes. This stretch of highway does not lead into a bottleneck, and the entrance ramps are controlled by traffic signals that are keyed to sensing devices embedded in the highway. These signals alternate red and green quickly to spread out the entering traffic and, when traffic on the highway is heavy, to permit vehicles to enter when there are gaps in the traffic flow. However, as the empirical results below demonstrate, the ramp signaling system does not guarantee that traffic never exceeds capacity. In short, this is a stretch of highway that carries heavy traffic, but it does not have built-in bottlenecks. Any bottleneck is created by the traffic itself.

The function to test for the presence of hypercongestion and bottleneck effects is written as follows:

Table 3-1

Crosstabulations of Volume and Occupancy:
Eisenhower Expressway

Three-Lane Portion

Volume	Occupancy (Percentage) 12.80-17.78	17.78-22.76	22.76-27.74	27.74-32.72	32.72-37.70
4112-4527	2	0	1	6	6
4527-4942	7	0	3	14	6
4942-5356	9	2	4	15	2
5356-5771	4	1	8	2	0
5771-6186	0	2	6	0	0
Column mean	5017	5564	5432	4880	4616

Four-Lane Portion

Volume	Occupancy (Percentage) 5.40-13.84	13.84-22.28	22.28-30.72	30.72-39.16	39.16 47.60
2911-3773	10	0	0	0	0
3773-4636	6	0	1	1	4
4636-5498	27	1	2	11	16
5498-6361	21	6	5	13	1
6361-7223	6	9	9	1	0
Column mean	5153	6361	6183	5531	4944

$$V = b_0 + b_1D_1 + b_2OCC(D_1) + b_3lnOCC(D_1) + b_4OCC(D_2) + b_5V_{+1} + b_6OCC_{+1} + u, \qquad (2)$$

where OCC is occupancy at the station in question, D_1 is a dummy equal to one if occupancy is less than or equal to the occupancy OCC* at which maximum volume occurs (and zero otherwise), D_2 is a dummy equal to one if occupancy is greater than this value (zero otherwise), V_{+1} is traffic volume at the next station downstream, OCC_{+1} is occupancy at that downstream station, and u is a random error term. Inclusion of occupancy and its natural log permits nonlinearity with a maximum value, and is the best functional form found by Boardman and Lave (1977) to fit similar data.[1] The hypothesis of hypercongestion is that $b_4<0$. Indeed, the finding that $b_4<0$ might lead one simply to estimate

$$V = c_0 + c_1OCC + c_2lnOCC + c_3V_{+1} + c_4OCC_{+1} + u. \qquad (3)$$

In this model peak volume occurs at $OCC^* = -c_2/c_1$.

The presence of a bottleneck means that traffic volume upstream from the bottleneck is inhibited by the relatively low traffic volume and/or high occupancy level in the bottleneck. The data from the Eisenhower Expressway permit the inclusion of the two variables traffic volume (V_{+1}) and occupancy (OCC_{+1}) for the same hour at the next downstream monitoring station (located about 2.5 miles away). It has been suggested that only downstream occupancy is needed to test for the bottleneck effect. However, both downstream volume and occupancy variables are included so that downstream traffic conditions are characterized as completely as possible with the available data. Data for the monitoring station at the western end of the highway are excluded because downstream data are not available. This leaves 100 observations for the three-lane portion of the highway.

The level of occupancy at which hypercongestion might begin is, of course, unknown. The procedure followed is to specify alternative values of occupancy (OCC*) that define the dummy variables D_1 and D_2. These alternatives are 20%, 22%, 24% and 26%. Plots of the raw data suggest strongly that traffic volume reaches its maximum in this range of occupancy, so these alternatives for OCC* were chosen. As noted above hypercongestion does <u>not</u> exist if, controlling for downstream traffic conditions, coefficient b_4 in Eq. (1) is not statistically significantly different from zero. If coefficient b_4 is zero, then traffic volume given that the value of occupancy is above OCC* is simply

$$V = b_0 + b_5V_{+1} + b_6OCC_{+1} + u. \qquad (4)$$

This is a form of the bottleneck model; traffic volume is governed by capacity (b_0) and by downstream traffic conditions.

Estimates of Eq. (1) for the three-lane portion of the highway are shown in Table 3-2. The Breusch-Pagan (1979) test indicates the presence of heteroskedasticity, so the standard errors of all regression coefficients reported in this paper have been corrected using the White (1980) method for computation of the

Table 3-2

Volume-Occupancy Functions:
Eisenhower Expressway, Three-Lane Portion[a]

Independent Variables	OCC*=20	OCC*=22	OCC*=24	OCC*=26
Constant	4857.68	4170.93	5918.74	5653.17
	(8.36)	(5.56)	(9.84)	(8.05)
Occupancy<OCC* (dummy)	-56,576.30	-14,125.80	-22,476.40	-10,963.00
	(4.08)	(1.56)	(3.34)	(1.97)
Occupancy if < OCC*	-1999.51	-3.23	-554.96	-202.33
	(3.82)	(1.14)	(2.77)	(1.40)
lnOccupancy if < OCC*	31,512.80	6658.81	10,471.30	4338.75
	(3.93)	(1.36)	(2.95)	(1.54)
Occupancy if > OCC*	-48.55	-39.93	-89.11	-81.80
	(4.12)	(2.48)	(7.45)	(4.84)
Volume ahead one station	.37	.43	.37	.38
	(6.04)	(6.14)	(5.84)	(5.82)
Occupancy ahead one station	-20.60	-17.12	-13.05	-14.31
	(3.27)	(2.57)	(2.19)	(2.30)
R^2	.651	.611	.702	.688
Standard error	290.82	306.65	268.47	274.86
Log likelihood	-705.66	-710.96	-697.67	-700.02
Sample Size	100	100	100	100

[a]Unsigned t values are in parentheses. Standard errors of regression coefficients are corrected for heteroskedasticity.

variance matrix of the error term. All four of the regressions strongly confirm that volume declines as occupancy increases above OCC*, and that downstream volume and occupancy influence volume in the expected directions. The version of the model with the highest value for the likelihood function has OCC*=24. In this case an increase in occupancy of 1% reduces volume by 89 vehicles per hour, an increase in downstream volume of 100 increases volume by 37 vehicles per hour, and an increase in downstream occupancy of 1% reduces volume by 13 vehicles per hour. The simple correlation between occupancy at the station in question and the downstream occupancy is .59, but the results show that the data are able to distinguish between the effects of these two measures of occupancy. As one would expect, volume and downstream volume are also positively correlated (simple correlation of .56), but this correlation does not prevent the effects of the other variables from emerging.

The tests for the four-lane portion of the highway are shown in Table 3-3. In this case the downstream variables include volume, occupancy, and a dummy variable for the monitoring station just to the East of the point where the highway changes from four to three lanes. This dummy variable is included for two reasons; it distinguishes one station from the other two four-lane stations that are not adjacent to the point where the highway narrows, and it also controls for the fact that a substantial number of vehicles exit the highway just to the West of this station. It is clear that drivers have an incentive to avoid the bottleneck created by the narrowing of the highway, and the author has observed that many do so by making use of two exits between the station in question and the point where the highway narrows. These two effects work in opposite directions on traffic volume, so the expected sign of the dummy variable is ambiguous.

The results in Table 3-3 are very strong. Every coefficient in all four versions of the model is highly statistically significant. All four versions of the model have an R^2 of .78 and almost identical values for the log of the likelihood function. All four versions of the model show that volume declines as occupancy rises 1% above OCC* by about 50 vehicles per hour, that volume rises by 46 vehicles as downstream volume rises by 100, and that an increase in downstream occupancy of 1% reduces volume by 16 vehicles per hour. In addition, traffic volume is about 300 to 320 vehicles per hour greater at the station just to the East of the point where the highway narrows to three lanes. This is an estimate of the number of vehicles that exited the highway between the station in question and the point where the highway narrows. The simple correlation between occupancy and downstream occupancy is .77, but the data are able to distinguish the effects of the two variables. Also, the simple correlation between volume and downstream volume is .71, but this relatively high correlation does not mask the effects of the other variables.

The results in Tables 3-2 and 3-3 confirm the presence of hypercongestion. As suggested above, Eq. (2) is a more parsimonious model for traffic volume with hypercongestion. Estimates of three different versions of Eq. (2) are shown in Table 3-4 for the three-lane and four-lane portions of the highway. The first version of the model omits all downstream variables, the

Table 3-3

Volume-Occupancy Functions:
Eisenhower Expressway, Four-Lane Portion[a]

Independent Variables	OCC*=20	OCC*=22	OCC*24	OCC*=26
Constant	5122.29	5403.67	5331.76	5639.24
	(7.94)	(7.56)	(6.86)	(7.46)
Occupancy<OCC* (dummy)	-12,019.60	-11,738.10	-11,118.50	-11,867.70
	(7.58)	(7.55)	(7.68)	(8.00)
Occupancy if < OCC*	-321.25	-273.04	-228.03	-260.37
	(3.58)	(3.69)	(4.24)	(4.53)
lnOccupancy if < OCC*	5714.88	5265.21	4813.59	5170.00
	(5.64)	(5.79)	(6.36)	(6.51)
Occupancy if > OCC*	-44.48	-51.16	-49.83	-56.43
	(5.31)	(5.43)	(4.30)	(5.25)
Volume ahead one station	.46	.46	.46	.46
	(5.77)	(5.63)	(5.76)	(5.65)
Occupancy ahead one station	-15.58	-15.66	-15.95	-16.36
	(3.26)	(3.34)	(3.42)	(3.50)
Station ahead has one fewer lanes	303.94	313.70	322.75	320.33
	(3.03)	(3.12)	(3.26)	(3.24)
R^2	.777	.781	.779	.782
Standard error	451.96	449.14	451.28	448.30
Log likelihood	-1125.9	-1124.9	-1125.7	-1124.7
Sample size	150	150	150	150

[a]Unsigned t values are in parentheses. Standard errors of regression coefficients are corrected for heteroskedasticity.

Table 3-4
Determinants of Traffic Volume:
Eisenhower Expressway[a]

Independent Variables	Three Lanes (1)	(2)	(3)
Constant	-11036.20	-6325.30	-11758.10
	(5.12)	(3.01)	(5.75)
Occupancy	-373.71	-240.64	-378.68
	(7.94)	(5.08)	(8.36)
ln Occupancy	8011.55	4879.85	8498.27
	(7.61)	(4.45)	(8.49)
Volume ahead one station	--	.41	--
		(6.22)	
Occupancy ahead one station	--	-12.35	-31.23
		(1.97)	(4.73)
R^2	.459	.670	.561
Standard error	354.30	279.45	320.92
Log likelihood	-727.41	-702.68	-717.01
Sample size	100	100	100

	Four Lanes (1)	(2)	(3)
Constant	-4947.35	-4878.18	-5670.27
	(7.96)	(9.90)	(9.93)
Occupancy	-259.92	-177.56	-269.28
	(16.93)	(9.13)	(19.40)
ln Occupancy	5566.19	4136.51	6051.23
	(16.75)	(9.58)	(19.81)
Volume ahead one station	--	.49	--
		(6.30)	
Occupancy ahead one station	--	-18.50	-20.98
		(3.80)	(3.50)
Station ahead has one fewer lanes	--	347.43	85.88
		(3.49)	(1.08)
R^2	.628	.782	.698
Standard error	540.68	445.10	521.93
Log likelihood	-1155.30	-1124.60	-1149.00
Sample size	150	150	150

[a] Unsigned t values are in parentheses. Standard errors of regression coefficients are corrected for heteroskedasticity.

second version includes all downstream variables, and the third version omits the downstream volume variable.

All of the functions shown in Table 3-4 exhibit strong evidence of hypercongestion. The estimated peak volume on three lanes occurs at an occupancy of 21.4%, 20.3%, and 22.4% for the three versions of the model. The volume peaks on four lanes at an occupancy of 21.4%, 23.3%, and 22.5% for the three versions of the model. However, these estimated equations also show that a more complete explanation of traffic volume must include data on downstream traffic. The results in column 2 of Table 3-4 show that both downstream volume and occupancy have statistically significant effects on volume. Further, the results in column 3 of Table 4 show that the omission of downstream volume significantly reduces the explanatory power of the regression model.

E. CONCLUSION

This chapter has presented an empirical model of highway traffic flow that combines the continuous flow and the bottleneck models of traffic. The results for the Eisenhower Expressway in Chicago for the week of May 2, 1994 indicate that traffic flow at a monitoring station is strongly related both to the level of occupancy (i. e., traffic density) at that point and to the downstream volume and occupancy level. Furthermore, the evidence of hypercongestion remains very strong even after the downstream variables are included in the model. Hypercongestion is the phenomenon in which, beyond some point of maximum traffic volume, increases in occupancy (traffic density) cause a reduction in volume. Hypercongestion occurs at an occupancy level in the range of 20 to 24 percent. The occupancy level on the Eisenhower Expressway frequently is in excess of 30%. If vehicles are of uniform length, this means that hypercongestion is beginning if the vehicles are separated by a distance of three to four vehicle-lengths.

Footnote

1. An alternative is to use a simple quadratic function of occupancy. All of the models reported in this chapter were also estimated in this form, but the models that included occupancy and natural log of occupancy (rather than the square of occupancy) consistently have higher levels of explanatory power.

References

Arnott, R., A. de Palma, and R. Lindsey, 1990, Economics of a bottleneck, Journal of Urban Economics 27, 111-130.

Boardman, A. and R. Lave, 1977, Highway congestion and congestion tolls, Journal of Urban Economics 4, 340-359.

Breusch, T. and A. Pagan, 1979, A Simple test for heteroskedasticity and random coefficient variation, Econometrica 47, 1287-1294.

Ross, P., 1988, Traffic dynamics, Transportation Research B 22, 412-435.

Small, K., 1992, Urban Transportation Economics, Chur, Switzerland: Harwood Academic Publishers.

White, H., 1980, A heteroskedasticity consistent covariance matrix and a direct test for heteroskedasticity, Econometrica 48, 817-838.

PART II

COMMUTER CHOICE OF TOLLLWAYS VERSUS FREEWAYS

4 THEORY OF ROUTE CHOICE AND THE VALUE OF TIME

A. INTRODUCTION

The first section of this book has concentrated on the specification of the supply side of travel on urban highways. The demand side receives attention in this and the next chapter. Our purpose here is not to provide a comprehensive discussion of the demand for urban travel, but rather to concentrate on whether the commuter chooses a tollway for the drive to work. After some introduction to urban travel demand in general, this chapter examines the theory of route choice and the value of time. Chapter 5 is an empirical study of the choice of freeways versus tollways. A comprehensive theoretical and empirical survey of the demand for urban travel is provided by Small in his text "Urban Transportation Economics" (1992).

The study of the demand for urban transportation is usually undertaken in an individual urban area. The urban area is broken down into a set of small geographic zones. It is assumed that the location patterns by geographic zone of houses, jobs,and shopping opportunities, as well as other possible trip destinations, are fixed. Travel demand analysis is then broken down into four steps. The first step is to study the generation of trips by a geographic zone during a particular time of day (e.g., the morning rush hour). Each zone is both an origin and a destination for trips. The end of this first phase of the analysis yields models that explain (or predict) the number of trips that originate in a zone and the number of trips that have the zone as destination.

The second phase of a travel demand study, known as trip distribution analysis, is to model how the trips from each origin are distributed to the various destinations. A technique that is often used for this purpose is called the gravity model of spatial interaction. The gravity model says that the number of trips taken from an origin i to a destination j increases with the number of trips with origin at zone i and with the number of trips with zone j as destination. Also, the number of trips from i to j will depend upon the cost of the trip, which is often measured as the distance from i to j. The model is stated in logarithmic form as

$$\log T_{ij} = a \log O_i + b \log D_j + c \log d_{ij},$$

where T_{ij} is trips from i to j, O_i is the number of trips with i as origin, D_j is the number of trips with j as destination, and d_{ij} is the distance between zones i and j. The model must also be constrained to ensure that the totals for trip origins and destinations are in balance.

Given that a certain number of trips is being taken from origin i to destination j, how are those trips divided among the modes of travel? Models that explain these decisions are called mode split models. Small (1992) provides a detailed discussion of such models. The choice is presumed to be based on differences in time and money costs among the various modes available, but the choice is also influenced by mode-specific features. For example, the private auto is indeed private, but it also must be driven. Public transit is not private, but is driven by an employee.

The final step in the analysis of urban travel demand is to model the choice of route given that a particular mode has been chosen. In the model of mode choice it usually is assumed that there is only oneroute for each mode (with its time and money costs). This is often a reasonable assumption. However, there are situations in which the routes that might be chosen have quite different time and money costs. The choice of tollway versus freeway is a leading example of the case of alternate routes with different time and money costs. Theremainder of this chapter examines this problem in detail.

This discussion began with the statement that a set of travel demand models pertains to a particular time of day. Indeed, the problem of traffic congestion exists because of the concentration of demand in peak periods of the day. Further, in recent decades the total amount of travel, especially by auto, has grown much more rapidly than has the road and highway system. One implication of this growth in demand is that the rush hour period has become longer. It is clear that some people choose to leave for work early, and in some cases employers have altered their schedules to permit employees to try to "beat the traffic." Also, there is evidence that improvements in the urban transportation system lead to a shortening of the rush hour. It is clear that a model of urban travel demand should include the fact that, for at least some people, the time of travel is flexible to some degree.

Two types of models have been developed to address this issue of flexible travel times. The older type of model is a set of conventional demand functions, with a demand function specified for each period during the day. Each period has its own demand function in which travel during that period is a function of its own price during that period and the prices in adjacent periods. The adjacent periods are viewed as substitutes for the time period in question, so reducing the price in one time period will reduce demand in the adjacent time periods. For example, an improvement in a highway will reduce travel times during the peak of the rush hour, increase traffic during the rush hour, and reduce traffic in the adjacent periods. More empirical research is needed to determine the magnitudes of these "cross-price" effects (i.e., the cross-elasticities of demand). This approach is utilized in Chapters 8 through 10 to study optimal congestion tolls with peak period demand.

The second approach has been developed more recently, and it makes the time of departure for the trip a continuous variable. This type of model is discussed extensively by Small (1992). The model is based on the assumption that a cost is imposed on a person who arrives at a time other than the "desired" time. Work begins at 9 A.M. Early arrival means that there is some time spent at work that is neither as productive as regular working hours nor as pleasurable as leisure time at home. The cost of early arrival is a function of the amount of time spent in this state of limbo. The penalty for early arrival at work may not be very much, but the penalty for late arrival can be sizable. The worker can lose pay and, ultimately, be fired for lateness. Commuters know the function that describes the cost of being early and being late. They also know that the time spent to make the trip to work will be shorter if they avoid the peak of the rush hour. They can decide to go early, reduce travel time, and arrive early. Alternatively, they can decide to go later, reduce travel time, and arrive late. They make the choice of departure time, which is a continuous variable, based on a balancing of these two costs; the time cost of travel versus the cost of arriving early (or late). It would seem that more people decide to arrive early than choose to arrive late because of the potentially higher costs of arriving late. While considerations of this nature are implicit in the older peak period demand models, this newer approach provides a more explicit explanation for the timing of urban travel demand.

B. A MODEL OF GENERALIZED TRAVEL COST AND TIME VALUE

We assume that a route is chosen on the basis of what is called generalized travel cost, which combines the time and money costs of a particular route into a single function. The value of time is a critical component of the generalized travel cost function. The commuter selects the route with the lowest generalized cost.

In order to conduct a simple derivation of a commuter's generalized travel cost function, consider a household that consists of only one individual who works at a center of employment. Assume that the individual has a utility function which can be written

$$U = U(X,L,N,C,H), \qquad (1)$$

where X is a composite good, L is land consumption, N is leisure time, C is commuting time, and H is time spent at work. Land consumption and land rent are included in the model to provide a simple rationale for the existence of benefits derived from additional commuting distance. The utility function is ordinal, continuous, real valued, and twice differentiable. Utility is maximized subject to money and time constraints. The Lagrangian is written

$$L^* = U(X,L,N,C,H) + n[wH-X-r(u)L-t(u)] + m(T-N-C-H), \tag{2}$$

where w is the after tax wage, n and m are Lagrange multipliers, u is travel distance to work, r(u) is the rental price of land, and t(u) is the money cost of commuting.

The first-order conditions found by differentiating with respect to X, L, N, H,and u are

$$U_X - n = 0, \tag{3}$$

$$U_L - nr(u) = 0, \tag{4}$$

$$U_N - m = 0, \tag{5}$$

$$U_H + nw - m = 0, \tag{6}$$

and

$$U_c(C_u) - n[r'(u)L+t'(u)] - m(C_u) = 0, \tag{7}$$

respectively, where C_u is partial differentiation of C with respect to u, travel distance. Simple manipulations of these equations yield

$$-r'(u)L = t'(u) + (C_u)[w + (U_H-U_c)/U_X] \tag{8}$$

and

$$-r'(u)L = t'(u) + (C_u)(U_N-U_c)/U_X. \tag{9}$$

These conditions state that the marginal benefit of added commuting distance -r'(u)L equals the marginal cost of commuting distance (i.e., marginal generalized travel cost). Marginal generalized travel cost consists of the marginal money cost t'(u) plus the marginal value of time times C_u ,the time cost of a marginal unit of distance (i.e., the inverse of speed).

The marginal value of commuting time can be expressed either as

$$V' = w + [(U_H-U_c)/U_X], \tag{10}$$

or as

$$V' = (U_N-U_c)/U_X. \tag{11}$$

The former expression is the net cost of giving up a marginal unit of work time, while the latter is the net cost of giving up a unit of leisure time. If we assume that neither commuting time nor work time produces utility, then the marginal value of time reduces to $w = U_N/U_X$, the after tax wage rate.

A large number of empirical studies of the value of commuting time contradict the conclusion that the after-tax wage is the correct value. The large number of estimates reviewed by Bruzelius (1979) and Small (1992) are almost all below 70% of the gross wage, and many are less than 40% of the gross wage. In the context of the model under consideration here, this result has three possible explanations:

- Commuting may be a good, meaning that $U_C/U_X > 0$;
- There may be a constraint imposed on hours of work which makes

$$w > (U_N\text{-}U_H)/U_X; \text{ or}$$

- Work time may produce disutility, meaning that $U_H/U_X < 0$

However, the hypothetical constraint on hours worked implies that workers wish to work more than they do currently. It is not clear why workers should not be able to work more hours if they so wish. Also, while it is possible that there is disutility in work at the margin, it should be realized that $U_H < 0$ means that the individual prefers to have his or her total time budget (the life span) reduced to working the marginal hour at no pay. Obviously the individual would rather have leisure than work at no pay, but it is doubtful that the individual would opt to have his or her life shortened. Thus, if we assume that all uses of time contribute to utility in the relevant range, we are left with the notion that $U_C/U_X > 0$ is the best explanation for the observed empirical results.

It seems reasonable to consider the marginal value of time to be

$$V' = (U_N - U_C)/U_X.$$

This formulation has important implications for the form of the marginal generalized travel cost function. As commuting time increases, the marginal value of time may be expected to increase because it is likely that U_N/U_X, the marginal value of leisure time, rises and that U_C/U_X, the marginal value of commuting time, falls as C increases. Also, an increase in income can be expected to increase U_N/U_X and have an ambiguous effect on U_C/U_X. (For example, it is possible that higher income people own more expensive autos which are more "fun" to drive.) In summary, the basic model of time allocation for commuters presented in this section leads to the hypotheses that the marginal value of travel time may increase with the length of the trip and with income.

It is also worth noting that the slope of the land-rent function can be written simply as

$$r'(u) = -(1/L)[t'(u) + (C_u)(U_N-U_c)/U_x]. \tag{12}$$

This is a version of the well-known condition that the negative slope of the (bid) rent function for a household is equal to marginal transportation cost divided by the amount of land occupied. Similarly, the slope of the (bid) rent function in percentage terms is

$$r'/r = -(1/rL)[t'(u) + (C_u)(U_N-U_c)/U_x]. \tag{13}$$

C. CONCLUSION

This chapter has presented a model of a household in urban space from which we obtain a model of generalized travel cost. We hypothesize that routes are chosen on the basis of generalized travel costs. Generalized travel cost at the margin is a function of

- the marginal monetary cost of distance,
- the time cost of distance at the margin, and
- the marginal value of commuting time.

The monetary cost of distance depends upon vehicle operating costs and tolls paid for the use of the highway. The time cost of distance depends upon the size and quality of the highway facilities and the level of traffic congestion. The marginal value of commuting time is possibly a positive function of income and of the total time spent commuting. These hypotheses regarding the marginal value of commuting time are tested empirically in the next chapter. The hypothesis that routes are chosen on the basis of generalized travel costs is also tested in Chapter 5.

References

Bruzelius, N. 1979, The Value of Travel Time: Theory and Measurement, London: Croom Helm.

Small, K., 1992, Urban Transportation Economics, Chur, Switzerland: Harwood Academic Publishers.

5 AN EMPIRICAL STUDY OF THE CHOICE OF TOLLWAY OR FREEWAY

A. INTRODUCTION

The previous chapter examined the theory of marginal generalized travel cost and the value of time from the perspective of the individual commuter. The purpose of this chapter is to present an empirical study of route choice using data on commuters in the Chicago metropolitan area who had the option of using a tollway or a freeway. The empirical study provides estimates of the value of reductions in commuting time and the responsiveness of commuter choice to changes in tolls and trip times. These empirical estimates of commuter behavior will then be used in subsequent chapters that examine the issue of optimal congestion tolls in the presence of substitute routes.

The empirical study shows that commuters are sensitive both to tolls and to the amount of time that can be saved by taking the tollway. The commuters in the sample revealed that, in 1972, they had an average value of travel time savings of 3.27 cents per minute. The study shows that the value of travel time savings is larger the longer is commuting time. Therefore, holding the toll and time saved on the tollway constant, commuters with larger travel times are more likely to take the tollway. In short, tollway users will tend to be long distance commuters. Commuters with shorter travel times have lower values of travel time savings and will therefore tend to respond to tolls by seeking out free routes. Another finding of the study is that the value of time saved does not vary with household income.

B. A STOCHASTIC MODEL OF INDIVIDUAL CHOICE

This section presents a simple version of the stochastic binary choice model as developed by Domencich and McFadden (1975). Assume that the total generalized cost of the commuting trip on route i for the jth person is

$$GC_{ij} = M_{ij} + (V_{ij}/C_{ij})C_{ij} + u_{ij}, \qquad (1)$$

where M_{ij} is the money cost, C_{ij} is commuting time, (V_{ij}/C_{ij}) is the average value of commuting time (with V_{ij} = the total value of commuting time), and u_{ij} is the random component of generalized cost. As Hausman and Wise (1978) have discussed, there are two possible explanations for the random component. It may be that individuals behave randomly so that the individual does not make the same choice when repeatedly faced with the same choice set. The second, and better, explanation is to argue that u_{ij} represents variables that are not observed by the researcher but influence the generalized cost. Equation (1) is a translation of the equation for marginal generalized travel cost from Chapter 4.

For the problem at hand the choices for the commuter are only two; the commuter may select to drive on a free street or highway, or to drive on a tollway. If the tollway is chosen, the commuter saves time at the expense of paying a toll. The commuter will choose the tollway if

$$GC_{fj} > GC_{tj}, \tag{2}$$

where f and t refer to freeway and tollway, respectively. Substituting for GC_{fj} and GC_{tj} from equation (1) produces

$$u_{fj} - u_{tj} > (M_{tj}-M_{fj}) + [(V_{tj}/C_{tj})C_{tj} - (V_{fj}/C_{fj})C_{fj}]. \tag{3}$$

The probability that the tollway is chosen can thus be written

$$P_t = \text{Prob}\{u_{fj}-u_{tj} > (M_{tj}-M_{fj}) + [(V_{tj}/C_{tj})C_{tj} - (V_{fj}/C_{fj})C_{fj}]\}, \tag{4}$$

or

$$P_t = 1 - F\{(M_{tj}-M_{fj})+[(V_{tj}/C_{tj})C_{tj} - (V_{fj}/C_{fj})C_{fj}]\}, \tag{5}$$

where F{ } is the cumulative distribution function of $(u_{fj}-u_{tj})$. In this problem F{ } is assumed to be a normal distribution with mean zero. Because 1 - F(x) = F(-x), equation (5) becomes

$$P_t = F\{-(M_{tj}-M_{fj}) - [(V_{tj}/C_{tj})C_{tj} - (V_{fj}/C_{fj})C_{fj}]\}. \tag{6}$$

Now consider the functional form for (V_{ij}/C_{ij}), the average value of commuting time. It is assumed that the average value of time is possibly a linear function of commuting time and income, or

$$(V_{ij}/C_{ij}) = v_0 + v_1 C_{ij} + v_2 Y_{ij}, \tag{7}$$

where Y_{ij} is income of the jth person if the ith route is chosen,and v_0, v_1, and v_2 are the parameters of the function. This function implies that the marginal value of time is

$$V'_{ij} = v_0 + 2v_1 Cij + v_2 Y_{ij}. \tag{8}$$

Substitution of equation (7) for the tollway and freeway users into equation (6) yields

$$P_t = F\{-(M_{tj}-M_{fj})-v_0(C_{tj}-C_{fj})-v_1(C^2{}_{tj}-C^2{}_{fj})-v_2(Y_{tj}C_{tj}-Y_{fj}C_{fj})\}. \tag{9}$$

Now variables $(M_{tj}-M_{fj})$ and $(C_{tj}-C_{fj})$ are simply the differences in money and time costs of the two routes; the variables that are conventional to this type of analysis. The variables $(C^2{}_{ij}-C^2{}_{fj})$and $(Y_{tj}C_{tj}-Y_{fj}C_{fj})$ are the additions to the specification implied by the hypotheses discussed in Chapter 4 that the average value of time varies with trip time and income.

Given the F{ } is a normal distribution, probit analysis can be used as the estimation technique. The convention in probit analysis is to assume that the underlying error term (or threshold level) is distributed as a standard normal variable (unit variance). Thus the distribution function to be estimated is that of $(u_{fj}-u_{tj})/s$, where s is the standard error of $(u_{fj}-u_{tj})$. Equation (9) becomes

$$P_t = F\{-(1/s)(M_{tj}-M_{fj}) - (v_0/s)(C_{tj}-C_{fj})- (v_1/s)(C^2{}_{tj}-C^2{}_{fj}) - (v_2/s)(Y_{tj}C_{tj}-Y_{fj}C_{fj})\}, \tag{10}$$

where F{ } now has a unit variance. This equation is estimated.

The function for the value of time can be obtained from the estimate of equation (10). For example, if the average value of time is specified simply to be v_0, then an estimate of v_0 is obtained by dividing the coefficient of $(C_{tj}-C_{fj})$ by the coefficient of $(M_{tj}-M_{fj})$; i.e., the estimate of v_0 is found as

$$v_0 = (v_0/s)/(1/s).$$

Similarly, if the average value of time is assumed to be

$$v_0 + v_1 C_{ij},$$

then the estimate of this function is found as

$$[(v_0/s) + (v_1/s)]/(1/s).$$

The marginal value of time is estimated in this case as

$$[(v_0/s) + 2(v_1/s)]/(1/s).$$

Similar computations are performed if the average value of time is as shown in equation (7).

C. THE DATA AND EMPIRICAL RESULTS

The data used involve a choice situation for commuters who drive a private auto to work and who do not carry any passengers. The commuters have the choice of taking a tollway (a faster trip) or using free streets and highways (a slower trip). Individuals who face this choice are not difficult to find because, assuming people value their time, tollways should be less congested than freeways. Commuters filled out a questionnaire at their suburban places of work. If the commuter used the tollway, he was asked to specify the amount of time saved. If the commuter used the freeway, he was asked to specify the amount of the toll that he avoids (if a tollway is relevant to him) and how much time is added to the trip to avoid the toll. Some 900 persons at 17 different firms filled out the questionnaire, and 115 persons indicated that they face the tollway-freeway choice (and responded to the other questions). The sample of 115 is used for the results reported here. The survey was conducted in May 1972 for the Northwest Conference of Mayors, a group of mayors from towns in the northwestern area of Cook County, Illinois (Chicago metropolitan area).

The variables used in the analysis are:

C_{tj} = trip time for journey to work if tollway is chosen (minutes),
C_{fj} = trip time for journey to work if freeway is chosen (minutes),
M_{tj}-M_{fj} = the toll on the tollway (cents),
Y_{fj} = household income (cents/day), and
Y_{tj} = household income (cents/day) minus the toll on thetollway.

The income variables used in the analysis are not net of vehicle operating costs because these data are not available. However,the correlation between income and trip time on the freeway (one measure highly correlated with trip length in miles and operating costs) is low (R^2 = 0.008). Thus the failure to adjust income for vehicle operating costs essentially creates a minor problem of random measurement error in the income variable, which is probably already subject to some measurement error.

The analysis is conducted assuming that the toll is the only difference in monetary expenditures between the tollway and freeway choices. This assumption is reasonably accurate because the tollway users purchase a somewhat faster trip, but not a shorter trip. In the area of the study there are always parallel free streets and highways in the close vicinity of the tollway. Also, the toll of 30 cents or more was, as of 1972, large in relationship to possible differences in vehicle operating costs associated with differences in speed. Furthermore, drivers probably do not perceive these small differences in operating costs. Means and standard deviations for the basic variables are shown in Table 5-1.

Table 5-1
Route Choice Data:
Variables, Means, and Standard Deviations

	Mean	Standard Deviation
Tollway user	.40	
Trip time if freeway is chosen (min.)	48.15	18.47
Toll if tollway is chosen (cents)	40.04	20.91
Household income (dollars/yr)	15,330	5758
Time saved if tollway is chosen (min.)	10.64	8.04
Sample size	115	

Estimates of alternative formulations of equation (10) are shown in Table 5-2. In column 1 only the toll on the tollway and $(C_{tj}-C_{fj})$, negative the amount of time saved on the tollway, are included as independent variables. Both variables have coefficients that are highly statistically significant, and the value of a reduction in commuting time is estimated to be 3.27cents per minute, or $1.96 per hour in 1972. This figure is $6.50 in 1997 dollars. However, the

Table 5-2
Probit Analysis of Route Choice
(Dependent variable is 1 for tollway, 0 for freeway.)

Independent Variable	(1)	(2)	(3)
Toll on tollway	-.0213	-.0259	-.0259
	(4.07)	(4.47)	(4.46)
Time saved on tollway x -1	-.0697	.0481	.0474
	(3.86)	(1.38)	(1.03)
$C^2_{tj} - C^2_{fj}$	--	-.0012	-.0012
		(3.97)	(3.97)
$Y_{tj}C_{tj} - Y_{fj}C_{fj}$	--	--	$-.2\text{x}10^{-7}$
			(0.02)
Log of likelihood function	-70.159	-60.817	-60.817
Sample size	115	115	115

Unsigned t values are in parentheses.

addition of the other variables implied by equation (7) for the average value of time, the results of which are shown in columns 2 and 3 of Table 5-2, significantly increases the log of the likelihood function from -70.16 to -60.82.

This change is statistically significant at the 99% level. In particular, from the results in columns 2 and 3, it is clear that the only additional variable that makes a significant contribution is $(C^2_{tj}-C^2_{fj})$. The other variable which incorporates the hypothesis that the average value of time is a function of income is not at all significant.

Recall that the average value of commuting time is estimated to be \$1.96 per hour (in 1972 dollars), and the econometric results for the sample also show that this value does not vary with household income. How does this value of time compare to the wage rate? Hourly wage data are not available for the workers in the sample, but data from County Business Patterns show that the average hourly wage for the first quarter of 1972 was \$3.98 per hour in the two suburban counties adjacent to the area of the study. The value of travel time saving is 49% of this before-tax wage rate. Given that the value of commuting time is estimated not to vary with household income, it is reasonable to conclude that the value of time found in this study is at least 50% of the average after-tax wage rate, a result that is consistent with previous studies. Our finding is in rather sharp contrast to the results obtained in a recent study by Calfee and Winston (1998). Their finding is that the value of commuting time is only 19% of the before-tax wage rate.

As discussed above, the estimates in column 2 can be used to form the expression for the marginal value of commuting time,which can be written in 1972 values as

$$V'_{ij} = [(-0.0481 - 0.0024C_{ij})/0.0259] \text{ cents/min.}$$

Evaluated at the mean of C_{fj} of 48.15 minutes, the marginal value of time is 2.61 cents per minute. More importantly, perhaps, the marginal value of time increases by .0927 cents per minute as commuting time increases by one minute. In other words, two commuters who travel 30 or 60 minutes for the journey to work value a one-minute reduction in commuting time at .92 and 3.70 cents per minute, respectively.

D. IMPLICATIONS FOR CHOICE BEHAVIOR

The results in Table 5-2 can be used to describe how commuters make the choice between tollway and freeway routes in the area of the study. Throughout this discussion we shall make use of the function estimated in column 2 of Table 5-2, which is

$$P_t = F\{-.0259(M_{tj}-M_{fj}) + .0481(C_{tj}-C_{fj}) - .0012(C^2_{tj}-C^2_{fj})\},$$

where F{ } is a unit normal probability distribution function with a unit normal probability density function f{ } that has a mean of zero. These assumptions mean that F{0} = 0.5; for example, if the freeway and the tollway have identical money and time costs, then the probability of choosing the tollway is 0.5. Note that the function for P_t includes the toll and the trip times on both the tollway and freeway routes. An increase in the toll on the tollway will tend to reduce P_t, of course, but the reduction in traffic on the tollway may cause trip times on the tollway to fall and trip times on the freeways to increase as commuters seek out alternate routes. The net effect of these changes on P_t can be estimated via this equation.

One method for examining how the equation works is to insert the mean values for the three independent variables and computethe P_t implied. The mean values are:

$M_{tj}-M_{fj}$	40.04 cents
$C_{tj}-C_{fj}$	-10.64 minutes
$C^2_{tj}-C^2_{fj}$	-1026.06 minutes squared

These values imply that P_t = F{-.283}, or .283 standard deviations below the mean, which translates into a probability of choosing the tollway of .389. The actual probability of choosing the tollway for the members of the sample is .40, so the model comes very close to replicating the behavior of the commuters in the study as a group.

The model says that, starting with a "tollway" with no toll ,a tollway and a freeway for which travel times are equal, and an equal distribution of commuters between the two, the imposition of a toll of 40.04 cents, coupled with a time saving of 10.64 minutes, will reduce the proportion of commuters who take the tollway by .111 (from .50 to .389). Table 5-3 is drawn up to show the effects of various combinations of toll and travel time differences on the split between tollway and freeway use. It is assumed that trip time on the freeway is 40 minutes. A different table must be computed for other values of trip time. The table shows that, for example, a toll of 20 cents and a time difference of 10 minutes generate a probability of taking the tollway of .446.

Table 5-3
Probability of Choosing the Tollway
(Assuming travel time on freeway is 40 minutes.)

		Toll (cents)					
		0	10	20	30	40	50
Time	0	.500	.397	.301	.218	.149	.097
Saved	5	.587	.484	.382	.289	.208	.141
	10	.649	.550	.446	.347	.257	.181
	15	.685	.589	.486	.384	.290	.208
	20	.698	.603	.500	.397	.302	.229

E. SUMMARY

Previous studies of urban commuters have not concentrated on the choice of tollway versus freeway. This choice is one which must be understood if we wish to consider the policy of imposing congestion tolls in a world in which it may not be possible to levy a toll on some portions of the highway and road network. The model of generalized cost minimization used in this chapter is based on the hypothesis that commuters regard a tollway and a freeway with equal generalized cost as perfect substitutes. The study of commuters in suburban Chicago who faced this choice shows that, as hypothesized, they are sensitive both to the toll and to the time that can be saved by taking the less congested tollway. The study finds that the value of time saved is larger the longer is commuting time. Therefore, holding the toll and time saved constant, commuters who have longer travel times are more likely to opt for the tollway. Also, the finding that the average value of commuting time is at least 50% of the average after-tax wage rate is consistent with previous studies.

References

Calfee, J. and C. Winston, 1998, The value of automobile travel time: Implications for congestion policy, Journal of Public Economics 69, 83-102.

Domencich, T and D. McFadden, 1975, Urban Travel Demand, Amsterdam: North Holland.

Hausman, J. and D. Wise, 1978, A conditional probit model for qualitative choice: Discrete decisions recognizing interdependence and heterogeneous preferences, Econometrica 46, 403-426.

PART III

CONGESTION PRICING IN THE SHORT RUN

6 CONGESTION PRICING IN THE SHORT RUN: THE BASIC MODEL

A. INTRODUCTION

The purpose of this chapter is to present briefly the conventional rationale for congestion pricing. The basic model dates back to the first edition of Pigou's "Economics of Welfare" (1920), and it was discussed by Knight (1924), Beckman, McGuire, and Winsten (1955), and others. The analysis begins with the basic production function model of highway traffic flow presented in Chapter 2, turns the production function into a cost function, adds a demand function, and generates traffic equilibria. The model pertains to a single route for a particular time of day. We assume either that the route in question is the only route, or that any other route that exists is not subject to congestion. As we emphasize in the next four chapters, we believe that neither assumption is tenable.

The model presented here leads to the conclusion that economic efficiency will be improved by a congestion toll that equals the difference between the marginal cost and the average cost of the marginal trip on the route. This difference is equal to the marginal congestion cost attributable to the marginal trip. The marginal congestion cost is, of course, a classic example of a negative externality.

The chapter concludes with a critical examination of a recent article by Evans (1992) that presented a diagrammatic approach to highway congestion. The problem with the Evans model is that it is based on a misspecification of the quantity that is demanded by highway users. Following Else (1981), Evans argues that the true demand curve relates traffic density to the cost of the journey, but we argue that road users demand miles of travel, which is (from Chapter 2) equivalent to traffic volume. Indeed, we demonstrated in Chapter 2 that traffic density is a measure of the variable input driver and vehicle time used to produce travel. Further detailed study of the Else (1981)/Evans (1992) model is contained in Chapter 15 and in the appendix to this book. Traffic density can be a relevant measure of demand for trips if all of the trips are being taken simultaneously.

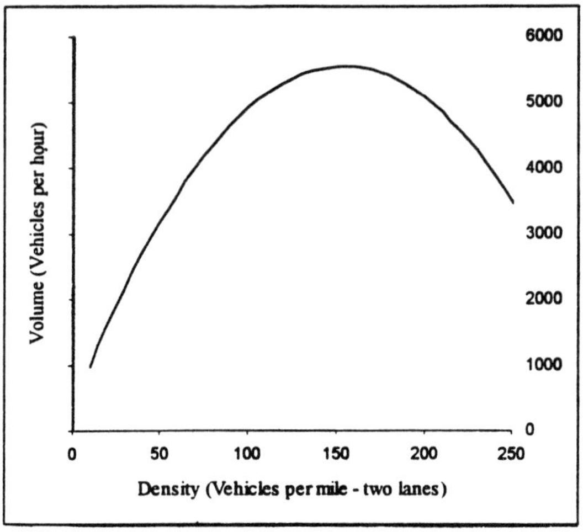

Figure 6-1
The Fundamental Diagram of Traffic

B. THE STANDARD MODEL OF ROAD CONGESTION AND TOLLS

The standard model is one in which average cost, marginal cost, and demand price are depicted as functions of traffic volume. (Actually, some presentations show two levels of average cost for a given amount of traffic volume. To be mathematically precise, average and marginal cost are related to traffic volume.) Recall from Chapter 2 that average variable cost measured in units of time (ignoring vehicle operating cost) is the inverse of speed;

$$AVC = (1/S) = D/V, \tag{1}$$

where S is average speed, D is traffic density, and V is traffic volume per unit of time. Average variable cost in units of time can be converted to money by using the average value of time. Then average vehicle operating costs can be added to obtain average trip costs as they depend upon traffic volume.

The Fundamental Diagram of Traffic (repeated as Figure 6-1) dictates the shape of the AVC curve. As traffic density rises from zero, traffic volume increases. As shown in Figure 6-2, initially D and V rise in proportion and AVC is constant. Traffic moves at the speed limit. However, at some level of density, the increase in traffic volume for an increase in density is less than proportional. Speed begins to fall with increases in density, so AVC rises as speed falls. If density rises to the point of maximum traffic volume shown in Figure 6-1, then additional increases in density reduce traffic volume. This means that two levels of average variable cost are associated with one traffic volume. Figure 6-2 shows that the AVC curve bends back (turns from positive to negative slope) at that point of maximum traffic volume.

The next step is to derive the marginal cost of traffic volume, given the average variable cost. Marginal cost in the short run is defined as the change in total variable cost as output increases by one unit;

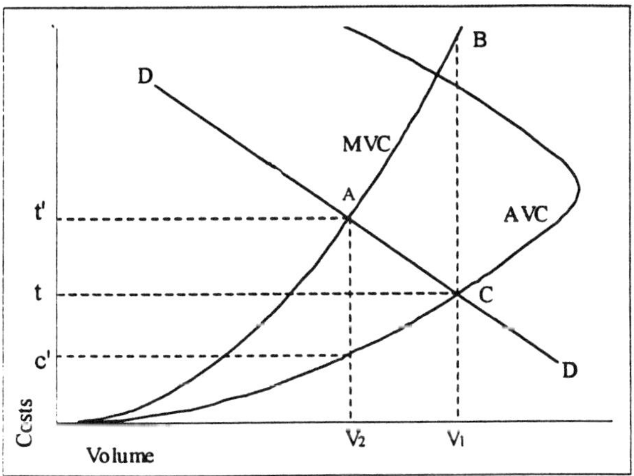

Figure 6-2
Cost, Demand, and Traffic Volume

$$MC = dVC/dV = d(AVC x V)/dV. \tag{2}$$

This marginal change consists of two parts, so that

$$MC = AVC + V(dAVC/dV). \tag{3}$$

This is a crucial result; it says that the marginal cost of output (traffic volume) is equal to average variable cost plus the change in average variable cost with respect to traffic volume times the traffic volume. Average variable cost rises as traffic volume rises (up to the maximum traffic volume), and this increase in cost (arising from the drop in speed) is multiplied by the total traffic volume. This term is the difference between AVC and MC, i.e.,

$$MC - AVC = V(dAVC/dV). \tag{4}$$

The marginal cost curve for the positively-sloped portion of the AVC curve is also plotted in Figure 6-2. The marginal cost curve for the negatively-sloped portion of the AVC curve (the backward bending portion) is not shown because it falls into the negative quadrant.

Now consider the external cost involved in traffic congestion. An external cost involves a cost that is imposed directly on others by, in this case, an individual traveler. An increase in traffic volume has a cost equal to the marginal cost shown above, but the individual traveler does not pay all of that cost. In fact, the individual traveler makes the trip at average variable cost. In the absence of a toll, this is the cost that the traveler sees and is the price that the traveler uses to make the decision whether to travel on the highway at that time. The external cost is therefore the difference between marginal cost and average variable cost; or

$$\text{marginal external cost} = V(dAVC/dV).$$

The external cost is the increase in cost imposed on each traveler (dAVC/dV) times the number of travelers (V). Recall that AVC is indeed the cost that each traveler sees.

The demand for trips on the highway during the time period in question is also shown on Figure 6-2 as DD. As discussed in Chapter 2, quantity demanded is also measured as traffic volume, and is expressed as a function of the cost of the trip that must be borne by the individual traveler. Travelers as a group will generate an equilibrium traffic volume of V_1, where the demand curve intersects the average variable cost. At this point the marginal benefit of the trip, as measured by the height of the demand curve at V_1, is just equal to the cost borne by the last traveler, which is AVC at volume V_1.

We can see immediately that V_1 is an inefficient level of output because the marginal cost of the last unit of output exceeds its marginal benefit (MB). In fact, the marginal cost exceeds the marginal benefit by the size of the marginal external cost, or

$$MC - MB = MC - AVC = V_1(dAVC/dV). \qquad (5)$$

The efficient level of output in Figure 6-2 is V_2, where the marginal benefit of the output equals the marginal cost, which includes the marginal external cost. If the level of traffic volume could be cut back from V_1 to V_2, a dead-weight loss equal to triangle ABC would be eliminated. The resources devoted to producing trips V_1-V_2 (driver and vehicle time and operating expenses) can be better used in some other pursuits. What are those other pursuits? They perhaps include producing trips at other times of day, or they may include other uses of travelers' time entirely.

For many years urban economists have advocated the use of tolls to cut back on traffic congestion. Note that the efficient level of traffic volume in Figure 6-2, which is V_2, still involves traffic congestion in the sense that the marginal external cost is not zero. A toll equal to the marginal external cost at efficient traffic volume V_2 would make the cost borne by the marginal traveler equal to the true marginal cost of that person's trip. The toll is shown as amount tt', which is expressed in monetary units. Toll tt' is an efficient toll provided that travelers who are induced not to use the highway at the time in question do not create more traffic congestion at some other location or at some other time, and provided that the collection of the toll can be accomplished costlessly. Note that the efficient toll tt' is larger than the reduction in the average variable cost of producing travel tc'. The toll must be larger than the reduction in average variable cost so that the price of travel rises and travel volume is reduced. Yang and Huang (1998) have shown that the same result holds for efficient tolls in a general road network. The efficient toll in each link i in the network is still

$$t_i = V_i(dAVC_i/dV_i).$$

However, as we show in great detail in Chapters 7 and 8, this result does not hold if efficient tolls cannot be charged on all links in the network.

The argument for the use of toll tt' in Figure 6-2 is that it is a policy which creates an efficient allocation of resources. The efficient toll produces an allocation of resources that is Pareto efficient. A reallocation of resources (away from traffic volume V_2) cannot be accomplished without reducing the welfare of at least one person, while holding the welfare of all other people constant. For example, if traffic volume were to increase beyond V_2, the costs of the additional trips would exceed the benefits of those trips. Suppose that the value of the benefits of the added trip are $2.00 to the traveler, but that the cost of the added trip is $2.10. Further suppose that the consumer of the added trip actually pays $2.00, so that this person remains at the same level of utility as before. However, the additional cost of the trip of $.10 must have been imposed on someone, who is worse off by that amount. The movement away from Pareto-efficient traffic volume V_2 to inefficient traffic volume V_1 thus involved imposing dead-weight loss of triangle ABC on the group.

The argument in favor of the toll tt' is somewhat more complex if we take as given traffic volume V_1, which is an inefficient allocation of resources. The imposition of the toll means that toll revenue (in amount tt' times V_2) will be collected from those travelers who continue to travel on the highway at the time in question. These travelers have, of course, experienced an increase in the price of their trips in order to accomplish the reduction in traffic volume from V_1 to V_2. The toll has reduced traffic volume and eliminated the dead-weight loss of area ABC, but it has also made the remaining travelers worse off unless some form of compensation can be arranged for them. We suppose that no form of compensation can be arranged because we think that no compensation could be paid to congestion toll payers that could not be seen to be tied to tollway use. If compensation were tied to tollway use, the compensation would defeat the purpose of having the toll in the first place. The fact is that those who continue to use the highway during the peak period (and pay the toll) are worse off with the toll regime than without it. What is the argument in favor of a policy that makes some people worse off?

The argument is that the benefits of the policy outweigh the costs; there is a potential Pareto improvement. Hypothetically it is possible that those upon whom costs are imposed can be compensated out of the benefits of the program, with something left over. Those upon whom costs are imposed are not in fact compensated, but more than sufficient benefits exist to do the job. The benefits of the congestion toll policy consist of the elimination of deadweight-loss area ABC. Because the toll causes a reduction in traffic volume, a reduction in the cost of producing the trips results. This cost reduction is the reduction in AVC of amount tc' times the traffic volume V_2. This reduction in AVC comes in the form of lower travel times, and it means that the travelers (and their vehicles) are available for other activities. Real resources are saved. At the same time the tollway users pay toll tt', which means that the price that they pay has increased by amount c't'

The critical point is that the real cost of traffic volume V_2 has declined at the same time toll revenue tt' times V_2 has been collected from the tollway users. The toll revenue is only money that has been redistributed from tollway users to the tollway authority (i.e., the government, or society at large). In the process real resources in the form of person and vehicle time have been freed up to engage in other activities with economic value. The toll revenue is not a cost to society as a whole, but only a redistribution of income. If society is neutral about the net effect of this redistribution of income, then the congestion toll policy generates net benefits of area ABC. Obviously more than enough toll revenue exists to compensate the tollway users for their loss of c't' times V_2. The problem is that this compensation cannot be paid without destroying the incentive to conserve on the use of the congested highway.

The lessons of this section are standard applications of welfare economics, but these basic points are not always applied clearly. A recent study of the value of travel time by Calfee and Winston (1998, p. 83) concludes that, "It appears that even high-income commuters ... simply do not value travel time savings enough to benefit substantially from tolls." Calfee and Winston (1998) are concerned with the lack of political support for congestion toll policy. The basic idea of a congestion toll is, of course, to cut back on traffic at critical times and places by making the marginal commuter who pays the toll worse off. It could be that a some commuters have a high value of time and benefit from the combination of toll and reduction in travel time. But congestion toll policy by its very nature cannot be "sold" to commuters in general by claiming that they will be better off. Society will be better off if we regard a potential Pareto improvement as making society better off. Calfee and Winston (1998, pp. 93-94) discuss some simulation experiments in which, in one case, an optimal toll of 27 cents per mile leads on average to a 13 minute travel time reduction for a commute of 60 minutes. This example is based on a value of time of 50% of the wage rate. If commuting distance is 25 miles (typical for 60 minutes), then the toll is $6.75. Only commuters with a value of time of 52 cents per minute ($31.15 per hour) or more will benefit from this combination of toll and time saving. If commuters value time savings at 50% of the wage, then a value to time of $31.15 per hour translates into an annual salary of about $125,000.

C. HYPERCONGESTION EQUILIBRIA

Figure 6-2 depicts the standard "backward bending" average variable cost curve that corresponds to the short-run production function with a region of negative marginal product for a variable input. The purpose of this section is to consider cases of traffic equilibria that include the backward bending portion of the average variable cost curve -- the cases known as hypercongestion.

It is helpful to assume that the highway in question is a small link in a very large urban highway system. Assume that this highway is only one of several routes that can be used by travelers. In other words, the demand for the services of the highway in question are perfectly elastic at equilibrium cost. Furthermore, following Knight (1924), it is assumed for simplicity that the alternative routes are not congested (and that traffic diverted from or to the highway in question will not change the time cost on those other routes).

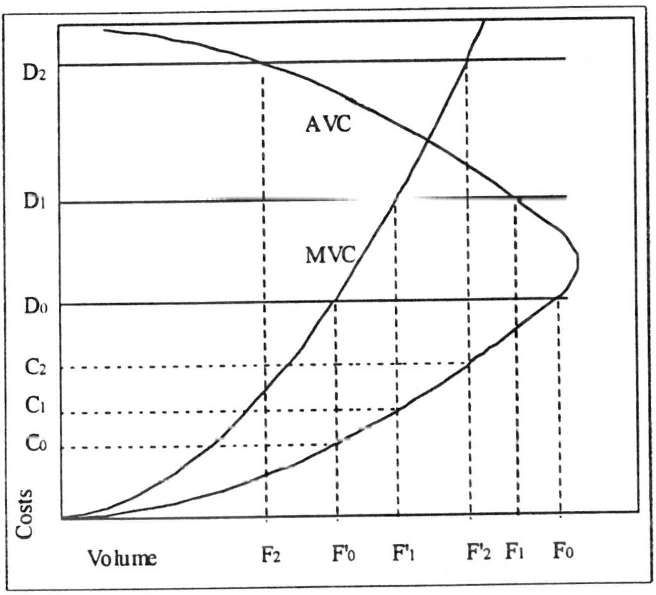

Figure 6-3
Hypercongestion Equilibria

Three cases for demand are of interest and are shown in Figure 6-3. If the demand for traffic flow on the highway is D_0, the standard textbook model of traffic congestion applies. Congestion toll D_0 - C_0 will produce an efficient allocation of traffic; traffic amount F_0 - F'_0 will be diverted to other routes. The congestion toll produces a welfare gain because the toll revenue simply represents a redistribution of money income from the users of the highway in question to others, but these users gain a real resource - their own time (and vehicle time, as well) with a value equal to the toll revenue.

Consider demand curve D_1. At this relatively high cost level the highway in question is operating at a high level of density, and traffic flow F_1 is below capacity. In this case a congestion toll equal to D_1 - C_1 will induce highway users to equate demand to marginal cost, and traffic flow F'_1 is the result. The highway in question produces a smaller output ($F'_1 < F_1$) at a lower average cost. Given the previous assumptions, the decrease in output on the highway does not change the cost of travel on any other route. As before, the toll revenue is simply a redistribution of money income from the users of the highway depicted to others, and thus constitutes no net benefit. The welfare gain arises from the saving of driver and vehicle time with value equal to the toll revenue.

Lastly, consider demand curve D_2. At this very high cost level the highway in question is operating at a very high level of density, and traffic flow F_2 is far below capacity. A congestion toll of D_2 - C_2 will induce traffic flow of F'_2. The highway produces a larger output ($F'_2 > F_2$) at a lower average cost. As we have assumed, the increase in output on the highway does not change the cost of travel on other routes. As before, the toll revenue is just a redistribution of money income from users to others and constitutes no net benefit. The welfare gain once again arises from the saving of driver and vehicle time.

Knight (1924) pointed out that a private owner of the highway depicted in Figure 6-3 would set a toll equal to the efficient congestion toll. To see this note that toll revenue TR can be written

$$TR = F(D_i - AVC), \tag{6}$$

where D_i is equal to D_0, D_1, or D_2. Maximization of TR proceeds as follows:

$$dTR/dF = D_i - AVC - F(dAVC/dF) = 0, \text{ or} \tag{7}$$

$$D_i = AVC + F(dAVC/dF) = MC. \tag{8}$$

$$\text{Toll} = F(dAVC/dF).$$

However, the specific model used by Knight (1924) should be used with caution because it assumes that there is no congestion on other routes. This assumption is relaxed in Chapters 7-10.

D. HYPERCONGESTION ON THE EISENHOWER EXPRESSWAY

Do highways really operate in the region of negative marginal product of the variable input? Some prominent transporation economists such as Arnott (1990), Small (1992), Chu and Small (1997), and Yang and Huang (1998) argue that urban highways that seem to be operating in the region of negative marginal product of the variable input (i.e., backward bending average variable cost) are actually highways with bottlenecks causing traffic jams upstream from the bottlenecks. They argue that, if we could remove the bottlenecks, the backward bending average variable cost curve would not be observed. The purpose of this section is to present some clear and simple empirical results from the Eisenhower Expressway in metropolitan Chicago, a road that is reasonably free of bottleneck problems. The data used here were also studied in Chapter 3. Some simpler empirical results are discussed briefly here because they show clearly that traffic flow declines as traffic density (measured as the percentage of the highway occupied during an hour) rises above a critical level.

As we noted in Chapter 3, the Eisenhower Expressway runs a distance of 14 miles from downtown Chicago to the West. The highway has four lanes in each direction for the first seven miles, and three lanes thereafter. This study considers only the outbound side of the highway, and concentrates on its three-lane portion. At its western end the highway splits into two sections, each with two lanes. Each of these two sections then leads almost immediately into various options with more lanes. In short, the three-lane portion of the Eisenhower is not subject to a downstream bottleneck problem. Indeed, the bottleneck is located upstream where the highway narrows from four to three lanes. In addition, traffic lights on the entrance ramps are used to control entry to the three-lane portion of the highway used in this study.

Traffic flow and density are monitored by the Illinois Department of Transportation (IDOT) at six stations during the morning and afternoon rush periods. The monitoring stations are located about 2.5 miles apart, and three of the stations are located along the three-lane portion of the highway. Traffic flow per hour is recorded along with occupancy, the percentage of time that a detector is occupied by vehicles. IDOT provided the data on traffic flow and occupancy for the week of Monday, May 2 to Friday, May 6, 1994. This was a week in which there was no rain or other weather conditions that impeded traffic. Hourly data for 5 AM to 10 AM and 2 PM to 7 PM were provided for the three monitoring stations, yielding a total of 30 observations on outbound flow and occupancy per day for the three-lane portion of the highway.

The mean traffic flow for the morning hours ws 5165 vehicles per hour (or 1722 per lane per hour), and the mean occupancy was 22.0%. The afternoon hours had a mean traffic flow of 5272 vehicles per hour (1757 per lane per hour) and a mean occupancy of 25.6%. In other words, traffic flow and occupancy were only slightly lower in the morning hours compared to the afternoon hours. The Eisenhower Expressway provides access to the areas of rapid employment growth in west-suburban DuPage County. The range of traffic flow was 4048 to 6235 vehicles per hour, and the range of occupancy was 12.80% to 37.70%. A plot of the data shows clearly that traffic volume rises with occupancy, reaches a maximum at an occupancy rate of about 22%, and then declines.

Regression results (corrected for heteroskedasticity) are as follows:

$$\begin{array}{l} \text{Vol} = -18{,}008.5 - 522.38\ \text{Occ} + 11{,}393.7\ \ln(\text{Occ}), \\ \qquad\qquad (11.3) \quad (15.2) \qquad\qquad (14.8) \end{array}$$

where Vol = traffic volume per hour, Occ = occupancy rate for that hour, unsigned t values are in parentheses, $R^2 = .614$, and the sample size is 150. The estimated equation implies that

$$\text{dVol/dOcc} = -522.38 + 11{,}393.7/\text{Occ}.$$

Therefore, traffic volume is at a maximum of 5718 vehicles per hour where the occupancy rate is 21.8%. The mean occupancy rate for morning and afternoon rush periods combined was 23.8%. At an occupancy rate of 30% the estimated traffic volume is 5072, and at an occupancy rate of 37% the estimated traffic volume falls to 3808 vehicles per hour (only 1269 vehicles per lane per hour).

The data on the morning and afternoon rush periods for a typical week on the Eisenhower Expressway show that this particular facility was operating in the region of negative marginal produce more than 50% of these time periods. The section of the highway that was studied was selected to minimize the possibility that a bottleneck was causing the slowdown in traffic.

E. THE EVANS MODEL OF TRAFFIC CONGESTION

The recent article by Evans (1992) is a critique of the basic model that is being presented in this book, so it is necessary to respond to that criticism. Evans agrees that traffic flow is a function of traffic density as in Figure 6-1. However, he argues that the demand for travel is property expressed as a demand for traffic density rather than traffic flow. Evans (1992, p. 212) states that

> "But whereas consumers choose whether to buy goods given the price, they do not choose traffic flow given the price. The traffic flow is an endogenous variable resulting from the characteristics of the road and the interactions among road users. They actually make a choice whether, given the cost of a journey, they should put their vehicles on the road. Thus the decision to undertake a journey affects the number of vehicles on the road, or density, directly and traffic flow only indirectly. So the true demand curve relates traffic density (the number of vehicles on the road) to the

cost of the journey, including the time costs imposed by congestion."

As we discussed in Chapter 2, we maintain that there are two demand curves; the consumer of travel demands miles of travel, and the demand for traffic density is a derived demand for the variable input; driver and vehicle time. The decision to place your vehicle on the road is the decision to employ you and your vehicle in the business of producing miles of travel. This decision is determined by the productivity of these (joint) inputs, which is the average speed on the highway.

In this section we compare the Evans (1992) model to our model, which we regard as the standard approach in the case of steady-state traffic flow. We can write out our basic model in equation form as

$F = F(D)$ (short-run production function),

$MPD = F'(D)$ (marginal product of traffic density),

$APD = F/D = S$ (average product of traffic density),

$MCF = w/MPD$ (marginal cost of traffic flow),

$AVCF = w/APD = wS$ (average variable cost of flow),

$Fd = Fd(AVCF) = Fd(wS)$ (demand for traffic flow),

where all notation is obvious except that w is the cost of a unit of driver and vehicle time (i.e., a wage rate). If it is assumed that $w = w^*$, a constant, then the set of six equations can be solved by first setting

$$F(D) = Fd(w^*S).$$

The equilibrium rate of traffic flow $F^*(D)$ determines D and S (through $F=DS$), which in turn determine MPD and MCF.

Evans (1992) argues that the model should be specified as

$F = F(D)$,

$Fd = Fd(D)$ (demand as a function of density),

$MCD = c(D)$ (marginal cost of density), and

$AVCD = C(D)/D$ (average cost of density),

where c(D) is marginal cost and C(D) is total variable cost. As we have argued, this approach is inconsistent with the notion that the service being provided by the highway is the traffic flow, which is same type of output measure that is used conventionally in the economic analysis of production. The Evans (1992) model can be justified as a model in which there is a demand for trips of equal length over a time period that varies with traffic density. The implications of this approach are explored in depth in Chapter 15 and in the appendix to this book.

F. CONCLUSION

This chapter has presented the standard model of congestion pricing in the short run in order to focus on both the equilibrium and welfare properties of the model. We see that the normal case of imposition of an efficient congestion toll on a highway that has no toll creates a potential Pareto improvement in welfare. But in all likelihood a congestion toll will not generate an actual Pareto improvement because the drivers who continue to use the highway in question will pay a higher cost for use of the highway. This likelihood no doubt is an important source of opposition to congestion tolls among urban commuters, unless the toll can provide the driver with access to additional road capacity, a topic that is examined in detail in Chapter 10.

This chapter has also examined the case of hypercongestion both theoretically and empirically. We argue that urban expressways suffer from hypercongestion a good deal of the time during the normal rush hour periods. The western half of the Eisenhower Expressway in metropolitan Chicago, an expressway that does not suffer from any obvious bottlenecks, operated in May 1994 in the region of negative marginal product of traffic density over 50% of the time during the rush periods. The chapter concluded with a critique of the Evans (1992) model of traffic congestion. We argue that Evans (1992) specifies the quantity that is demanded and supplied by highway users, traffic density, can be justified as the demand for "trips" of equal length over a time period that varies with traffic density. Further analysis of this model is contained in Chapter 15 and in the appendix to the book.

References

Arnott, R., 1990, Signalized intersection queuing theory and central business district auto congestion, Economics Letters 33, 197-201.

Beckman, M., C. McGuire, and C. Winsten, 1955, Studies in the Economics of Transportation, New Haven: Yale University Press.

Calfee, J., and C. Winston, 1998, The value of automobile travel time: Implications for congestion policy, Journal of Public Economics 69, 83-102.

Chu, X., and K. Small, 1997, Hypercongestion, Paper presented at annual meeting of AREUEA, New Orleans.

Else, P., 1981, A reformulation of the theory of optimal congestion taxes, Journal of Transport Economics and Policy XV, 217-232.

Evans, A., 1992, Road congestion: The diagrammatic analysis, Journal of Political Economy 100, 211-217.

Knight, F., 1924, Some fallacies in the interpretation of social cost, Quarterly Journal of Economics 38, 582-606.

Pigou, A., 1920, The Economics of Welfare, London: Macmillan.

Small, K., 1992, Urban Transportation Economics, Chur, Switzerland: Harwood Academic Publishers.

Yang, H. and H. Huang, 1998, Principle of marginal cost pricing: How does it work in a general road network? Transportation Research A 32, 45-54.

7 URBAN HIGHWAY CONGESTION: AN ANALYSIS OF SECOND-BEST TOLLS

A. INTRODUCTION

The use of tolls to improve the efficiency with which urban highways are used is no longer just a fanciful proposal of academic economists. A popular book by Downs (1992) is serving to introduce the idea of congestion pricing to a wider audience. As we have noted in the Introduction to this volume, State Route 91 in California, Singapore, a highway in France, and three cities in Norway already have some form of congestion pricing, congestion pricing projects are being planned for several other cities around the world, and the U. S. Federal Highway Administration is conducting demonstration projects to test the viability of congestion tolls in various circumstances. Congestion pricing is being taken seriously by transportation policy makers.

No one believes that the implementation of congestion pricing schemes will be easy. Small (1992a, p. 290) raises cautionary notes about demonstration projects when he states that

> Demonstration projects have disadvantages, also. Because they are limited, they may generate troublesome traffic spillovers onto roads that are not part of the project.

He goes on to suggest that

> A type of project deemed far less likely to succeed as a demonstration is pricing a city street network. Reasons include the complexity of the charging mechanism, the possibilities for traffic diversion, and the strong tradition of free access to local streets.

The purpose of this chapter is to argue that it is not just demonstration projects that have these problems. The problems of technical complexity and traffic spillover and the tradition of free access to local streets make the implementation of congestion pricing inherently difficult. It simply may be true that there will be portions of the urban road network that cannot be subject to congestion pricing. Does this constraint on policy mean that there are no gains to be made from a congestion pricing scheme? This chapter will show that the answer to this question is "no," but it will also show that the optimal congestion pricing policy can be very different if there are major portions of the road network left out of the toll scheme.

The chapter first presents an economic model of a simple urban highway system consisting of just two routes, both of which are subject to congestion. A congestion toll can be imposed on one route, but the other route must remain a free road. The model is a simplified version of a model first introduced by Levy-Lambert (1968) and Marchand (1968), and derives what economists call a "second-best optimum," the best that can be done given that efficient congestion tolls cannot be imposed on both routes. The basic theoretical result is that the toll on the tollway should be reduced (relative to the first-best optimum) if the two routes are considered substitutes by urban travelers, and the toll should be increased if the two routes are complements. Crew and Kleindorfer (1986) and Sherman (1989) provide surveys of the extensive literature on optimal pricing in second-best situations.

The next section contains numerical examples designed to explore the differences between the second-best toll scheme and two other regimes, the case in which no toll is imposed and the case in which efficient tolls are imposed on both routes. A principal lesson is that it is usually incorrect to impose what appears to be the efficient textbook toll on only a portion of the road system. Indeed, it is possible that users of an uncongested or lightly congested "tollway" should be paid so that congestion on the free road can be reduced.

B. THE MODEL

The issues indentified in the previous section can be examined through the use of a simplified model of road congestion and route choice. The model is the static model of road congestion that is widely used for pedagogical and policy purposes. See Small (1992b) for a survey of static and dynamic traffic congestion models. The model presented here is a version of the model introduced by Levy-Lambert (1968) and Marchand (1968), and is a more general version of the model first introduced by Pigou (1920) and Knight (1924). The alternative routes are considered to be substitutes by Levy-Lambert (1968) and Marchand (1968), an assumption that is relaxed in this section.

Consider two routes that are both subject to traffic congestion. In the general case it is assumed that these routes can be substitutes or complements for urban travelers. If the two routes are substitutes, additional trips on one route reduce the benefits of trips on the other. Complementary routes mean that additional trips on one route increase the benefits of trips on the other. The extreme cases are those of perfect substitutes and perfect complements. For example, two routes are perfect substitutes if they have the same origin and destination and travelers care only about the (time and money) cost of the trip. This case is used to examine the problem of traffic diversion mentioned in the introduction. Two routes are perfect complements if, for example, the user must use both routes to travel to the desired destination. In this example, using only the first route brings the traveler to an intermediate destination that is of no value in itself. The situation is similar to the standard textbook case of the demands for left shoes and right shoes.

The model is now formulated for the general case; the special cases of perfect substitutes and perfect complements are examined after the general case is discussed. One route is a tollway and, because of technical and/or political constraints, the other route must remain a free road (i. e., no toll can be charged). The marginal benefit of trips (traffic volume per time period) during a particular peak period on the tollway is $B_t(v_t, v_f)$, where v_t is traffic volume on the tollway and v_f is traffic volume on the free road. The usual assumption is made that marginal benefit (B_t) declines with traffic volume on the tollway (v_t). In order to simplify the model somewhat, this marginal benefit (or demand) function is assumed to possess an income effect of zero. In other words, for the price changes contemplated in this article, it is assumed that the income effects of the price changes are zero. This assumption means that the marginal benefit function is also the compensated (or Hicksian) demand function. Similarly, the marginal benefit function for trips on the free road is $B_f(v_t, v_f)$, which is assumed to decline with traffic volume on the free road (v_f) and to have zero income effect.

As shown in Layard and Walters (1978, pp. 141-142) and other texts in microeconomic theory, given the assumption of zero income effects, these demand functions have the further property that

$$\partial B_t/\partial v_f = \partial B_f/\partial v_t, \tag{1}$$

or that the cross-partial effects are equal. This property is known as the integrability condition, and means that the solution for the maximization of the benefits of travel does not depend upon the path taken to evaluate the relevant line integral. This technical matter is discussed extensively in this context by Pressman (1970) and Silberberg (1972), is included in standard texts such as Crew and Kleindorfer (1986) and Sherman (1989), and is discussed in the appendix to this article.

Recall that both routes are subject to congestion delays during the peak period. It is also possible that there are other external costs associated with traffic on these two routes (e. g., traffic passing through residential areas, air pollution, etc.), but these other costs are not considered here. Denote the average cost of travel on the tollway (free road) as c_t (c_f). Average cost on a route is a function only of traffic volume on that route. The constraint on the pricing of the free road is that $p_f = c_f = B_f$, or that the price to the users (p_f) equals average cost (c_f), which in turn equals marginal benefit (B_f). The price of the trip on the tollway is

$p_t = c_t + t = B_t$, where t is the congestion toll. The problem is to find the second-best optimum traffic volumes and toll t*, given that $c_f = B_f$.

The problem can be solved by setting up a conventional Lagrangian function L, written

$$L = \int B_t(v_t, v_f)dv_t + \int B_f(v_t, v_f)dv_f - v_t c_t(v_t) - v_f c_f(v_f) - \lambda[B_f(v_t, v_f) - c_f]. \qquad (2)$$

The integrals in the Lagrangian function are the total benefits of travel - the integrals of the marginal benefit function evaluated along some path from 0 to v_t^* and 0 to v_f^*, the equilibrium traffic volumes. As noted above and discussed in the appendix, the value of the sum of the two integrals does not depend upon the path used to evaluate the integrals as long as $\partial B_t/\partial v_f = \partial B_f/\partial v_t$. In the appendix the model is written with linear demand functions and the path selected is (0,0) to $(v_t^*,0)$ and then $(v_t^*,0)$ to (v_t^*,v_f^*). The total costs of travel are $v_t c_t + v_f c_f$, and the total benefits minus the total costs are maximized subject to the constraint that $B_f(v_t, v_f) = c_f$.

Maximization of L with respect to v_t, v_f, and λ produces the set of first-order conditions

$$\partial L/\partial v_t = B_t(v_t, v_f) - (c_t + v_t c_t') - \lambda(\partial B_f/\partial v_t) = 0, \qquad (3)$$

$$\partial L/\partial v_f = B_f(v_t, v_f) - (c_f + v_f c_f') - \lambda(\partial B_f/\partial v_f - c_f') = 0, \qquad (4)$$

and

$$\partial L/\partial \lambda = B_f(v_t, v_f) - c_f = 0. \qquad (5)$$

The new notation is $c_t' = dc_t/dv_t$ and $c_f' = dc_f/dv_f$. As is discussed in the appendix, $\partial B_t/\partial v_f = \partial B_f/\partial v_t$ implies that

$$(\partial/\partial v_t^*)[\int B_t dv_t + \int B_f dv_f] = B_t \text{ and} \qquad (6)$$

$$(\partial/\partial v_f^*)[\int B_t dv_t + \int B_f dv_f] = B_f; \qquad (7)$$

so the first-order conditions follow.

Now $t = B_t - c_t$ and $B_f = c_f$. These conditions can be substituted into equations (3) and (4), and then the two equations can be solved for t to yield

$$t^* = v_t c_t' + (\partial B_f/\partial v_t)[v_f c_f'/(c_f' - \partial B_f/\partial v_f)]. \qquad (8)$$

This is the pivotal result. The second-best optimum toll t* equals the marginal congestion cost on the tollway ($v_t c_t'$) plus an adjustment term. The sign of the adjustment term is determined as follows. The term $v_f c_f'$ (marginal congestion cost on the free road) is assumed to be greater than zero. Furthermore, the denominator (c_f'-$\partial B_f/\partial v_f$) is positive because $c_f' > 0$ and $\partial B_f/\partial v_f < 0$. These conditions mean that the sign of the adjustment term is determined by the sign of $\partial B_f/\partial v_t$, the cross-partial effect. The standard assumptions is that $\partial B_f/\partial v_t < 0$ if the two routes are substitutes, and $\partial B_f/\partial v_t > 0$ if the two routes are complements.[1] In short, equation (8) shows that the optimum second-best toll involves a downward adjustment from the marginal congestion cost on the tollway if the two routes are substitutes, and an upward adjustment if the two routes are complements. But note that the congestion toll cannot be computed until the equilibrium values for v_t and v_f are found. Several special cases are of interest.

Consider first the case of perfect substitutes. This case is particularly relevant for the problem of traffic diversion in congestion toll schemes that cover only a portion of the road system. As is well known, the demand function for a good that is a perfect substitute is discontinuous, so separate differentiable marginal benefit functions for v_t and v_f cannot be specified. However, in this instance there is really only one marginal benefit function B(v), where $v = v_t + v_f$, total trips taken. Function B(v) can be assumed to be differentiable. In this case it must be that $\partial B/\partial v_t = \partial B/\partial v_f = \partial B/\partial v = B' < 0$, where B' is the slope of the demand curve. Equilibrium requires that

$$c_t + t = c_f, \tag{9}$$

or that travelers face equal costs on the two routes. Following Levy-Lambert (1968), equation (8) becomes

$$t^* = v_t c_t' + B'[v_f c_f'/(c_f'-B')]. \tag{10}$$

Three special cases of equation (10) are of particular interest.

The case considered by Pigou (1920) and Knight (1924) is the case in which the free road is uncongested ($c_f' = 0$); the case in which the optimum toll equals the marginal congestion cost on the tollway. As equation (8) shows, this result also holds if the two routes are not perfect substitutes. Secondly, in the special case of an uncongested tollway ($c_t' = 0$), users of the tollway are subsidized under second-best pricing. The subsidy amount is

$$-t^* = -B'[v_f c_f'/(c_f'-B')] \tag{11}$$

Indeed, from equation (8), tollway users are subsidized if the tollway is a substitute for the free road ($\partial B_f/\partial v_t < 0$) and

$$-(\partial B_f/\partial v_t)[v_f c_f'/(c_f'-\partial B_f/\partial v_f)] > v_t c_t'. \tag{12}$$

(Presumably advanced tollway technology can be adapted to pay users.)

Thirdly, the case of perfect substitutes and fixed total travel demand is of particular interest. Assume the demand for travel is fixed at some level v^T and the problem is reduced to one of optimal assignment to the two routes. In this case only one toll is needed to achieve a first-best optimum assignment. If demand is fixed, $B' = -\infty$ and

$$t^* = v_t c_t' + v_f c_f'/[(c_f'/B') - 1]$$

$$= v_t c_t' - v_f c_f'. \quad (13)$$

Since marginal trip costs to society can be written $MC_t = c_t + v_t c_t'$ and $MC_f = c_f + v_f c_f'$,

$$t^* = MC_t - c_t - (MC_f - c_f). \quad (14)$$

The equilibrium assignment must satisfy the condition in equation (9), so $MC_t = MC_f$. As before, the optimal toll is the difference between the average costs on the tollway and the free road, but this toll achieves a first-best optimum in the special case of fixed demand. This optimal toll may be positive, zero, or negative. In the route assignment problem with fixed demand, it is not necessary for a first-best optimum to impose tolls equal to marginal congestion cost on all routes. Indeed, if the two routes have identical cost functions, the optimal toll is zero.

Consider finally the case in which the two routes are perfect complements. The user cannot travel to the desired destination unless both routes are used. For example, a user crosses the only bridge over the river, and then travels on a congested free road. What should be the toll on the bridge? In this case a first-best optimum again can be achieved, but there is one complication. In the case of perfect complements it is not possible to specify a demand function with zero income effect from a price change. As texts in microeconomic theory show, a reduction in the price of one of the two goods that are perfect complements must increase the consumption of both goods (by an equal amount, of course), and these changes in consumption are income effects. There is no substitution effect. However, the demand for perfectly complementary goods can be specified as a single function, where the relevant own price is the price of the goods taken together (e. g., the price of a pair of shoes; or the price of traveling from home to the bridge, plus the price of crossing the bridge, plus the price of traveling from the bridge to the desired destination). The marginal benefit function is assumed to be B(v), where v is traffic volume on both routes. An income effect of zero is assumed. The relevant maximand is the equation for net benefits,

$$NB = \int B(v) - (c_t + c_f)v, \quad (15)$$

The first-order condition is

$$d(NB)/dv = B(v) - (c_t+c_f) - v[(dc_t/dv) + (dc_f/dv)] = 0. \quad (16)$$

The traveler pays toll t and average cost on both routes. In equilibrium it must be that marginal benefit equals the price of the entire trip, or $B(v) = t + c_t + c_f$, so the optimal toll is

$$t^* = v[(dc_t/dv) + (dc_f/dv)], \tag{17}$$

or the toll imposed on the tollway portion of the trip equals the marginal congestion costs on both the tollway and the free road portions of the trip. Once again, note that the actual toll cannot be found until v is known.

C. NUMERICAL EXAMPLES

Does the second-best toll, and its accompanying traffic volumes and costs, differ appreciably from the first-best solution? How much does the failure to impose tolls on all routes matter? This question is examined using numerical examples for the case in which the routes are perfect substitutes. The case of perfect substitutes is particularly important because, as noted in the introduction, traffic diversion is likely to be a serious problem with congestion toll schemes that cover only a portion of the road system.

The numerical examples assume a linear marginal benefit function (demand function) for trips, written

$$B = A - bv, \tag{18}$$

where $v = v_t + v_f$ as before in the case of perfect substitutes, and -b is the slope of the marginal benefit function. Further it is assumed that there are two routes with linear average cost curves

$$c_t = \alpha_t + \delta_t v_t \text{ and} \tag{19}$$

$$c_f = \alpha_f + \delta_f v_f. \tag{20}$$

Three regimes are compared; the case of no tolls, the case of first-best tolls on both routes, and the case of the optimum second-best toll on the tollway.

The case in which no toll is imposed is easy to compute. Setting $B = c_t = c_f$, equations (19) and (20) imply the set of equations written as

$$\begin{aligned} (-b-\delta_t)v_t - bv_f &= \alpha_t - A \\ -bv_t + (-b-\delta_f)v_f &= \alpha_f - A \end{aligned} \tag{21}$$

These equations yield solutions for v_t and v_f as they depend upon the parameters in the demand and cost functions. The case of the first-best tolls on both routes is also easy to compute. Setting B equal to marginal cost on each route ($c_t + v_t c_t'$ and $c_f + v_f c_f'$) generates the set of equations

$$(-b-2\delta_t)v_t - bv_f = \alpha_t - A$$
$$-bv_t + (-b-2\delta_f)v_f = \alpha_f - A \tag{22}$$

Given solutions for v_t and v_f, the optimum first-best tolls are $\delta_t v_t$ and $\delta_f v_f$.

Now consider the second-best toll case. The first step is to set up the Lagrangian function

$$L = \int(A - bv)dv - (\alpha_t+\delta_t v_t)v_t - (\alpha_f+\delta_f v_f)v_f - \lambda[(A - bv) - (\alpha_f+\delta_f v_f)]. \tag{23}$$

The integral is evaluated from zero to equilibrium traffic volume. The first-order conditions are

$$\partial L/\partial v_t = [A-b(v_t+v_f)] - (\alpha_t+2\delta_t v_t) + \lambda b = 0, \tag{24}$$

$$\partial L/\partial v_f = [A-b(v_t+v_f)] - (\alpha_f+2\delta_f v_f) + \lambda(b+\delta_f) = 0, \tag{25}$$

and

$$\partial L/\partial \lambda = -[A-b(v_t+v_f)] + (\alpha_f+\delta_f v_f) = 0. \tag{26}$$

These equations can be written as

$$(-b-2\delta_t)v_t - bv_f + b\lambda = \alpha_t - A,$$
$$-bv_t + (-b-2\delta_f)v_f + (b+\delta_f)\lambda = \alpha_f - A, \text{ and} \tag{27}$$
$$bv_t + (b+\delta_f)v_f = A - \alpha_f.$$

Solutions for v_t and v_f can then be used to solve for the optimum toll as in equation (10) above.

The computations require knowledge of five parameters - the slopes of the average cost functions (δ_t and δ_f), the slope of the demand function (b), and the intercept of the demand function minus the intercepts of the cost functions ($A-\alpha_t$ and $A-\alpha_f$). A discussion of each parameter follows, but the reader is reminded that the sets of equations (21), (22) and (27) can be used to simulate traffic volumes and optimal tolls for any set of parameter values one wishes to use. Also, comparative static analysis can be performed on sets of equations (21), (22) and (27) to determine the effects of marginal changes in parameter values on equilibrium traffic volumes and optimal tolls. Instead the approach taken here is to use a small number of numerical examples.

The model has been set up to examine the effects of alternative cost functions for the two routes. Four alternatives are considered; these are

1) both routes have three lanes, and speeds on the two routes are equal if traffic volumes are equal,

2) tollway has four lanes, free road has two lanes, and speeds are equal if traffic volume on the tollway is twice as great as on the free road,

3) both routes have three lanes, but speed on the tollway is 22 mph faster than on the free road if traffic volumes are equal, and

4) tollway has four lanes, free road has two lanes, and speed on tollway is 22 mph faster if it carries twice the traffic volume of the free road.

Values for the slopes of the average cost functions can be obtained from the function used by Decorla-Souza and Kane (1992), written in minutes as

$$\text{Average time per mile} = 4.29/[1+(1\text{-}V/K)^{.5}], \qquad (28)$$

where V/K is the volume-to-capacity ratio. For example, average time per mile is 3.25 minutes when V/K = .90. The derivative of average time per mile with respect to V/K is

$$2.145(1\text{-}V/K)^{-.5}/[1+(1\text{-}V/K)^{.5}]^2,$$

which equals 3.92 when V/K = .90. Following Decorla-Souza and Kane (1992, p. 301), if the value of time is 8.3 cents per minute ($5.00 per vehicle hour), then the derivative equals 32.54 cents. The derivative dc/dV is needed, so

$$\delta = dc/dV = [dc/d(V/K)][d(V/K)/dV] = 32.54/K. \qquad (29)$$

If the two routes have a total of six lanes and the capacity of each lane is 2000 vehicles per hour, then K is 2000 times the number of lanes. If lanes equal 4, 3, or 2, then δ is .00407, .0054, or .00814. The cost function used by Decorla-Souza and Kane (1992) was taken from a Federal Highway Administration (1982) study, but others could have been used. Small (1992b, pp. 61-74) provides a survey of empirical congestion cost functions.

The intercept of the average cost function is average cost when traffic volume in zero. In the function used by Decorla-Souza and Kane (1992), the free speed is 28 mph because average time cost is 2.145 minutes per mile when V/K = 0. However, the average cost function is clearly nonlinear (or piecewise linear). In this study a linear approximation of the average cost function is used to examine alternative scenarios in the neighborhood of a benchmark case with no tolls. Therefore, the intercepts (α_t and α_f) in the linear approximations to the average cost functions are not the free speeds.

Decorla-Souza and Kane (1992, p. 300) indicate that a reasonable assumption for demand elasticity is e=-.30. The slope of the demand curve is

$$dB/dv = -b = (1/e)(B/v), \tag{30}$$

Assume that the two routes have a total of six lanes so that capacity is 12,000 vehicles per hour. If traffic volume is 90% of capacity (10,800) and, according to the above average time cost function, B = 26.97 (3.25 times 8.3), then

$$b = -(1/e)(.0025) = .0083. \tag{31}$$

The intercepts of the demand and cost functions are found by using the first case with no toll as a benchmark. If the two routes have identical cost functions, then equations (21) imply that $v_t = \delta(A-\alpha)/[(b+\delta)^2+b^2]$. In this case the two routes are identical with three lanes each ($\delta = .0054$). Total traffic volume is 10,800 vehicles per hour (90% of capacity) and traffic volume on each route is 5400. Given these assumptions and b = .0083, the value for $(A-\alpha)$ is 118.8. Two of the cases examined below involve lowering α_t by enough to increase speed at any traffic volume by 22 mph. The required value for $(A-\alpha_t)$ is 126.69 because increasing speed by 22 mph means lowering cost by .95 minutes per mile, or 7.89 cents per mile (with a value of time of 8.3 cents per minute). Table 7-1 displays the assumptions used in the numerical examples.

The results of the comparisons of the three regimes for each of the cost-function cases are shown in Table 7-2. In the first case the two routes are identical with three lanes and equal speeds if traffic volumes are equal. As noted above, it is assumed that total traffic volume with no toll is 10,800 and each route carries 5400 vehicles per hour. With an efficient congestion toll imposed on both routes total traffic volume is reduced to 8668 vehicles per hour, or 80.3% of the traffic volume in the regime with no tolls. Traffic again is split evenly between the two routes; 4334 vehicles per hour. The congestion toll is computed as $\delta v_t = \delta v_f = 23.4$ cents per mile. If a congestion toll can only be imposed on one route (the tollway), the second-best traffic volume is 10,557 vehicles per hour, or 97.8% of the traffic

Table 7-1
Assumptions Used in Numerical Examples

	Case 1	Case 2	Case e3	Case 4
Slope of demand function (b)	-.0083	-.0083	-.0083	-.0083
Slope of ave. cost				
Tollway (δ_t)	.0054	.00407	.0054	.00407
Freeway (δ_f)	.0054	.00814	.0054	.00814
Difference in intercepts				
$(A - \alpha_t)$	118.8	118.8	126.69	126.69
$(A - \alpha_f)$	118.8	118.8	118.8	118.8

volume in the regime with no toll. However, traffic volume on the tollway has been reduced to 4700 vehicles per hour. And the traffic volume on the free road is now 5857 vehicles per hour. In other words, the imposition of the toll on the tollway reduces traffic volume on that route by 700 vehicles per hour and increases traffic volume on the free road by 457 vehicles per hour, for a net reduction of 243 vehicles per hour. The optimum second-best toll is computed as in equation (10) as

$$t^* = \delta_t v_t - b[\delta_f v_f/(\delta_f + b)], \tag{32}$$

which equals 6.2 cents per mile.

The constraint that a congestion toll can be imposed only on one route makes a sizable difference in this case. The second-best toll is only 6.2 cents per mile compared to the first-best toll of 23.4 cents per mile, and the resulting reduction in total traffic volume compared to the regime with no toll is small - only 2.25%. The first-best reduction in traffic volume is 19.74%. The second-best toll diverts traffic from the tollway to the free road; the free road carries 8.5% more traffic and the tollway carries 13.0% less traffic compared to the regime with no toll.

The results for the other cost-function cases shown in Table 7-2 suggest that the above conclusions are not particularly sensitive to variations in the parameters of the underlying cost functions. In the second case the tollway is four lanes, the free road is two lanes, and and speeds are equal if the tollway carries twice the traffic volume as the free road. Total traffic volumes under the three toll regimes are very close to the volumes in the first case, and the first-best and second-best tolls are 23.5 cents per mile and 8.3 cents per mile, respectively. Traffic volumes on the tollway (free road) in this case are, of course, appreciably larger (smaller) than in the first case.

In the third case shown in Table 7-2 both routes have three lanes, but the tollway has a speed that is 22 mph faster than the free road if they carry equal traffic volumes. This "improvement" in the tollway compared to the first case induces slightly higher total traffic volumes and generates appreciably higher traffic volumes on the tollway itself in each of the three toll regimes. However, the first-best and second-best tolls do not change very much. The first-best toll on the tollway is now 26.1 cents per mile, and the first-best toll on the free road is 22.2 cents per mile. The second-best toll is 9.9 cents per mile, and change of only 3.7 cents per mile compared to the first case. However, this change is an increase of 60% in the toll compared to the first case.

The fourth case shown in Table 7-2 may be regarded as particularly relevant. In this case the tollway has four lanes and a 22 mph faster speed if it carries twice the traffic volume as the free road. The free road has only two lanes and a slower speed. This case is intended to depict a situation in which drivers are induced by the congestion toll to substitute an arterial city street for a limited-access highway. In this case total traffic volume is 11,263 with no tolls, and the "tollway" carries 72.4% of the traffic. The first-best optimum tolls are 25.8 cents

Table 7-2
Comparison of Congestion Toll Regimes:
Two Routes Are Perfect Substitutes*

	Traffic Volumes Total	Tollway	Free Road	Tolls (cents)	Potential Welfare Gain ($)
Case 1: Both routes - 3 lanes and equal speeds at equal volumes					
No toll	10,800	5400	5400	0	
Toll on both routes	8,668	4334	4334	23.4	$310.85
Toll on one route	10,557	4700	5857	6.2	25.55
Case 2: Tollway - 4 lanes, free road - 2 lanes, and equal speeds if tollway has twice the volume					
No toll	10,785	7190	3595	0	
Toll on both routes	8,655	5770	2885	23.5	$311.65
Toll on one route	10,292	6183	4109	8.3	71.59
Case 3: Both routes - 3 lanes, tollway has 22 mph faster speed at equal volumes					
No toll	11,160	6311	4849	0	
Toll on both routes	8,957	4844	4113	26.4 (t) 22.2 (f)	$346.33
Toll on one route	10,757	5197	5560	9.9	79.34
Case 4: Tollway - 4 lanes, free road - 2 lanes, tollway has 22 mph faster speed if it has twice the volume					
No toll	11,263	8155	3108	0	
Toll on both routes	9,038	6349	2689	25.8 (t) 21.9 (f)	$352.71
Toll on one	10,563	6734	3829	11.7	144.84

per mile on the tollway and 21.9 cents per mile on the free road, and these tolls result in a reduction of total traffic volume to 9038 vehicles per hour, or a reduction of 19.75%. Traffic volume on the tollway is reduced by 22.15%, and traffic volume on the "free road" is reduced by 13.48%. The second-best toll is computed to be 11.7 cents per mile, which is almost double the 6.2 figure in the first case in which the two routes are identical. This toll on the tollway results in a reduction of total traffic volume to 10,563 vehicles per hour, or a reduction of 6.22%. Compared to the regime with no toll, the second-best toll results in a reduction in traffic volume on the tollway of 17.42% and an increase in traffic volume on the free road of 23.2%.

The results in Table 7-2 show that an ability to impose a toll on a larger portion of the road system (in the case of perfect substitutes) results in a larger reduction in total traffic volume compared to the regime with no toll. Comparing the first and second cases, the reductions in total traffic volume with the second-best toll are 2.25% and 4.57%, respectively. Recall that the tollway has four lanes in the second case compared to three lanes in the first case. The comparison of the third and fourth cases goes in the same direction. Total traffic volume is reduced by the second-best toll by 3.61% in the third case (tollway with three lanes), while the reduction is 6.22% in the fourth case (tollway with four lanes).

One final question needs to be answered. What are the magnitudes of the potential welfare gains implied by the first-best and second-best pricing schemes? And therefore how much of the potential welfare gain is lost because of the constraint that the free road cannot have a congestion toll? From equation (23), the net benefits of traffic volume v* are

$$NB = \int (A - bv^*)dv - c_t^* v_t^* - c_f^* v_f^*, \tag{33}$$

where the integral is evaluated from zero to v* and average costs are evaluated at the equilibrium traffic volumes v_t^* and v_f^*. Computation of the integral produces

$$NB = (A - bv^*)v^* + .5b(v^*)^2 - c_t^* v_t^* - c_f^* v_f. \tag{34}$$

For a change in traffic volume $\Delta v = \Delta v_t + \Delta v_f$, the change in net benefits can be written

$$\Delta NB = (A - bv^*)\Delta v + .5b(\Delta v)^2 - [\Delta v_t c_t + \Delta c_t(v_t^* - \Delta v_t)] - [\Delta v_f c_f + \Delta c_f(v_f^* - \Delta v_f)]. \tag{35}$$

The changes in the traffic volumes are shown in Table 7-2, and the changes in average costs are based on the parameter values shown in Table 7-1 for each case.

The results of these computations are shown in Table 7-2 under the heading potential welfare gain. In the first case use of the first-best pricing scheme results in a welfare gain of $310.85 per hour, but the second-best pricing scheme only yields a welfare gain of $25.55 per hour. In this example most (92%) of the welfare gain is lost because of the constraint that the free road cannot have a congestion toll. In the other examples the situation is not quite so stark. In fact, in the fourth case the welfare gain with first-best pricing is $352.71 per hour and the second-best pricing scheme yields a welfare gain of $144.84, or 41% of the possible gain. These results show that the welfare gain with the second-best pricing scheme is greater when the tollway is a larger and a higher-speed facility compared to the free road.

D. CONCLUSIONS

This chapter has used economic theory and numerical examples to explore the question of optimal congestion pricing in the case in which a significant portion of the urban road system cannot be subjected to a congestion toll. The main theoretical result is that the optimal congestion toll is, in general, not equal to the marginal congestion cost on the tollway. This standard textbook result holds only if the free road portion of the system is **not** subject to congestion or if the demands for the tollway and the free road are independent of each other. If the free road substitutes for the tollway, then the optimal toll on the tollway is below its marginal congestion cost. Indeed, if the free road is subject to congestion and the tollway is not, the the optimal policy is to pay people to use the tollway. And if the free road is complementary with the tollway, then the optimal toll on the tollway is above its marginal congestion cost.

The numerical examples presented in this article set up a simple situation of two routes that are perfect substitutes. The two routes are permitted to have different congestion cost functions, however. In these examples the optimal policy is to set a relatively small congestion toll on the tollway that cuts back total traffic volume only slightly (up to 6.2% in the examples). The toll on one route causes traffic to switch to the other. Indeed, it is the ease with which traffic can switch to the free road that keeps the toll relatively low. If a congestion toll could also be imposed on the free road, the (first-best) optimum tolls would be much larger and total traffic volume would be cut back substantially (by 19.7% in the examples).

The basic message of this chapter is really quite clear. A failure to impose a congestion toll on a substantial portion of the urban road system makes the computation of optimum second-best tolls a complex matter. Furthermore, this failure is costly in terms of potential welfare gains of congestion pricing that are lost. Ways and means for removing the technical and political constraints on reasonably complete schemes for congestion pricing should be pursued. In the meantime, congestion pricing policy should be designed with the lessons of this chapter in mind.

Footnote

1. Note that the pricing constraint on the free road, which is $B_f(v_t,v_f) = c_f$, can be totally differentiated to give

$$(\partial B_f/\partial v_t)dv_t + (\partial B_f/\partial v_f)dv_f = c_f' dv_f.$$

This equation can be solved to read

$$dv_f/dv_t = (\partial B_f/\partial v_t)/(c_f' - \partial B_f/\partial v_f).$$

This result means that equation (8) can be written

$$t^* = v_t c_t' + (dv_f/dv_t)(v_f c_f'),$$

which means that the second-best toll involves an adjustment to the first-best toll that equals the change in traffic volume on the free road per unit change in traffic volume on the toll road times the marginal congestion cost on the free road. The sign of dv_f/dv_t indicates directly whether the two routes are substitutes or complements. This result clearly is related to the standard result in the theory of optimal commodity taxation that, if there is an untaxed commodity, the good that is most complementary with the untaxed good should be taxed most heavily. See Atkinson and Stiglitz (1980, pp. 370-376) for a proof.

References

Atkinson, A. and J. Stiglitz, 1980, Lectures on Public Economics, New York: McGraw-Hill.

Crew, M. and P. Kleindorfer, 1986, The Economics of Public Utility Regulation, Cambridge: MIT Press.

Decorla-Souza, P. and A. Kane, 1992, Peak period tolls: Precepts and prospects. Transportation 19, 293-311.

Downs, A., 1992, Stuck in Traffic: Coping with Peak-Hour Traffic Congestion, Washington, D. C.: Brookings Institution.

Federal Highway Administration, May 1982, Final Report on the Federal Highway Cost Allocation Study.

Knight, F., 1924, Some fallacies in the interpretation of social cost. Quarterly Journal of Economics 38, 582-606.

Layard, P. and A. Walters, 1978, Microeconomic Theory, New York: McGraw-Hill.

Levy-Lambert, H., 1968, Tarification des services a qualite variable - application aux peages de circulation, Econometrica 36, 564-581.

Marchand, M., 1968, A note on optimal tolls in an imperfect environment, Econometrica 36, 575-581.

Pigou, A., 1920, The Economics of Welfare, London: Macmillan.

Pressman, I., 1970, A mathematical formulation of the peak load pricing problem, Bell Journal of Economics 1, 304-326.

Sherman, R., 1989, The Regulation of Monopoly, Cambridge: Cambridge University Press.

Silberberg, E., 1972, Duality and the many consumer's surpluses, American Economic Review 62, 942-952.

Small, K., 1992a, Guest editorial. Transportation 19, 287-291.

Small, K., 1992b, Urban Transportation Economics, Chur, Switzerland: Harwood Academic Publishers..

Appendix

Application of the Line Integral Theorem

The model is formulated above in equation (2) as a Lagrangian function that includes a two-dimensional function for consumers surplus, which can be written

$$CS = \int_{F(\mathbf{0},\mathbf{v})} \sum B_i(v_t,v_f)dv_i, \tag{A-1}$$

where consumers' surplus is represented as a line integral along some curve $F(\mathbf{0},\mathbf{v})$ connecting the origin to the vector $\mathbf{v}$. In general the value of the integral depends upon the path chosen to integrate from $\mathbf{0}$ to $\mathbf{v}$. The independence of path theorem for line integrals states that the value of the integral will be independent of the path chosen if and only if $\partial B_t/\partial v_f = \partial B_f/\partial v_t$, and that there exists a function $Z(v_t,v_f)$ such that $dZ = B_t dv_t + B_f dv_f$ and with the property that

$$\partial Z/\partial v_t = B_t \text{ and } \partial Z/\partial v_f = B_f.$$

See Pressman (1970) and Silberberg (1972). The use of this theorem will be illustrated.

Consider the model in equation (2) written in linear form as

$$L = \int_{F(\mathbf{0},\mathbf{v})} \sum (A_i+b_iv_i+cv_j)dv_i - v_t(\alpha_t+\delta_tv_t) - v_f(\alpha_f+\delta_fv_f)$$
$$- \lambda[(A_f+b_fv_f+cv_t) - (\alpha_f+\delta_fv_f)], \tag{A-2}$$

where $i = t$ and f, and $j = f$ and t. The theorem says that the value of the integral is independent of the path of integration because $\partial B_i/\partial v_j = c$ for $i = t$ and f and $j = f$ and t. In this case the path selected is $(0,0)$ to $(v_t^*,0)$ and then $(v_t^*,0)$ to (v_t^*,v_f^*). The Lagrangian becomes

$$L = \int(A_t+b_tv_t+0)dv_t + \int(A_f+b_fv_f+cv_t)dv_f - v_t(\alpha_t+\delta_tv_t)$$
$$- v_f(\alpha_f+\delta_fv_f) - \lambda[(A_f+b_fv_f+cv_t) - (\alpha_f+\delta_fv_f)]. \tag{A-3}$$

Use of indefinite integrals produces

$$L = H_t+A_tv_t+(b_t/2)(v_t)^2 + H_f+A_fv_f+(b_f/2)(v_f)^2+cv_tv_f$$
$$- v_t(\alpha_t+\delta_tv_t) - v_f(\alpha_f+\delta_fv_f) - \lambda[(A_f+b_fv_f+cv_t)-(\alpha_f+\delta_fv_f)], \tag{A-4}$$

where H_t and H_f are constants of integration. The first-order conditions for the model are

$$\partial L/\partial v_t = A_t+b_tv_t+cv_f - (\alpha_t+2\delta_tv_t) - \lambda c = 0, \tag{A-5}$$

$$\partial L/\partial v_f = A_f+b_fv_f+cv_t - (\alpha_f+2\delta_fv_f) - \lambda(b_f-\delta_f) = 0, \tag{A-6}$$

and

$$\partial L/\partial\lambda = -(A_f+b_f v_f+cv_t) + (\alpha_f+\delta_f v_f) = 0. \quad \text{(A-7)}$$

The other obvious option for the path of integration is (0, 0) to (0, v_f*) and then (0, v_f*) to (v_t*, v_f*). Clearly the first-order conditions would be identical if this path were chosen.

Use of the condition that the optimum second-best toll is

$$t^* = (A_t+b_t v_t+cv_f) - (\alpha_t+\delta_t v_t) \quad \text{(A-8)}$$

produces the basic result that

$$t^* = \delta_t + c[v_f\delta_f/(\delta_f-b_f)]. \quad \text{(A-9)}$$

The first-order conditions, equations (A-5), (A-6), and (A-7), can be used to solve for v_t, v_f, and t*.

8 MATHEMATICAL FORMULATION OF A MULTIPLE-PERIOD CONGESTION PRICING MODEL

A. INTRODUCTION

Congestion pricing, as Downs (1992) indicates, is one of the demand-side strategies that focus on behavior. Congestion pricing aims at alleviating congestion by altering travel behavior - by encouraging people to travel during less congested time periods, by less congested routes, by alternative modes, or not at all. In the previous chapter, we studied the second-best congestion pricing problem using the model for a two-route network and a single period. The one-period model allows us to analyze the effects of congestion pricing on traveler's route choice behavior.

In this chapter, we extend the one-period model to two time periods - a peak period and an off-peak period (called the two-period model hereafter). We wish to make our model more realistic because the urban traveler does have some discretion over the choice of time of day for the trip. The major advantage of the two-period model is that it can handle both spatial and temporal effects of congestion pricing. The two-period model is able to deal with the question of how much congestion can be relieved by shifting peak period traffic to off-peak periods. The two-period model also creates another policy instrument, the toll in the off-peak period.

The two-period model combines the economic theories of the second-best pricing of transportation systems and peak-load pricing. The theory of second-best pricing considers the question of efficient prices given some constraint that prevents the use of a complete set of first-best marginal cost prices. As discussed in the previous chapter, second-best pricing of urban highway systems has been studied by many researchers including the original work by Levy-Lambert (1968) and Marchand (1968); recent studies by Berstein and El Sanhouri (1994) and Braid (1996) on the use of dynamic bottleneck model to deal with the pricing of a transportation facility with an unpriced substitute; and work by Verhoef et al. (1996) and Chapter 7 above using a two-link static equilibrium model to study the second best one-route congestion pricing in the presence of an untolled alternative.

On the other hand, the theory of peak-load pricing was developed by

Mohring (1970) and Pressman (1970), and permits the study of the temporal effects of congestion pricing. In particular, Pressman (1970) makes a distinct contribution to the formulation of peak-load pricing problems. Pressman (1970) uses more realistic period demand functions in which the demand for a good or service depends upon the prices of all the goods and/or services demanded in the multi-period problem involved. For example, for a regulated telephone utility that sells a single service in two distinct periods (known as the peak and off-peak periods), each demand function would be a function of both the peak and off-peak prices. With the dependent demand functions, Pressman generalized the notion of consumers' surplus by using the line-integral calculus. Although the paper is intended for the peak-load pricing problems in public utilities, the ideas also apply to the formulation of the multiple-period congestion pricing problem.

This chapter presents a mathematical formulation of the two-period congestion pricing model. The following section describes the transportation system considered in our study, including the network, travel cost and demand characteristics. The focus of this section is on demand properties, which are crucial to the formulation of gross benefits. Given the theoretical framework in that section, we then present mathematical formulations of the second-best congestion pricing problem and two alternative problems: the first-best and no-toll cases. This presentation is followed by an examination of road pricing under profit maximization.

B. THE TRANSPORTATION SYSTEM

The Network Representation

We consider an urban highway network consisting of two routes connecting an origin (e.g., home) and a destination (e.g., workplace), the network used in the previous chapter. This network has been used by other researchers, e.g., Arnott et al. (1990b), Ben-Akiva et al. (1986), and Marchard (1968). The main reason for choosing such a system is that the network is simple enough to conduct an economic analysis of traveler's route choice behavior. The routes considered here have no specific engineering configuration and are assumed to be perfect substitutes. In the system one route is a toll route and, due to technical and/or political constraints, the other route must remain untolled.

In addition to the spatial framework, we consider two time periods, peak and off-peak periods, to describe traveler's departure time choice. To be more specific, the study considers the problem of the morning commute. The capacity for each route is assumed to be fixed and to be the same for two periods. Each traveler can travel either early during the pre-peak period, or during the peak period. During each period the trip from the origin to the destination can be made on either route.

Travel Costs

Because of the focus of the study is congestion, only short run costs related to congestion will be considered. The cost borne by an individual traveler consists of *travel time cost*, *vehicle operating cost*, and *schedule-related cost*. Travel time and vehicle operating costs are caused by congestion in either the peak or pre-peak period. Schedule-related cost, as defined in Small (1992), is a cost of putting up with non-ideal travel schedules for a traveler who makes a trip in the pre-peak period. This concept is a special case of schedule delay costs used in previous studies. The schedule delay (the difference between actual and desired arrival time) was initially introduced by Vickrey (1969) and is normally related to endogenous scheduling. Small (1982, 1992) further develops this concept and estimates the value of schedule delay. Arnott et al. (1990a, 1990b) use the concept in models of traffic bottlenecks and endogenous scheduling. Unlike the endogenous formulation in the previous studies, the schedule-related cost considered in this study is assumed to be an exogenous value, which represents an average monetary value of schedule-related times borne by every commuter traveling in the off-peak period.[1]

An individual traveler can travel either in the peak period and incur potentially higher congestion (travel time and vehicle operating) costs and no schedule-related costs, or in the pre-peak period and avoid higher congestion costs but bear schedule-related costs. These three costs together constitute *average cost*, which is assumed to be a function of the traffic volume on the route in the period:

$$c_{ir}(v_{ir}),\ i=1,2;\ \ r=t,f. \tag{1}$$

where index i represents time period, i=1 for the peak, i=2 for the pre-peak; index r represents route, r=t for the toll route, r=f for the free route; and v_{ir} is traffic volume on route r in period i. The average cost is assumed to be a monotonically increasing function of the traffic volume:

$$c'_{ir}(v_{ir}) = dc_{ir}(v_{ir})/dv_{ir} > 0,\ i=1,2;\ r=t,f \tag{2}$$

The cost of an additional unit of traffic volume, *marginal cost*, is

$$MC_{ir} = d[v_{ir}c_{ir}(v_{ir})]/dv_{ir} = c_{ir}(v_{ir}) + v_{ir}c'_{ir}(v_{ir}),\ i=1,2;\ r=t,f. \tag{3}$$

The *total cost* consists of the costs borne by all travelers (for each route and for

---

1. Since we assume an exogenous (or constant) schedule-related cost, the effects of having the schedule-related cost could alternatively be modeled (without changing the simulations) by having the schedule-related cost be equal to 0 and changing the parameters of demand functions. These issues will be discussed later in the chapter.

each time period) in the system and is defined as:

$$C = [v_{1t}c_{1t}(v_{1t}) + v_{1f}c_{1f}(v_{1f})] + [v_{2t}c_{2t}(v_{2t}) + v_{2f}c_{2f}(v_{2f})]. \quad (4)$$

Without loss of generality, assume the two periods are of equal length and are normalized to length one.

Demand Characteristics

The aggregate demand for one period, called *period demand*, is the total traffic volume from the origin to the destination in that period. The demand in one period is a function of trip prices in both peak and pre-peak periods. Income effects are assumed to be negligible. The demand functions for the peak (i=1) and pre-peak (i=2) periods are given by:

$$v_1 = f_1(P_1,P_2),\ v_2 = f_2(P_1,P_2). \quad (5)$$

where v_i is aggregated traffic volume and P_i is trip price for period i. For demand functions (5), the following assumptions are made regarding dependency:
1. Negative own-price effect:

$$\partial v_1/\partial P_1 < 0, \text{ and } \partial v_2/\partial P_2 < 0. \quad (6)$$

$$\partial v_1/\partial P_2 > 0, \text{ and } \partial v_2/\partial P_1 > 0. \quad (7)$$

The purpose of introducing the dependency of period demands is to study the peak shifting problem, i.e., the diversion of the peak period trips to the pre-peak period, by considering the response of the peak period demand to the pre-peak trip price, and vice versa.

From (5), the *inverse period demand* function, i.e., the trip price for one period, can be derived as a function of the traffic volume in both the peak and pre-peak periods, or

$$P_1 = P_1(v_1,v_2), \text{ and } P_2 = P_1(v_1,v_2). \quad (8)$$

Given the inverse demand functions (8), the *gross benefit* for the system, denoted by B, can be expressed as a line integral

$$B = \int_{(0,0)}^{(v_1,v_2)} P_1(w_1,w_2)\ dw_1 + P_2(w_1,w_2)dw_2 \quad (9)$$

Without loss of generality, assume the two periods are of equal length and are normalized to length one.

However, there are two major problems associated with the expression

(9). The first problem relates to the definition of the line integral because it depends on the particular path on which the integral is calculated and is thus not unique. The second one relates to the differentiability of the line integral. As stated in Pressman (1970), both problems are solved by assuming the following integrability condition:

$$\partial P_1/\partial v_2 = \partial P_2/\partial v_1. \tag{10}$$

This condition says that the effect on the peak period trip price resulting from a change in the pre-peak traffic volume is the same as the effect on the pre-peak trip price resulting from a change in the peak traffic volume. Condition (10) is one of the fundamental properties associated with the compensated (or Hicksian, i.e., cost-minimizing demand function) demand function. Since this study assumes the demand function has an income effect of zero, the demand function can be regarded as the Hicksian demand function which satisfies integrability condition (10).

Under condition (10), the line integral is uniquely defined and is independent of the path chosen; and the first derivative of the line integral with respect to the traffic volumes for one period is equal to the inverse period demand function, i.e., the trip price for that period. Pressman (1970) provides a complete discussion of this integrability condition; the results are given by the following theorem.

Theorem 1: Suppose $P_i(v_1,v_2)$ (i=1,2), and $\partial P_i/\partial v_j$ (i,j=1,2) are continuous and single valued at every point of a simply connected region. Then, if and only if $\partial P_1/\partial v_2 = \partial P_2/\partial v_1$ will the line integral

(a) be independent of the path from (0,0) to (v_1,v_2);

(b) be zero around every closed curve in the region;

(c) be such that there exists a function $B(v_1,v_2)$ for which:

$$dB = P_1 dv_1 + P_2 dv_2, \text{ and} \tag{11}$$

(d) be such that the following equations are satisfied:

$$\partial B(v_1,v_2)/\partial v_1 = P_1(v_1,v_2),\ \partial B(v_1,v_2)/\partial v_2 = P_2(v_1,v_2). \tag{12}$$

This theorem implies that if integrability (10) is satisfied, then the line integral (9) is uniquely defined and thus can be calculated along any path from (0,0) to(v_1,v_2). For example, two special paths can be selected to calculate the line integral:

$$B = \int_{(0,0)}^{(v_1,v_2)} P_1(w_1,w_2)dw_1 + P_2(w_1,w_2)dw_2 \tag{13}$$

$$= \int_0^{v_1} P_1(w_1, 0)dw_1 + \int_0^{v_2} P_2(v_1, w_2)dw_2$$

which is calculated along the path I: $(0,0) \rightarrow (v_1,0)$ and $(v_1,0) \rightarrow (v_1,v_2)$; or

$$B = \int_{(0,0)}^{(v_1,v_2)} P_1(w_1, w_2)dw_1 + P_2(w_1, w_2)dw_2 \tag{14}$$

$$B = \int_0^{v_1} P_1(w_1, v_2)dw_1 + \int_0^{v_2} P_2(0, w_2)dw_2$$

which is calculated along the path II: $(0,0) \rightarrow (0,v_2)$ and $(0,v_2) \rightarrow (v_1,v_2)$.

C. MATHEMATICAL FORMULATION OF CONGESTION PRICING MODELS

In this section, we present formulations of two sets of congestion pricing models: welfare-maximizing congestion pricing models and profit-maximizing congestion pricing models.

Formulation of Welfare-Maximizing Congestion Pricing Models

A Second-Best Congestion Pricing Model

Given the theoretical framework in the previous sections, a second-best congestion pricing problem (model SB) can thus be formulated as a constrained optimization program. The problem is to maximize net benefits, or

$$\max W = B - C \tag{15}$$

$$= \int_{(0,0)}^{(v_1,v_2)} P_1(w_1, w_2)dw_1 + P_2(w_1, w_2)dw_2$$

$$- [v_{1t}c_{1t}(v_{1t}) + v_{1f}c_{1f}(v_{1f})] - [v_{2t}c_{2t}(v_{2t}) + v_{2f}c_{2f}(v_{2f})],$$

subject to

$$P_1(v_1,v_2) = c_{1f}(v_{1f}) = c_{1t}(v_{1t}) + \tau_{1t}, \tag{16}$$

$$P_2(v_1,v_2) = c_{2f}(v_{2f}) = c_{2t}(v_{2t}) + \tau_{2t}, \tag{17}$$

$$v_1 = v_{1t} + v_{1f};\ v_2 = v_{2t} + v_{2f}, \tag{18}$$

$$v_{1t} \geq 0,\ v_{1f} \geq 0,\ v_{2t} \geq 0,\ v_{2f} \geq 0,\ v_1 \geq 0,\ v_2 \geq 0. \tag{19}$$

where congestion tolls on the toll route are denoted by τ_{1t} and τ_{2t}. Equation (16) is the constraint on the pricing of the free route in the peak period. In the peak period the equilibrium price of a trip on either route is equal to the average cost on the free route. The equilibrium price of the trip on the toll route is the average cost plus the congestion toll in the peak period. Equation (17) is the similar condition for the pre-peak period. Equation (18) states that the total traffic volume in a period is the sum of the volumes on the toll route and the free route. Equation (19) is the nonnegativity condition for traffic volumes.

By solving the model for optimal traffic volume allocation ($v_{1t}, v_{1f}, v_{2t}, v_{2f}, v_1, v_2$), the second-best congestion tolls (τ_{1t}, τ_{2t}) on the toll route for the peak and pre-peak periods are determined by:

$$\tau_{1t} = P_1(v_1,v_2) - c_{1t}(v_{1t}), \text{ and } \tau_{2t} = P_2(v_1,v_2) - c_{2t}(v_{2t}). \tag{20}$$

The Lagrangian of the second-best problem is written as:

$$\begin{aligned} L(v_{1t},v_{1f},v_{2t},v_{2f},v_1,v_2) = {} & B(v_1,v_2) - C(v_{1t},v_{1f},v_{2t},v_{2f}) \\ & - \lambda_1[P_1(v_1,v_2) - c_{1f}(v_{1f})] - \lambda_2[P_2(v_1,v_2) - c_{2f}(v_{2f})] \\ & - \mu_1[v_1 - v_{1t} - v_{1f}] - \mu_2[v_2 - v_{2t} - v_{2f}] \end{aligned} \tag{21}$$

By Theorem 1, the first-order conditions for (21) are derived as follows:

$$\partial L/\partial v_{1t} = -MC_{1t} + \mu_1 = 0 \tag{22}$$

$$\partial L/\partial v_{1f} = -MC_{1f} + \lambda_1 c'_{1f}(v_{1f}) + \mu_1 = 0 \tag{23}$$

$$\partial L/\partial v_{2t} = -MC_{2t} + \mu_2 = 0 \tag{24}$$

$$\partial L/\partial v_{2f} = -MC_{2f} + \lambda_2 c'_{2f}(v_{2f}) + \mu_2 = 0 \tag{25}$$

$$\partial L/\partial v_1 = P_1 - \lambda_1 P_{11} - \lambda_2 P_{21} - \mu_1 = 0 \tag{26}$$

$$\partial L/\partial v_2 = P_2 - \lambda_1 P_{12} - \lambda_2 P_{22} - \mu_2 = 0 \tag{27}$$

$$\partial L/\partial \lambda_1 = -P_1(v_1,v_2) + c_{1f}(v_{1f}) = 0 \tag{28}$$

$$\partial L/\partial \lambda_2 = -P_2(v_1,v_2) + c_{2f}(v_{2f}) = 0 \tag{29}$$

$$\partial L/\partial \mu_1 = -v_1 + v_{1t} + v_{1f} = 0 \tag{30}$$

$$\partial L/\partial \mu_2 = -v_2 + v_{2t} + v_{2f} = 0 \tag{31}$$

$$v_{1t}\geq 0,\ v_{1f}\geq 0,\ v_{2t}\geq 0,\ v_{2f}\geq 0,\ v_1\geq 0,\ v_2\geq 0 \tag{32}$$

where MC_{ir} is the marginal cost on route r in period i, defined in (3), and P_{ij} represents the partial derivative of $P_i(v_1,v_2)$ with respect to v_j:

$$P_{ij} = \partial P_i/\partial v_j,\ \ i,j=1,2. \tag{33}$$

By eliminating v_1, v_2, λ_1, λ_2, μ_1, μ_2, conditions (22)-(32) can be simplified to the following system of equations for $(v_{1t},v_{1f},v_{2t},v_{2f})$:

$$P_1(v_1,v_2) = MC_{1t} + \lambda_1 P_{11} + \lambda_2 P_{21} \tag{34}$$

$$P_1(v_1,v_2) = c_{1f}(v_{1f}) \tag{35}$$

$$P_2(v_1,v_2) = MC_{2t} + \lambda_1 P_{12} + \lambda_2 P_{22} \tag{36}$$

$$P_2(v_1,v_2) = c_{2f}(v_{2f}) \tag{37}$$

$$v_{1t}\geq 0,\ v_{1f}\geq 0,\ v_{2t}\geq 0,\ v_{2f}\geq 0. \tag{38}$$

where v_1, v_2, λ_1, λ_2 are substituted respectively by:

$$v_1 = v_{1t}+v_{1f};\ \ v_2 = v_{2t}+v_{2f},\ \text{and} \tag{39}$$

$$\lambda_1 = (MC_{1f} - MC_{1t})/c'_{1f}(v_{1f});$$

$$\lambda_2 = (MC_{2f} - MC_{2t})/c'_{2f}(v_{2f}). \tag{40}$$

Equations (34)-(38) are the optimality conditions of model SB for each route and for each period. Among them, (34) and (36) are the optimality conditions of the trip prices for the toll route in the peak and pre-peak periods, respectively. Equation (34) ((36)) says that the trip price on the toll route for the peak (pre-peak) period is equal to the marginal cost plus two adjustment terms for the peak (pre-peak) period. In general, it is difficult to solve equations (34)-(38) analytically. Hence, in chapter 9, some special cost and demand functions will be utilized to solve these equations numerically.

By substituting (34) and (36) into (20), the second-best congestion tolls can be expressed as follows:

$$\tau_{1t} = v_{1t}\, c'_{1t}(v_{1t}) + \lambda_1 P_{11} + \lambda_2 P_{21},\ \text{and} \tag{41}$$

$$\tau_{2t} = v_{2t} c'_{2t}(v_{2t}) + \lambda_1 P_{12} + \lambda_2 P_{22}.$$

Equation (41) indicates that: (1) the second-best tolls are endogenously determined by the traffic volumes; and (2) the second-best toll for each period is equal to the marginal congestion cost plus two adjustment terms. As explained earlier, because it is rather difficult to find the traffic volume analytically, the congestion tolls can only be computed in a numerical way or by simulation.

Two Alternative Congestion Pricing Models

To evaluate the second-best congestion pricing scheme, it is necessary to study two other regimes for the system: the first-best problem (model FB), in which congestion tolls can be imposed on both routes; and the no-toll problem (model NT) in which congestion tolls cannot be imposed on any route. For the first-best problem, there are no pricing constraints. In this case, net benefits B-C in (15) are maximized:

$$\max W = B - C$$

$$= \int_{(0,0)}^{(v_1,v_2)} P_1(w_1,w_2)dw_1 + P_2(w_1,w_2)dw_2$$

$$- [v_{1t}c_{1t}(v_{1t}) + v_{1f}c_{1f}(v_{1f})] - [v_{2t}c_{2t}(v_{2t}) + v_{2f}c_{2f}(v_{2f})],$$

$$= B(v_1,v_2) - C(v_{1t},v_{1f},v_{2t},v_{2f}) \tag{42}$$

subject to traffic volume constraints (18) and nonnegativity condition (19).

The Lagrangian of the first-best problem is written as:

$$L_1(v_{1t},v_{1f},v_{2t},v_{2f},v_1,v_2) = B(v_1,v_2) - C(v_{1t},v_{1f},v_{2t},v_{2f}) - \mu_1[v_1 - v_{1t} - v_{1f}] - \mu_2[v_2 - v_{2t} - v_{2f}] \tag{43}$$

By Theorem 1, the first order conditions of (43) lead to the following system of equations for $(v_{1t},v_{1f},v_{2t},v_{2f})$:

$$P_1(v_1,v_2) = MC_{1t} \tag{44}$$

$$P_1(v_1,v_2) = MC_{1f} \tag{45}$$

$$P_1(v_1,v_2) = MC_{2t} \tag{46}$$

$$P_2(v_1,v_2) = MC_{2f} \tag{47}$$

$$v_{1t}\geq 0,\ v_{1f}\geq 0,\ v_{2t}\geq 0,\ v_{2f}\geq 0, \tag{48}$$

where v_1, v_2 are equal to.

$$v_1 = v_{1t}+v_{1f};\ \ v_2 = v_{2t}+v_{2f}. \tag{49}$$

Equations (44)-(48) are the optimality conditions of model FB for each route and for each period. These conditions says that the trip price for each route and for each period is given by its marginal cost. From (44)-(47), and the notation in (3), the first-best congestion tolls can be derived as follows:

$$\tau_{1t} = P_1(v_1,v_2) - c_{1t}(v_{1t}) = v_{1t}c'_{1t}(v_{1t}) \tag{50}$$

$$\tau_{1f} = P_1(v_1,v_2) - c_{1f}(v_{1f}) = v_{1f}c'_{1f}(v_{1f})$$

$$\tau_{2t} = P_2(v_1,v_2) - c_{2t}(v_{2t}) = v_{2t}c'_{2t}(v_{2t})$$

$$\tau_{2f} = P_2(v_1,v_2) - c_{2f}(v_{2f}) = v_{2f}c'_{2f}(v_{2f}),$$

where $c_{ir}(v_{ir})$ ($i=1,2$; $r=t,f$) is the average cost for a traveler; $v_{ir}c'_{ir}(v_{ir})$ is called the *marginal congestion cost*, which represents the cost that the traveler imposes on all other travelers by adding to the level of congestion.

For the no-toll problem, no maximization is involved. Traffic volumes are determined by the following equilibrium conditions:

$$P_1(v_1,v_2) = c_{1t}(v_{1t}) = c_{1f}(v_{1f}), \text{ and} \tag{51}$$

$$P_2(v_1,v_2) = c_{2t}(v_{2t}) = c_{2f}(v_{2f}). \tag{52}$$

with traffic volume constraints (18) and nonnegativity condition (19).

Formulation of Profit-Maximizing Congestion Pricing Models

Profit maximization is a plausible assumption when a highway network (part or entire) is operated by a private company which holds a partial monopoly as in the California State Route-91 (SR-91) case. In this case, we only consider the short run costs, the long run capital costs are ignored. Instead of maximizing B-C from (15), the monopolist maximizes profits (i.e., toll revenues):

$$\begin{aligned} \max R &= v_{1t}(P_1-c_{1t}) + v_{1f}(P_1-c_{1f}) + v_{2t}(P_2-c_{2t}) + v_{2f}(P_2-c_{2f}) \\ &= v_1P_1(v_1,v_1) + v_2P_2(v_1,v_1) \\ &\qquad - [v_{1t}c_{1t}(v_{1t}) + v_{1f}c_{1f}(v_{1f})] - [v_{2t}c_{2t}(v_{2t}) + v_{2f}c_{2f}(v_{2f})] \end{aligned} \tag{53}$$

As in the welfare-maximizing models, the profit-maximizing models can also be classified as one-route toll and two-route toll models. The one-route toll model is to maximize R subject to the constraints (16)-(19). The Lagrangian of the one-route toll model is:

$$\begin{aligned} L(v_{1t},v_{1f,}v_{2t,},v_{2f,}v_1,v_2) = R &- \lambda_1[P_1(v_1,v_2) - c_{1f}(v_{1f})] \\ &- \lambda_2[P_2(v_1,v_2) - c_{2f}(v_{2f})] \\ &- \mu_1[v_1 - v_{1t} - v_{1f}] - \mu_2[v_2 - v_{2t} - v_{2f}]. \end{aligned} \tag{54}$$

The first order conditions of (54) lead to the following system of equations for $(v_{1t}, v_{1f}, v_{2t}, v_{2f})$:

$$P_1(v_1,v_2) = MC_{1t} + (\lambda_1 - v_1)P_{11} + (\lambda_2 - v_2)P_{21} \quad (55)$$

$$P_1(v_1,v_2) = c_{1f}(v_{1f}) \quad (56)$$

$$P_2(v_1,v_2) = MC_{2t} + (\lambda_1 - v_1)P_{12} + (\lambda_2 - v_2)P_{22} \quad (57)$$

$$P_2(v_1,v_2) = c_{2f}(v_{2f}) \quad (58)$$

$$v_{1t} \geq 0,\ v_{1f} \geq 0,\ v_{2t} \geq 0,\ v_{2f} \geq 0. \quad (59)$$

where P_{ij} is given by (33), and v_1, v_2, λ_1, λ_2 are substituted for, respectively, by

$$v_1 = v_{1t} + v_{1f};\ v_2 = v_{2t} + v_{2f}, \text{ and} \quad (60)$$

$$\lambda_1 = (MC_{1f} - MC_{1t})/c'_{1f}(v_{1f});$$

$$\lambda_2 = (MC_{2f} - MC_{2t})/c'_{2f}(v_{2f}). \quad (61)$$

The profit-maximizing two-route toll model is to maximize R subject to traffic volume constraints (18) and nonnegativity condition (19). The Lagrangian is:

$$L_2(v_{1t}, v_{1f}, v_{2t}, v_{2f}, v_1, v_2) = R - \mu_1[v_1 - v_{1t} - v_{1f}] - \mu_2[v_2 - v_{2t} - v_{2f}]. \quad (62)$$

The first order conditions of (62) lead to the following system of equations for $(v_{1t}, v_{1f}, v_{2t}, v_{2f})$:

$$P_1(v_1,v_2) + v_1P_{11} + v_2P_{21} = MC_{1t} = MC_{1f} \quad (63)$$

$$P_2(v_1,v_2) + v_1P_{12} + v_2P_{22} = MC_{2t} = MC_{2f} \quad (64)$$

$$v_{1t} \geq 0,\ v_{1f} \geq 0,\ v_{2t} \geq 0,\ v_{2f} \geq 0, \quad (65)$$

and v_1, v_2 are given by (60). Equations (63) and (64) simply state that marginal revenue equals marginal cost.

D. SUMMARY

In this chapter, we present the mathematical formulations of two sets of congestion pricing models: welfare-maximizing and profit-maximizing congestion pricing models. For welfare-maximizing models, three models, model SB (second-best), model FB (first-best), and model NT (no-toll) are considered. And for each of the three models, the first-order conditions are equivalent to the system of equations for the traffic volume allocation. However, it is in general difficult to obtain analytical solutions of these equations without specifying the cost and demand functions. Therefore, there is a need to conduct a simulation study and this will be the task for chapter 9.

References

Arnott, R., A. dePalma, and R. Lindsey, 1990a, Economics of a bottleneck, Journal of Urban Economics 27, 111-130.

Arnott, R., A. dePalma, and R. Lindsey, 1990b, Departure time and route choice for the morning commute, Transportation Research 24B, 209-228.

Ben-Akiva, M., A. dePalma, and P. Kanaroglou, 1986, Dynamic model of peak period traffic congestion with elastic arrival rates, Transportation Science 20, 164-181.

Berstein, D. and I. El Sanhouri, 1994, Congestion pricing with an untolled alternative, draft paper, MIT, Cambridge, MA.

Braid, R., 1996, Peak-load pricing of a transportation route with an unpriced substitute, Journal of Urban Economics 40, 179-197.

Downs, A., 1992, Stuck in Traffic: Coping with Peak-Hour Traffic Congestion, Washington, D. C.: The Brookings Institution.

Levy-Lambert, H., 1968, Tarification des services a qualite variable: Application aux peages de circulation, Econometrica 36, 564-574.

Marchand, M., 1968, A note on optimal tolls in an imperfect environment, Econometrica 36, 575-581.

Mohring, H., 1970, The peak load problem with increasing returns and pricing constraints, American Economic Review 60, 693-705.

Pressman, I., 1970, A mathematical formulation of the peak-load pricing problem, Bell Journal of Economics 1, 304-324.

Small, K., 1982, The scheduling of consumer activities: Work trips, American Economic Review 72, 467-479.

Small, K., 1992, Urban Transportation Economics, Chur, Switzerland: Harwood Academic Publishers.

Verhoef, E., P. Nijkamp, and P. Rietveld, 1996, Second-best congestion pricing: The case of an unpriced alternative, Journal of Urban Economics 40, 279-302.

Vickrey, W., 1969, Congestion theory and transportation investment, American Economic Review, Papers and Proceedings 59, 251-261.

9 A SIMULATION STUDY OF PEAK AND OFF-PEAK CONGESTION PRICING

A. INTRODUCTION

In chapter 8, we derived the first-order conditions for both welfare-maximizing and profit-maximizing congestion pricing models. The welfare-maximizing congestion pricing models include model SB (second-best), model FB (first-best), and model NT (no-toll). For each of the three models, we demonstrate that the first-order conditions are equivalent to the system of equations for traffic volume allocation ($v_{1t}, v_{1f}, v_{2t}, v_{2f}$): equations (34)-(38) for model SB, (44)-(48) for model FB, and (51)-(52) for model NT, respectively. This chapter provides solution methods to solve the equivalent systems of equations for the three models. The solution procedure also applies to the profit-maximizing congestion pricing models.

In this chapter, we focus our attention on welfare-maximizing congestion pricing models only. The study of the profit-maximizing congestion pricing models was conducted in Liu and McDonald (1998). The next section will specify the cost and demand functions, and describe solution methods for the simulation study. Following that, we will make an extensive analysis of the simulation results of traffic volume allocations, congestion tolls, and social welfare properties for different cost and demand scenarios.

B. SPECIFICATION OF COST AND DEMAND FUNCTIONS

Specification of Cost Functions

The average cost $c_{ir}(v_{ir})$, defined in (1) in chapter 8, includes travel time costs, vehicle operating costs and schedule-related costs, and applies the FHWA function (Branston (1976)):

$$c_{ir}(v_{ir}) = l_r[\gamma_r + \delta_r(v_{ir}/K_r)^4] + S_i, \quad i=1,2; \quad r=t,f, \tag{1}$$

where l_r is the length of route r (miles); $\gamma_r=\alpha T_r^0+\beta$; $\delta_r=0.15\ \alpha T_r^0$, where α is the value of travel time (cents per minute) and is equal to 10.6 (Small (1982)), β is the operating costs (cents per mile) and is equal to 6.8 (Small (1992)), and T_r^0 is the uncongested travel time (minutes) per mile on route r; K_r is the level of capacity (vehicles per hour) on route r. Since K_r is less than the maximum flow of route r, traffic volume v_{ir} may exceed K_{ir}. S_i is the schedule-related cost (cents) for period i, S_1=0 for the peak period and S_2 is equal to 33 for the off-peak period (Small (1992)).[1]

From (1), the derivative of the average cost function, $c'_{ir}(v_{ir})$, and the marginal cost function MC_{ir}, can be calculated from (2) and (3) respectively, as follows:

$$c'_{ir}(v_{ir}) = 4(l_r\delta_r/K_r)(v_{ir}/K_r)^3,\quad i=1,2;\ r=t,f. \tag{2}$$

$$MC_{ir} = l_r[\gamma_r + 5\delta_r(v_{ir}/K_r)^4] + S_i,\quad i=1,2;\ r=t,f. \tag{3}$$

In order to conduct the simulation study, the parameters (T_t^0, T_f^0, K_t, K_f) need to be assigned values. The simulation study is designed to solve the models for different *cases*, which represent different scenarios in the study network (i.e., the supply side). A basic assumption is that the toll route has a free flow travel time lower than or equal to the free route, i.e., $T_t^0 \leq T_f^0$. Given this assumption, four cases are considered:

Case 1: The toll route has a lower free flow travel time than the free route; and two routes have identical capacities: $T_t^0 = 1$, $T_f^0 = 2$, $K_t = K_f = 2000$.

Case 2: The toll route has a lower free flow travel time and a larger capacity than the free route: $T_t^0 = 1$, $T_f^0 = 2$, $K_t = 2000$, $K_f = 1000$. This case represents the scenario in which congestion tolls can be imposed in a major portion of the network.

Case 3: The toll route has a lower free flow travel time and a smaller capacity than the free route: $T_t^0 = 1$, $T_f^0 = 2$, $K_t = 1000$, $K_f = 2000$. This case represents the scenario in which congestion tolls can be imposed only in a small portion of the network.

Case 4: This is a special case in which the two routes have identical free flow travel times and capacities: $T_t^0 = T_f^0 = 2$, $K_t = K_f = 2000$.

For Cases 1-4, the two routes are assumed to have the same lengths which are equal to one mile, i.e., $l_t = l_f = 1$.

Specification of Demand Functions

The demand functions for the peak and pre-peak periods are assumed to be linear:

$$v_1 = Q_1 - \beta_{11} P_1 + \beta_{12} P_2, \text{ and}$$
$$v_2 = Q_2 + \beta_{21} P_1 - \beta_{22} P_2. \tag{4}$$

where Q_i is the potential demand in period i, and $Q_1 > Q_2$, i.e., the potential demand in the peak period is higher than the off-peak. Coefficients $\beta_{ij} > 0$, indicating negative own-price effect and positive cross-price effect. As implied by the integrability condition (10) in chapter 8, the cross-price effects are equal: $\beta_{12} = \beta_{21}$. It is also assumed that the own-price effects outweigh the cross-price effects: $\beta_{11}\beta_{22} - \beta_{12}\beta_{21} > 0$.

From (4), the inverse demand functions are also linear:

$$P_1 = A_1 - b_{11}v_1 - b_{12}v_2, \text{ and } P_2 = A_2 - b_{21}v_1 - b_{22}v_2. \tag{5}$$

where coefficients $b_{12} = b_{21}$ because $\beta_{12} = \beta_{21}$.

For the base case simulation, the demand parameters are based on Wohl and Hendrickson (1984). The values of Q_1 and Q_2 (vehicles per hour) are set to 7500 and 4000 respectively. And β_{ij} is given by: $\beta_{11} = 21$, $\beta_{12} = \beta_{21} = 15$, and $\beta_{22} = 25$.

Solution Methods

After specifying the cost and demand functions, we can obtain the optimal traffic volume allocations by solving the nonlinear systems of equations, which are presented in chapter 8: (34)-(38) for model SB, (44)-(48) for model FB, and (51)-(52) for model NT, respectively. The solutions to the three models: second-best (SB), first-best (FB), and no-toll (NT), can be computed numerically by applying the Newton's method, to each of the four cases considered in the cost functions. For each case, the output includes, (1) optimal traffic volume allocations; (2) congestion tolls, equilibrium average cost, and trip prices; and (3) social welfare, welfare gains, and relative welfare improvement, for models SB, FB and NT, respectively. The results of Cases 1-4 with the base parameters are presented in Tables 1-4 respectively. For each table, rows 1-4 are traffic volumes, rows 5-8 are tolls, costs and trip prices, and rows 9-12 are welfare characteristics.

C. ANALYSIS OF SIMULATION RESULTS

In this section we first describe the simulation results with the base parameters and then presents the results of sensitivity analyses of some key cost and demand parameters.

Analysis of Traffic Volume Allocations

As shown in Tables 9-1 to 9-4, the imposition of congestion tolls in models FB and SB has three major impacts on the traffic volume allocations: (1) diversion of the peak period traffic to the free route in Model SB; (2) shift of the peak period traffic to the pre-peak period; and (3) reduction in total traffic volumes.

First, under the SB regime, the peak period traffic is diverted to the free route because there is a toll on the toll route and the free route is untolled. In Tables 9-1 to 9-4 (rows 1-4), by comparing the (v_{1t}, v_{1f}) for the SB with that for the NT, it is shown that the peak traffic goes down on the toll route and goes up on the free route for all four cases. Under the FB regime, however, the peak traffic goes down on both routes compared to the NT regime because of the imposition of the tolls on the two routes.

It is worth noting that in Case 4, traffic volume is split evenly between the toll route and the free route in both the peak and the pre-peak periods for the NT and FB regimes. This property can be derived analytically as follows. From the equivalent system of equations (44)-(47), and (51)-(52) in chapter 8, the following equations hold for the FB and the NT respectively.
For the FB,

$$MC_{1t} = MC_{1f}; \quad MC_{2t} = MC_{2f}. \tag{6}$$

For the NT,

$$c_{1t}(v_{1t}) = c_{1f}(v_{1f}); \quad c_{2t}(v_{2t}) = c_{2f}(v_{2f}). \tag{7}$$

Substituting the marginal cost function (3) into (6), and the average cost function (1) into (7), the above equations become:
For the FB,

$$l_t[\gamma_t + 5\delta_t(v_{1t}/K_t)^4] = l_f[\gamma_f + 5\delta_f(v_{1f}/K_f)^4], \text{ and} \tag{8}$$

$$l_t[\gamma_t + 5\delta_t(v_{2t}/K_t)^4] = l_f[\gamma_f + 5\delta_f(v_{2f}/K_f)^4].$$

For the NT,

$$l_t[\gamma_t + \delta_t(v_{1t}/K_t)^4] = l_f[\gamma_f + \delta_f(v_{1f}/K_f)^4], \text{ and} \tag{9}$$

Table 9-1
Simulation Results of Case 1 with the Base Parameters

Case 1: $T_t^0 = 1$, $T_f^0 = 2$; $K_t = K_f = 2000$

Model	v_{1t}	v_{1f}	v_{2t}	v_{2f}	v_1	v_2	V
NT	4212	3193	3214	76	7405	3289	10694
FB	3555	2884	2379	1521	6439	3900	10340
SB	3809	3443	2273	1121	7252	3394	10645

	(τ_{1t},τ_{1f})	(τ_{2t},τ_{2f})	(c_{1t},c_{1f})	(c_{2t},c_{2f})	P_1	P_2
NT	(0, 0)	(0, 0)	(43.4, 43.4)	(54.5, 54.5)	43.4	54.5
FB	(65.9, 57.1)	(13.2, 4.4)	(27.5, 36.3)	(46.8, 55.6)	93.4	60
SB	(18.3, 0)	(8.6, 0)	(32.7, 51)	(46.3, 54.8)	51	54.8

	W ($)	ΔW ($)	RW (%)
NT	38813.17	0	
FB	39530.14	716.97	100
SB	39141.28	328.11	45.8

Notes: Units of traffic volumes are vehicle per hour; units of tolls, of costs and trip prices are cents per mile per vehicle. RW=Relative welfare gain.

Table 9-2
Simulation Results of Case 2 with the Base Parameters

Case 2: $T_t^0 = 1$, $T_f^0 = 2$; $K_t = 2000$, $K_f = 1000$

Model	v_{1t}	v_{1f}	v_{2t}	v_{2f}	v_1	v_2	V
NT	4893	1954	3225	461	6847	3686	10532
FB	4024	1656	2963	1149	5680	4111	9791
SB	4261	2154	2935	1012	6415	3947	10361

	(τ_{1t},τ_{1f})	(τ_{2t},τ_{2f})	(c_{1t},c_{1f})	(c_{2t},c_{2f})	P_1	P_2
NT	(0, 0)	(0, 0)	(70.1, 70.1)	(54.6, 54.6)	70.1	54.6
FB	(108.1, 99.3)	(31.8, 23)	(38, 46.8)	(51.4, 60.2)	146.1	83.2
SB	(48.1, 0)	(6.8, 0)	(45, 93.1)	(51.1, 58)	93.1	58

	W ($)	ΔW ($)	RW (%)
NT	36907.46	0	
FB	38232.15	1324.69	100
SB	37507.66	600.2	45.3

Notes: Units of traffic volumes are vehicle per hour; units of tolls, of costs and trip prices are cents per mile per vehicle. RW=Relative welfare gain.

Table 9-3
Simulation Results of Case 3 with the Base Parameters

Case 3: $T_t^0 = 1$, $T_f^0 = 2$; $K_t = 1000$, $K_f = 2000$

Model	v_{1t}	v_{1f}	v_{2t}	v_{2f}	v_1	v_2	V
NT	2553	4115	1724	2041	6668	3765	10433
FB	2073	3421	1579	2500	5494	4079	9573
SB	2234	4264	1568	2282	6508	3850	10358

	(τ_{1t}, τ_{1f})	(τ_{2t}, τ_{2f})	(c_{1t}, c_{1f})	(c_{2t}, c_{2f})	P_1	P_2
NT	(0, 0)	(0, 0)	(81.1, 81.1)	(58.1, 58.1)	81.1	58.1
FB	(121.8, 112)	(41, 32.2)	(41.4, 50.2)	(53.8, 62.6)	163.2	94.8
SB	(37.3, 0)	(6.6, 0)	(52.8, 90.2)	(53.5, 60.1)	90.2	60.1

	W ($)	ΔW ($)	RW (%)
NT	36036.66	0	
FB	37446.42	1409.76	100
SB	36304.79	268.13	19

Notes: Units of traffic volumes are vehicle per hour; units of tolls, of costs and trip prices are cents per mile per vehicle. RW=Relative welfare gain.

Table 9-4
Simulation Results of Case 4 with the Base Parameters

Case 4: $T_t^0 = T_f^0 = 2$; $K_t = K_f = 2000$

Model	v_{1t}	v_{1f}	v_{2t}	v_{2f}	v_1	v_2	V
NT	3584	3584	1717	1717	7168	3433	10601
FB	3076	3076	1919	1979	6153	3958	10110
SB	3329	3721	1849	1849	7049	3520	10570

	(τ_{1t},τ_{1f})	(τ_{2t},τ_{2f})	(c_{1t},c_{1f})	(c_{2t}, c_{2f})	P_1	P_2
NT	(0, 0)	(0, 0)	(56, 56)	(56.3, 56.3)	56	56.3
FB	(73.9, 73.9)	(12.7, 12.7)	(40.5, 40.5)	(57.7, 57.7)	114.4	70.3
SB	(14.2, 0)	(-0.8, 0)	(47.3, 61.5)	(56.9, 56.1)	61.5	56.1

	W ($)	ΔW ($)	RW (%)
NT	37836.48	0	
FB	38479.74	643.26	100
SB	37909.69	73.2	11.4

Notes: Units of traffic volumes are vehicle per hour; units of tolls, of costs and trip prices are cents per mile per vehicle. RW=Relative welfare gain.

$$l_t[\gamma_t + \delta_t(v_{2t}/K_t)^4] = l_f[\gamma_f + \delta_f(v_{2f}/K_f)^4].$$

From (1), $l_t = l_f$ and $T_t^0 = T_f^0$ lead to:

$$\gamma_t = \gamma_f, \ \delta_t = \delta_f. \tag{10}$$

From (10), (8) and (9) becomes:

$$(v_{1t}/v_{1f}) = (v_{2t}/v_{2f}) = (K_t/K_f), \text{ for both FB and NT} \tag{11}$$

which means that the ratio of the traffic between the two routes in each period is proportional to the ratio of the capacities in Case 4 where the two routes have equal free flow travel times.

Finally, by $K_t = K_f$, (11) gives:

$$v_{1t} = v_{1f}, \text{ and } v_{2t} = v_{2f}, \text{ for both FB and NT} \tag{12}$$

which indicates that the two routes attract the same traffic in each period if the two routes have identical free flow travel times and capacities.

Secondly, in the presence of the tolls (SB and FB), there is a shift of traffic from the peak to the pre-peak period. Tables 9-1 to 9-4 display that for each of the SB and FB, the peak traffic v_1 ($= v_{1t}+v_{1f}$) falls and the pre-peak traffic v_2 ($= v_{2t}+v_{2f}$) rises in comparison with the NT. In each case, the FB induces a larger shift of traffic from the peak to the pre-peak than the corresponding SB. The reason is that since the FB charges the tolls on both routes, the peak traffic which would be switched to the free route in the SB regime is now forced to the pre-peak period. Note that each decrease in the peak traffic may not be equal to the corresponding increase in the pre-peak because the total demand V is not fixed.

Thirdly, the imposition of the congestion tolls also reduces the total traffic volume. Tables 9-1 to 9-4 demonstrate the reduction in the total traffic V ($=v_2+v_2$) for the SB and the FB compared to the NT regime. In each case, the FB generates a larger reduction than the SB because the FB allows the tolls on both routes. This implies that the FB is more effective than the SB in alleviating congestion.

Analysis of Congestion Tolls

After analyzing the impacts of the tolls on the traffic volume allocations, it is necessary to examine the quantitative aspects of the tolls, the signs and the sizes of the tolls in relation to the resulting traffic volume allocations. The congestion tolls, the equilibrium average costs and trip prices for Cases 1-4 are presented in Tables 9-1 to 9-4 (rows 5-8).

As discussed in chapter 8, the congestion tolls are endogenously determined by the equilibrium traffic volume allocations. Recall that the congestion tolls are defined as the difference between the trip price and the average cost:

$$\tau_{ir} = P_i(v_1,v_2) - c_{ir}(v_{ir}),\ \ i=1,2;\ r=t,f. \tag{13}$$

For equation (13), the tolls in model NT are equal to zero since no tolls are allowed on both routes; the second-best tolls on the free route are equal to zero since no tolls are allowed on the free route.

From equations (50) in chapter 8 and (2), the first-best toll can be derived analytically:

$$\tau_{ir} = 0.6(l_r\alpha\, T_r^0)(v_{ir}/K_r)^4,\ \ i=1,2;\ \ r=t,f. \tag{14}$$

which indicates that the first-best toll is positively related to the free flow travel time and the ratio of traffic-volume to capacity.

The first property from (14) is that the FB peak toll dominates the pre-peak toll on each of the two routes. As T_r^0 and K_r are the same between the peak and pre-peak period, and the traffic in the peak is higher than the pre-peak, the FB toll on each route is larger in the peak than the pre-peak period:

$$\tau_{1t}^{FB} > \tau_{2t}^{FB}\ ;\ \tau_{1f}^{FB} > \tau_{2f}^{FB}. \tag{15}$$

Another property is the free flow travel time is an important factor that determines the first-best tolls. In Case 4, the first-best tolls are equal between the two routes in each period. This fact can be derived analytically. Since $T_t^0 = T_f^0$ in Case 4, so (11) holds and is equivalent to:

$$(v_{1t}/K_t) = (v_{1f}/K_f);\ \ (v_{2t}/K_t) = (v_{2f}/K_f). \tag{16}$$

Substituting (16) into (14), and by $T_t^0 = T_f^0$, the first-best tolls have the following property:

$$\tau_{1t}^{FB} = \tau_{1f}^{FB}\ ;\ \tau_{2t}^{FB} = \tau_{2f}^{FB}. \tag{17}$$

This property indicates that the two routes have the same first-best tolls in each period as long as they have identical free flow travel times.

Unlike Case 4, in Cases 1-3, the FB tolls on the toll route are larger than those on the free route in both the peak and the pre-peak periods. Note that the FB toll in Case 2 is lower than the corresponding FB toll in Case 3 because of the lower ratio of the traffic volume to the capacity. For instance, in Case 2, the ratio for the toll route in the peak period is 2.01, compared to 2.07 in Case 3.

A common property shared by both Models FB and SB is that the peak toll on each route dominates the pre-peak toll on that route because each route has higher traffic-volume/capacity ratio in the peak than the pre-peak period. However, the second-best tolls differ sizably from the first-best tolls. In Cases 1-3, the SB tolls on the toll route are much smaller than the FB tolls in both the peak and the pre-peak periods. For example, the peak period toll on the toll route in Case 2 is \$1.08 per mile in model FB versus \$0.48 per mile in model SB.

A noticeable result for Case 4 is that the SB toll in the pre-peak period is negative. For example, τ_{2t} (cents per mile per vehicle) is equal to -0.8. The negativity implies that under some circumstance (e.g., the two routes have equal free flow travel times, etc.), people are encouraged to travel in the pre-peak period by being subsidized instead of being tolled in order to achieve the second-best goal.

Analysis of Social Welfare Properties

In addition to the effectiveness in reallocating the traffic volumes, another important measure for assessing the second-best congestion pricing scheme is the social welfare values (social benefits minus social costs) generated from such a scheme. Similarly to the previous analyses, the no-toll solution is taken as a benchmark, and the welfare properties of the second-best and the first-best solutions are studied in comparison with the NT solution.

The basic welfare properties can be derived analytically. Denote W_{NT}, W_{FB} and W_{SB} as the social welfare under the NT, FB and SB policies, respectively. The social welfare function W, given the specified cost and demand functions (1) and (5), can be calculated as:

$$W = \int_{(0,0)}^{(v_1,v_2)} P_1(w_1,w_2)dw_1 + P_2(w_1,w_2)dw_2$$
$$- [v_{1t}c_{1t}(v_{1t}) + v_{1f}c_{1f}(v_{1f})] - [v_{2t}c_{2t}(v_{2t}) + v_{2f}c_{2f}(v_{2f})]$$

$$= A_1v_1 + A_2v_2 - b_{12}v_1v_2 - (b_{11}/2)v_1^2 - (b_{22}/2)v_2^2$$
$$- [v_{1t}c_{1t}(v_{1t}) + v_{1f}c_{1f}(v_{1f})] - [v_{2t}c_{2t}(v_{2t}) + v_{2f}c_{2f}(v_{2f})] \tag{18}$$

Thus, W_{NT}, W_{FB} and W_{SB} can be written as follows:

$$W_{NT} = W(v \subset C_0) = W(v^0), \tag{19}$$

$$W_{FB} = \max W(v \in C_1) = W(v^*),$$

$$W_{SB} = \max W(v \in C_2) = W(v^{**}).$$

where $v=(v_1,v_2,v_{1t},v_{1f},v_{2t},v_{2f})$, the superscript 0, *, ** stand for the optimal values for the NT, FB and SB, respectively; C_0, C_1 and C_2 represent the sets of constraints in chapter 8: (51)-(52) for model NT; (48)-(49) for model FB; and (16)-(19) for model SB, respectively. It is easy to see that:

$$C_0 \in C_2 \in C_1. \tag{20}$$

Thus,

$$W_{NT} \leq W_{SB} \leq W_{FB}. \tag{21}$$

which indicates that the social welfare under the second-best scheme is at least as high as under the no-toll scheme; the social welfare under the first-best scheme is at least as high as under the second-best scheme. The property (21) can be rewritten in terms of the welfare gains of the SB and FB policies from the NT policy, denoted by $\Delta W_p = W_p - W_{NT}$, p=SB,FB.

$$0 \leq \Delta W_{SB} \leq \Delta W_{FB}. \tag{22}$$

and the relative welfare improvement of the SB to the FB, denoted by RW_{SB}:

$$0 \leq RW_{SB} = (\Delta W_{SB} / \Delta W_{FB}) \leq 1. \tag{23}$$

Inequalities (22) and (23) mean that both the SB and FB policies have welfare gains against the NT, but the gains under the FB policy are at least as large as under the SB policy.

The above welfare properties are tested using the simulation results. The tables (rows 9-12) indicate both the second-best and the first-best policies outweigh the no-toll policy; in other words, both the second-best and the first-best have welfare gains ($\Delta W>0$) against the no-toll policy. As expected, the first-best generates larger welfare gains than the second-best scheme; and the relative welfare improvement (RW) of the SB to the FB varies between Cases 1-4.

Tables 9-1 to 9-4 exhibit, when the two routes are similar in size, e.g., have equal capacities as in Cases 1 and 4, the social welfare under the three policies are higher than those in Cases 2 and 3. The reason is that the two routes in Cases 1 and 4 have the highest total capacities (4000 vehicles per hour) among the four cases and therefore can supply the most total traffic volumes. However, in Cases 1 and 4, the welfare gains generated by the SB and the FB policies are smaller than those in Case 2. In Case 1, the welfare gain under the FB policy is \$716.97 and the SB pricing policy yields a welfare gain of \$328.11, or 45.8 percent of the possible gain, which is the highest relative welfare improvement among all cases. The situation in Case 4 is quite different: the use of the FB scheme results in a welfare gain of \$643.26, but the SB scheme only yields a welfare gain of \$73.2. In this case nearly 90 percent of the welfare gain is lost because of the constraint that the free route cannot have a congestion toll.

Unlike Cases 1 and 4, the two routes are different in size in Cases 2 and 3. In Case 2, where two-thirds of the highway system is subject to toll, the welfare gain under the FB policy is \$1324.69 and the SB policy yields a welfare gain of \$600.2, or 45.3 percent of the possible gain. In Case 3, where only one-third of the highway system is subject to toll, the use of the FB scheme results in a welfare gain of \$1409.76, but the SB scheme only yields a welfare gain of \$268.13. In this case 81 percent of the welfare gain is lost because of the constraint that the free route cannot have a congestion toll.

Therefore, the failure to impose a congestion toll on a major portion of the network results in a major loss of the potential welfare gains. Furthermore, in the results, the relationship between the welfare gain and the proportion of the highway system covered by a toll is nonlinear. Cases 2 and 3 show that imposing a toll on 1/3 (2/3) of the system yields 19 percent (45 percent) of potential welfare gains. These net benefits of a toll system must be compared to the cost of the electronic toll collection system to determine overall net benefits.

Sensitivity Analysis of Cost and Demand Parameters

The purpose of this section is to test whether the conclusions from the previous sections are still valid after altering the values of some cost and demand parameters in the base case, including (1) the schedule-related cost parameter S_i, (2) the demand coefficient parameters β_{ij}s, and (3) the demand intercept parameters Q_is. We use Case 2 to conduct the sensitivity analysis.

First, we discuss the sensitivity analysis of the schedule-related cost parameter S_i. As discussed in earlier in the chapter, we handle a commuter's travel in the off-peak period in a different way from the previous studies. The study by Arnott et al. (1990) uses endogenous scheduling to model traveler's departure time choice by assuming the total demand is constant. While the conventional peak-load pricing model such as Pressman (1970) employs different demand functions for different periods but an identical cost function in each period. We combine the above two methods by introducing an exogenous schedule-related cost S_2 to the average cost function in the pre-peak period to distinguish the pre-peak period travel from the peak period. In addition, we also consider two distinct demand functions for the peak and pre-peak periods. This section tests whether the conclusions from the previous sections are still valid by assigning S_2=0, i.e., the case in which the average cost function in each period is identical.

Table 9-5 summarizes the results of Case 2 with S_2=0. Compared to the base results for Case 2, the decrease in S_2 causes the total peak traffic v_1 to fall and the total pre-peak traffic v_2 to rise for both models FB and SB, resulting a net increase in total traffic volume V due to the lower pre-peak travel cost. On the other hand, as a result of the reduction in S_2, the congestion tolls for models FB and SB decrease in the peak period and increase in the pre-peak period. The welfare gain in the second-best case drops from 45 to 40 percent of the gain in the first-best case. Overall, the change in S_2 does not affect the main conclusions found in the previous sections.

Secondly, the sensitivity analysis of the demand parameters is conducted by altering the coefficients (β_{11},β_{12},β_{21},β_{22}) in the base case. In one case, β_{12}(= β_{21}) is reduced by one-third and β_{11} and β_{22} remain unchanged. In the second case, each β_{ij} is reduced by one-third. Table 9-6 presents the results of Case 2 with the two sets of β's. As exhibited in Table 9-6, lower values for β_{12} and β_{21} lead to the

Table 9-5
Simulation Results of Case 2 with $S_2 = 0$

Case 2: $T_t^0 = 1$, $T_f^0 = 2$; $K_t = 2000$, $K_f = 1000$

Model	v_{1t}	v_{1f}	v_{2t}	v_{2f}	v_1	v_2	V
NT	4709	1862	3382	932	6571	4313	10885
FB	3956	1626	3188	1265	5581	4453	10034
SB	4188	2055	3248	1228	6244	4476	10719

	(τ_{1t},τ_{1f})	(τ_{2t},τ_{2f})	(c_{1t},c_{1f})	(c_{2t},c_{2f})	P_1	P_2
NT	(0, 0)	(0, 0)	(61.7, 61.7)	(24.5, 24.5)	61.7	24.5
FB	(101, 92.2)	(42.6, 33.8)	(36.2, 45)	(21.6, 30.4)	137.3	64.2
SB	(38.2, 0)	(7, 0)	(42.7, 80.9)	(22.5, 29.5)	80.9	29.5

	W ($)	ΔW ($)	RW (%)
NT	38678.09	0	
FB	39624.7	946.61	100
SB	39054.69	376.6	39.8

Notes: Units of traffic volumes are vehicle per hour; units of tolls, of costs and trip prices are cents per mile per vehicle. RW=Relative welfare gain.

Table 9-6
Simulation Results of Case 2 with New Demand Parameters β_{ij}s

Case 2: $T_t^0 = 1$, $T_f^0 = 2$; $K_t = 2000$, $K_f = 1000$

$\beta_{11} = 21$, $\beta_{12} = \beta_{21} = 10$, $\beta_{22} = 25$

Model	v_{1t}	v_{1f}	v_{2t}	v_{2f}	v_1	v_2	V
NT	4782	1899	3214	73	6681	3287	9968
FB	3886	1594	2629	953	5481	3583	9063
SB	4141	2103	2606	854	6244	3460	9704

	(τ_{1t},τ_{1f})	(τ_{2t},τ_{2f})	(c_{1t},c_{1f})	(c_{2t},c_{2f})	P_1	P_2
NT	(0, 0)	(0, 0)	(64.9, 64.9)	(54.5, 54.5)	64.9	54.5
FB	(94.1, 85.3)	(19.7, 10.9)	(34.5, 43.2)	(48.4, 57.2)	128.6	68.1
SB	(45.3, 0)	(8.0, 0)	(41.3, 86.6)	(48.3, 56.3)	86.6	56.3

	W ($)	ΔW ($)	RW (%)
NT	20965.93	0	
FB	22263.88	1297.96	100
SB	21590.29	624.36	48.1

$\beta_{11} = 14$, $\beta_{12} = \beta_{21} = 10$, $\beta_{22} = 18$

Model	v_{1t}	v_{1f}	v_{2t}	v_{2f}	v_1	v_2	V
NT	4993	2003	3233	532	6996	3765	10761
FB	4206	1738	3008	1173	5944	4181	10125
SB	4469	2207	2943	1016	6676	3959	10635

	(τ_{1t},τ_{1f})	(τ_{2t},τ_{2f})	(c_{1t},c_{1f})	(c_{2t},c_{2f})	P_1	P_2
NT	(0, 0)	(0, 0)	(75.1, 75.1)	(54.8, 54.8)	75.1	54.8
FB	(129.1, 120.3)	(33.8, 25.0)	(43.3, 52.1)	(51.9, 51.9)	172.4	85.7
SB	(48.2, 0)	(6.8, 0)	(52.1, 100.3)	(51.2, 58.0)	100.3	58.0

	W ($)	ΔW ($)	RW (%)
NT	52841.07	0	
FB	54147.07	1306.00	100
SB	53345.50	504.42	38.6

Notes: Units of traffic volumes are vehicle per hour; units of tolls, of costs and trip prices are cents per mile per vehicle. RW=Relative welfare gain.

reductions in traffic volumes and congestion tolls for model FB in both the peak and pre-peak periods, but have virtually no effect on other results. The welfare gain in the second-best case is raised to 48 percent of the gain in the first-best case. Similarly, smaller values for each β_{ij} cause the traffic volumes and congestion tolls to increase in both peak and pre-peak periods for model FB. And the relative welfare gain for model SB is down to 39 percent.

Finally, the potential demand for trips during the peak period, Q_1, is decreased by 10 percent and 20 percent respectively from the base case and Q_2 is fixed. Table 9-7 presents the sensitivity analysis results for Case 2 with the reduced Q_1s. As one would expect, in both cases, the decrease in demand causes the total traffic volumes and the peak period tolls to fall for model FB, but the welfare gains in model SB rise from 45 percent to 48 and 54 percent respectively.

D. SUMMARY

In this chapter, we use a simulation study to examine the peak and off-peak congestion pricing problems in the instance in which it is not possible to levy a congestion toll on a major portion of the urban road system. This case is pertinent because of technical and/or political constraints. By analyzing the three congestion pricing problems: second-best, first-best, and no-toll for a number of case scenarios, we find that the second-best policy has three major impacts on the allocation of traffic volume: (1) diversion of peak period traffic to the free route; (2) shift of peak period traffic to the off-peak period; and (3) reduction in total traffic volume.

However, the second-best tolls are less efficient than the first-best tolls in reallocating traffic volumes. Furthermore, the optimal second-best tolls are appreciably smaller than the first-best tolls. Lastly, the study shows that the welfare gains from the second-best tolls are much smaller than the welfare gains that are possible with a complete set of first-best tolls.

The simulations reported in this chapter lead us to the following conclusions:

- Within the range of values tried out, overall results for various cost and demand parameters are not sensitive to these changes, but there are some differences worth noting.

- Cases 2 and 3 show that coverage of system with toll from 0, 1/3, 2/3, 1 generates a nonlinear percentage of potential welfare gains: 0, 19, 45, 100.

- Cases 1 and 4 show that the system with faster toll route yields higher percentage of welfare gains: 46% vs. 11%.

- Demand parameters consist of slopes and intercepts. For the assumed

Table 9-7
Simulation Results of Case 2 with New Demand Parameters Q_is

Case 2: $T_t^0 = 1$, $T_f^0 = 2$; $K_t = 2000$, $K_f = 1000$

$Q_1 = 6750$

Model	v_{1t}	v_{1f}	v_{2t}	v_{2f}	v_1	v_2	V
NT	4583	1798	3215	270	6381	3485	9866
FB	3813	1561	2823	1071	5374	3894	9268
SB	4040	1998	2769	926	6038	3695	9733

	(τ_{1t}, τ_{1f})	(τ_{2t}, τ_{2f})	(c_{1t}, c_{1f})	(c_{2t}, c_{2f})	P_1	P_2
NT	(0, 0)	(0, 0)	(56.5, 56.5)	(54.5, 54.5)	56.5	54.5
FB	(87.2, 78.4)	(26.2, 17.4)	(32.8, 41.6)	(50.0, 58.8)	120.0	76.2
SB	(36.1, 0)	(7.4, 0)	(38.5, 74.6)	(49.6, 56.9)	74.6	56.9

	W ($)	ΔW ($)	RW (%)
NT	32334.62	0	
FB	33275.62	941	100
SB	32788.16	453.55	48.2

$Q_1 = 6000$

Model	v_{1t}	v_{1f}	v_{2t}	v_{2f}	v_1	v_2	V
NT	4255	1621	3214	96	5877	3310	9186
FB	3584	1456	2689	991	5039	3680	8719
SB	3795	1822	2622	848	5617	3470	9088

	(τ_{1t}, τ_{1f})	(τ_{2t}, τ_{2f})	(c_{1t}, c_{1f})	(c_{2t}, c_{2f})	P_1	P_2
NT	(0, 0)	(0, 0)	(44.8, 44.8)	(54.5, 54.5)	44.8	54.5
FB	(68.0, 59.2)	(21.6, 12.8)	(28.0, 57.7)	(48.9, 48.9)	96.1	70.4
SB	(26.0, 0)	(7.8, 0)	(48.4, 56.2)	(48.4, 56.2)	58.4	56.2

	W ($)	ΔW ($)	RW (%)
NT	27947.31	0	
FB	28599.91	652.59	100
SB	28301.15	353.84	54.2

Notes: Units of traffic volumes are vehicle per hour; units of tolls, of costs and trip prices are cents per mile per vehicle. RW=Relative welfare gain.

slopes, the basic conclusions hold but more empirical studies are needed to obtain estimates of the slopes. For the intercepts it is shown that with the potential peak demand reduced, percentage of possible welfare gains rises; second-best tolls fall in the peak and rise in the off-peak period.

- There is a possibility of negative second-best toll in the off-peak period with low potential off-peak demand.

Footnote

1. For qualitative purposes, the value of 33 cents is based on the assumption that an average commuter's schedule delay is worth three minutes of in-vehicle travel time, which is lower than the seven minutes reported by Small (1992, p. 78).

References

Arnott, R., A. dePalma, and R. Lindsey, 1990, Departure time and route choice for the morning commute, Transportation Research 24B, 209-228.

Branston, D., 1976, Link capacity functions: A review, Transportation Research 10, 223-236.

Liu, L., and J. McDonald, 1998, Efficient congestion tolls in the presence of unpriced congestion: A peak and off-peak simulation model, Journal of Urban Economics 44, 252-265.

Pressman, I. , 1970, A mathematical formulation of the peak-load pricing problem, Bell Journal of Economics 1, 304-324.

Small, K., 1992, Urban Transportation Economics, Chur, Switzerland: Harwood Academic Publishers.

Wohl, M. and C. Hendrickson, 1984, Transportation Investment and Pricing Principles, New York: John Wiley & Sons.

10 THE CALIFORNIA SR-91 EXAMPLE OF VALUE PRICING

A. INTRODUCTION

Increasing levels of traffic congestion in many urban areas and the ineffectiveness of other anti-congestion approaches have brought much attention to the possible use of congestion pricing as a technique for creating a more efficient urban transportation system. The Intermodal Surface Transportation Efficiency Act (ISTEA) of 1991 mandated that the U. S. Department of Transportation undertake a series of studies and demonstration projects to evaluate congestion pricing. ISTEA has been followed in 1998 by the Transportation Equity Act for the 21st Century (TEA-21). One portion of TEA-21 replaces the congestion pricing pilot program authorized by ISTEA with funds to support the costs of implementing "value pricing" projects that are included in up to 15 new state and local projects. Value pricing means that drivers pay tolls to have access to road capacity that previously was not available to them. It is likely that most of the value pricing projects will involve allowing vehicles with only one occupant to use lanes reserved for high occupancy vehicles provided that a toll is paid. At the same time some states have begun to consider the policy of congestion pricing. Most prominent among these is California, which now has the only urban expressway in the U.S. that is (as of December, 1998) specifically subject to time-of-day congestion pricing.

The purpose of this chapter is to examine California State Route 91 (SR-91), the California highway that has been subject to congestion tolls since December, 1995. The crucial feature of SR-91 is that two of its six lanes (in each direction) were constructed in the median of the original highway by a private firm and are subject to a toll that varies by time of day. The other four lanes must remain without tolls. This feature raises serious issues:

- What improvement in traffic flow resulted from adding two lanes (in each direction)?

- What is the efficient congestion toll under the constraint that only one-third of highway capacity can be subject to a toll? How does the efficient toll compare to the actual toll?

Our purpose therefore is to shed some light on the question of efficient pricing in situations that involve value pricing as defined above. The results presented here are relevant to the value pricing projects that will be undertaken in the coming years as part of TEA-21.

The plan of the chapter is first to describe the origins and operation of the SR-91 facility. Then the issue of efficient pricing is examined using the theory presented in Chapter 7. We show that the SR-91 facility combines two critical features; the two lanes upon which tolls are imposed are substitutes for the four original lanes, but the terminus of the facility is not the final destination for commuters who must continue on other free highways and arterials to their final destinations. The model that is relevant for SR-91 pricing includes both substitute routes and complementary routes. Assuming that traffic congestion exists on all relevant routes, the determination of the optimal second-best toll is difficult.

If it can be assumed that there is little or no traffic congestion on the complementary routes, then the simulation model of Chapters 8 and 9 can be used to study efficient second-best tolls and welfare gains. The details of the model are outlined, and the simulation results are presented. The basic result of the simulations is that, because a large fraction (two thirds) of the facility cannot be subject to a congestion toll, the second-best efficient peak-period toll is quite low and the welfare gains from this toll are modest. However, this conclusion holds only if there is little or no congestion on the complementary routes. Traffic congestion on complementary routes requires that efficient second-best tolls be higher than those computed in this chapter - perhaps much higher.

B. THE ORIGINS OF THE SR-91 FACILITY

California SR-91 is a six-lane expressway (in each direction) that connects residential Riverside County with employment centers in Orange County. The highway is ten miles in length and, because it runs through a mountainous area, is entered and exited only at its end points. SR-91 has four free lanes in each direction that are heavily congested in the peak hours, and the State of California had planned to build two additional lanes in each direction for high-occupancy vehicles (HOV) in the median of the highway. High-occupancy vehicles are cars (or other vehicles) that carry three or more people. The State of California discovered that it did not have the money to build these lanes, so it was decided to permit a private company (California Private Transportation Co. - CPTC) to build them and charge a toll for their use. The company issued bonds to pay most of the construction costs based on their projections of toll revenue. The State of California owns the land and the road itself, but has given the company a 35 year lease. The company sets the tolls to maximize profits, subject to a rate-of-return constraint. It should be noted that the company is not attempting to maximize social welfare. They are trying to maximize profits! The SR-91 Express Lanes opened on Dec. 27, 1995, and the use of the lanes has run well ahead of the company's forecast. See W. Reinhardt (1995) and D. Rizzo (1996) for details.

The build-transfer-operate franchise agreement for SR-91 was negotiated by the California Department of Transportation (CALTRANS) in 1990 and awarded in December, 1990. Three other experimental privatization agreements were negotiated in 1990, and SR-91 is the first project to be completed. The controlling shares of CPTC were originally held by CRSS, Inc., but these shares were sold in 1992 to Peter Kiewit Sons' Company, Inc. of Omaha and the private French toll owner-operator Cofiroute.

Financing was arranged in July, 1993 when the lead investor, Peter Kiewit Sons', agreed to purchase the $35 million 17-year institutional tranche of the total of $100 million in project debt. Another investor (Prudential Power Funding) had pulled out of the deal, which necessitated the purchase of this block of debt by the lead equity investor. CIGNA Investments subsequently purchased the debt from Kiewit in 1994. The other original debt holders are Citicorp, Banque Nationale de Paris, and Société General. Deutsche Bank joined these investors in 1994. These four investors hold $65 million in 14.5-year term loans. Because the $100 million in debt is issued by a private company, the returns are taxable. Also, the Orange County Transportation Authority left $7 million in reimbursable design and other expenses as a loan to be repaid after completion at 9%. Total debt is therefore $107 million.

The amount of funded equity is $19 million, which makes the total cost of the SR-91 project $126 million (i.e., 85% of the project is financed by debt). However, lenders required that the general partners agree that there be a sizable amount of unfunded contingent equity in case traffic and revenue fall short of projections. The lenders also require a 12-month debt service reserve. These provisions, if fully utilized, would add approximately $17 million to equity and make the debt-equity ratio 3:1.

Most of the land acquisition and environmental permitting was completed by CALTRANS and the Orange County Transportation Authority before Kiewit took over the project. The land remains the property of the State of California, and the costs of environmental permitting became part of the debt of the project.

The four express lanes, transition zones at each end, and interchanges were built by Granite Construction Co. with a 29-month construction contract of $56.9 million. Granite is a 21% limited equity partner in CPTC. The project was completed on schedule and within budget even though there were difficulties involved in constructing median lanes and other features of the project while the highway was in use (up to 250,000 vehicles per day).

The contract that CPTC holds gives the company 35 years from December 20, 1995 to pay off the $107 million in debt and earn a return. The contract puts a cap on the rate of return of 17% to equity and debt "blended" together, but does not regulate toll levels. It turns out that the rate of return on equity allowed under the contract can be as high as 65%, depending upon the cost of debt and whether various incentives in the contract are earned.

C. OPERATION OF THE SR-91 FACILITY

The SR-91 express lanes have been in operation since December 27, 1995. This section is a brief review of the experience of operating the facility in its first two years.

What are the tolls and how are they collected? The peak hour toll was set initially at $2.50 per vehicle (or $.25 per mile). Here is the initial toll schedule for a weekday morning on the inbound portion of the highway:

up to 4 A.M.	$.25
4 to 5	1.50
5 to 9	2.50
9 to 10	1.50
10 to 11	1.00
11 to 7 P.M.	.50
7 P.M. to 4 A.M.	.25

Initially, no toll was charged to a high-occupancy vehicle (3 or more persons), motorcycles, or cars with special disabled licenses. (Heavy trucks are not permitted on the express lanes.) The company estimates that about 30% of the vehicles using the express lanes are high-occupancy vehicles. Each user of the express lanes, including vehicles exempt from the toll, first had to set up an account with the company and deposit some money in the account. The required deposit is $40 on a credit card or $80 in cash. Each user is issued a transponder that is mounted on the inside of the windshield of the car. The toll collection area is located at the mid-point of the 10-mile road and is three lanes in width (each way). Users drive through two of these lanes at normal speeds, their presence is recorded, and the proper toll is deducted from their accounts. The high-occupancy vehicles drive through the third lane, their presence is recorded, but no toll is charged. An employee of the company sits at the toll collection area to verify that those vehicles using the third lane are in fact carrying three or more people. At this time there is no other reliable method for counting the people in the cars.

The tolls charged have been increased slightly in the first two years of operation. The peak toll was increased to $2.75 on January 1, 1997, and then increased again to $2.95 on September 14, 1997. The weekday tolls on the inbound portion of the highway (beginning September 14, 1997) are:

up to 4 A.M.	$.60
4 to 5	1.60
5 to 7	2.85
7 to 8	2.95
8 to 9	2.85
9 to 10	1.60
10 to 11	1.10
11 to 6 P.M.	.85

Starting in January, 1998 those vehicles that were previously exempt from tolls were charged tolls equal to 50% of the above rates. Those vehicles include high occupancy vehicles (3 or more people), motorcycles, and cars with special disabled licenses. This last change was made easily because, as noted above, all users of the express lanes had to set up an account and be equipped with a transponder. Also, beginning in January, 1997, users could join the "91 Express Club" by paying $15 per month. Club members get a discount of $.60 on every toll (e.g., they travel free between 6 P.M. and 4 A.M. on the inbound lanes).

It is notable that CPTC decided to use a published toll schedule rather than variable tolls that depend upon actual traffic levels. Setting tolls to reflect minute-by-minute changes in traffic conditions is within the capability of the electronic toll system. However, marketing analysis by CPTC prior to the opening of the express lanes showed that potential customers were not comfortable with unpredictable tolls.

Enforcement of the toll and the speed limit and other traffic laws is provided by the California Highway Patrol, which is paid for its services by CPTC. Enforcement is backed up by video records of all license plates. Addresses of violators are sent from the state Department of Motor Vehicles to CPTC by a computer link. Tickets not issued by the Highway Patrol are sent by CPTC to express lane violators. The fines are pretty steep. Motorists who have not obtained a transponder or who have failed to keep a positive balance in their accounts pay $100 for the first offense, $250 for the second offense (within one year), and $500 for each additional violation. Violators are unable to renew their vehicle registrations until they pay their fines, fees, or tolls to CPTC.

The extent and nature of the use of the express lanes is being studied by a research team headed by Professor Edward C. Sullivan of the Civil and Environmental Engineering Department at California Polytechnic State University at San Luis Obispo. We now turn to some of their initial findings, as reported by Sullivan and El Harake (1998).

We turn first to the traffic flow data for SR-91 as reported by Sullivan and El Harake (1998). All figures will refer to the weekday evening peak period on the eastbound portion of the highway. In February, 1995, prior to the opening of the express lanes, traffic volume on the four-lane SR-91 normally reached a maximum of 1900 vehicles per lane per hour at 3 P.M. and declined to 1400 vehicles per lane per hour during the 5 P.M. to 6 P.M. period. Volume would then increase to about 1600 vehicles per hour during the 6 P.M. to 7 P.M. hour. This is, in our view, a "classic" pattern of a highway that is operating with hypercongestion (negative marginal product of the variable input traffic density) during the peak period. Traffic density and volume both increased up to 3 P.M., and then further increases in density caused volume to drop. Traffic volume then increased as density declined as the rush hour started to subside. Note that the maximum volume of 1900 vehicles per lane per hour is virtually identical to the 1906 observed for the Eisenhower Expressway in metropolitan Chicago (as discussed in Chapters 3 and 6). Average speed in the peak period was approximately 15 mph.

Sullivan and El Harake (1998) report that, after the express lanes had opened and a year had passed, a new peak period equilibrium had been reached. Average speed in the express lanes is reported to be 65 mph, while average speed in the other four lanes is about 32 mph. These figures mean that the users of the express lanes were saving 9.52 minutes for the trip of 10 miles. (Elsewhere in their report Sullivan and El Harake state that users of the express lanes saved up to 12-13 minutes.) Traffic volume in February, 1997 increased steadily during the afternoon hours, reached a maximum of 1500 vehicles per lane per hour (9000 vehicles per hour on six lanes) during the 5 P.M. to 6 P.M. hour, and then declined as the peak period subsided. In other words, the addition of the two express lanes meant that the highway was no longer operating under conditions of hypercongestion. The data for February, 1997 also indicate that the express lanes were carrying about the same traffic volume of 1500 vehicles per lane per hour (at 65 mph) as were the other lanes (at 32 mph).

These basic facts about traffic before and after the opening of the express lanes can be combined with a production function for traffic volume to produce a preliminary analysis of the effects of adding the toll lanes to the capacity of SR-91. For this purpose we make use of a version of the two-input production function that was introduced in Chapter 2. We assume that traffic volume is produced according to

$$V = [2bKD - b^2D^2]^{0.5}, \tag{1}$$

where V is traffic volume per hour, K is the capital input, and D is traffic density. The function is defined for densities in the range of 0 to 2K/b. As demonstrated below, we assume that capacity (K) is measured in the same units as maximum flow; i.e., the evidence above for the SR-91 prior to the opening of the express lanes is that maximum flow was 1900 vehicles per lane per hour, or 7600 vehicles per hour for four lanes. The first derivatives of the production function are

$$\partial V/\partial dD = [bK - b^2D]/V \tag{2}$$

and

$$\partial V/\partial K = bD/V. \tag{3}$$

At the point of maximum volume dV/dD = 0, so that for any given capacity K_0, the density at which volume is a maximum is given by

$$D_0 = (1/b)K_0. \tag{4}$$

Substitution for D in equation (1) shows that the maximum volume V_0 is equal to K_0. Note that, from equation (4), the parameter b is interpreted as the speed (V/D) at the point of maximum traffic volume.

Recall that, before the express lanes were opened, maximum volume was

7600 vehicles per hour, and that volume during the rush hour was 5600 vehicles per hour at an average speed of 15 mph. Assume that vehicles average 18 feet in length. The evidence from the Eisenhower Expressway in Chapter 6 is that volume is maximized if the occupancy rate is 21.8%, which translates into a traffic density of 63.95 vehicles per lane per mile if each vehicle is 18 feet in length (i.e., (.218)(5280)/18). Maximum volume on the Eisenhower is 1906 vehicles per lane, so average speed at maximum volume is 29.8 mph (i.e., 1906/63.95). We shall use 29.8 as our estimate of b, the parameter in the production function. Substitution of 29.8 for b, 7600 for K, and 5600 for V into equation (1) produces an equation for traffic density during the peak period of

$$2bKD - b^2D^2 = V^2,$$

$$2(29.8)(7600) - (29.8)^2D^2 = (5600)^2, \text{ or}$$

$$454{,}390.4\ D - 888.04\ D^2 = 31{,}360{,}000.$$

One solution to this quadratic equation is density of 429.45 vehicles per mile (107.36 vehicles per lane per mile). At this density, average speed is V/D = 5600/429.45 = 13.04 mph, a figure that agrees quite well with the estimate of 15 mph noted above. The other solution to the quadratic equation is D = 82.23 vehicles per mile (20.56 vehicles per lane per mile), which generates an average speed of 68.10 mph. This is the solution on the "other side" of the point of maximum volume at volume of 5600 vehicles per hour.

Now consider the statement that, after the opening of the express lanes, peak hour traffic in the other four lanes was 1500 vehicles per hour at 32 mph (with density of 1500/32 = 46.88 vehicles per lane, or 187.5 for four lanes). These figures are not consistent with the statement that, prior to the opening of the express lanes, the four lanes carried 5600 vehicles per hour at a speed of 13 mph (or 15 mph, for that matter). Clearly 32 mph is very close to the speed of 29.8 at which traffic volume is at a maximum of about 1900 vehicles per lane per hour (7600 per hour for four lanes). Using our production function, traffic volume of 6000 vehicles per hour on four lanes is consistent with a speed of only 15 mph (or 60 mph). One plausible explanation for this discrepancy is that the construction of the express lanes also involved improvements that facilitate traffic flow on the other lanes as well. CALTRANS had the CPTC contractors add some auxiliary lanes to the unrestricted lanes beyond the end points of the express lanes, so the before-and-after analysis is not completely clean. Apparently the production function was shifted upward by these improvements.

The statement that the express lanes carry about 1500 vehicles per hour at a speed of 65 mph is reasonably consistent with our production function model. For two lanes the model is:

$$V = [2bKD - b^2D^2]^{0.5}$$

$$= [59.6(3800)D - 888.04D^2]^{0.5}, \text{ so}$$

$$V^2 = 226{,}480D - 888.04D^2.$$

Since speed is stated as 65 mph, V=65D and

$$V^2 = 3484.3V - .2102V^2, \text{ and}$$

$$V = 2879 \text{ (or 1440 per lane).}$$

Note that if speed were actually 60 mph, traffic volume as computed in the model is 3027 per hour for two lanes.

The SR-91 project is a crucial test case of the financial viability of this type of privatization of highway services. The first annual report issued by CPTC indicated that toll revenues in the first year were sufficient to cover operating costs, but were not sufficient to cover amortized capital costs. This result was expected, but the increases in tolls that were implemented in 1997 were motivated by the need to cover debt service expenses. Clearly more revenues will be needed, although Sullivan and El Harake (1998, p. 3) state that, "It seems reasonable to expect that profitability will eventually occur." Perhaps it need not be said that "eventually" may not be sufficient. The extent to which the SR-91 project represents a financially profitable venture will be determined in the coming years.

D. THEORY OF OPTIMAL TOLLS APPLIED TO SR-91

The operation of the SR-91 facility and its toll system have been described, and we turn now to the question of optimal tolls in such a situation. We formulate an optimization model for a second-best toll that follows the theory presented in Chapter 7. The SR-91 case has two critical features:

- Tolls can be imposed on only two lanes in each direction. The other four substitute lanes have no tolls.
- The endpoint of the SR-91 facility is not the final destination for commuters. They reach the terminus and then proceed to their various final destinations on free highways and arterials. These free highways and arterials are complementary routes with SR-91.

The model must therefore include both a route that substitutes for the toll route and a route that is complementary with the toll route. In fact, the substitute route is a perfect substitute, and the complementary route is a perfect complement.

In order to simplify the model, we assume that SR-91 tollway and freeway users all reach the same intermediate point (the terminus of SR-91), and then all proceed to the same final destination. Denote traffic volume on the tollway v_t and traffic volume on the free portion of SR-91 as v_f. Traffic volume on the complementary route is $v_g = v_f + v_t$. The average cost of taking the free portion of SR-91 is $c_f + c_g$, and the average cost of taking the tollway portion of $c_t + c_g + t$, where c_g is the average cost of the second leg of the journey and t is the toll on the tollway portion of SR-91. Following the presentation in Chapter 7, the Lagrangian function to be maximized is

$$L = \int B_t(v_t,v_f)dv_t + \int B_f(v_t,v_f)dv_f - v_t(c_t+c_g) - v_f(c_f+c_g) + \lambda[B_f(v_t,v_f) - c_f - c_g]. \quad (5)$$

Maximization of L with respect to v_t, v_f, and lamda produces the first-order conditions

$$B_t - [(c_t+c_g) + v_t(c_t'+c_g')] - \lambda(\partial B_f/\partial v_t - c_g') = 0, \quad (6)$$

$$B_f - [(c_f+c_g) + v_f(c_f'+c_g')] - \lambda[\partial B_f/\partial v_f - c_f' - c_g'] = 0, \quad (7)$$

and

$$B_f(v_t,v_f) = c_f + c_g \quad (8)$$

Also, we note that the toll is

$$t = B_t - c_t - c_g. \quad (9)$$

As before, we substitute these two conditions into the other two first-order conditions and solve for the optimal toll to yield

$$t^* = v_t(c_t'+c_g') + [(\partial B_f/\partial v_t) - c_g'][v_f(c_f'+c_g')/(c_f' + c_g' - \partial B_f/\partial v_f)]. \quad (10)$$

$$= v_t(c_t'+c_g') + (dv_f/dv_t)[v_f(c_f'+c_g')]. \quad (11)$$

This result states that the optimal second-best toll involves two adjustments to the usual first-best toll of v_tc_t'. One adjustment is an addition to the first-best toll equal to v_tc_g', which is the marginal congestion cost on the complementary route. The second adjustment is subtraction from the first best toll caused by traffic diversion to the substitute route. Consequently, we cannot in general determine whether the second-best toll in this sort of situation should be greater than or less than the first-best toll. Determination of the optimal second-best toll requires knowledge of traffic conditions both on the routes that are substitutes for and the routes that are complementary with the tollway in question. Information is readily available about the substitute route for the SR-91 case because the only relevant substitute is the free portion of the same highway. However, the adjustment to take account of complementary routes will require study of traffic conditions beyond the termini of SR-91. This is something that can be done, of course.

Precisely why the computation of efficient tolls requires such data is, we believe, pointed out here for the first time.

E. THE SIMULATION MODEL

The economic theory of congestion pricing that is used in this chapter has been presented in detail in Chapter 8. The full cost of a trip on a congested road includes not just the traveler's own time and vehicle operating costs, but also the costs that the traveler imposes on all other travelers by adding to the level of congestion. A congestion price can thus be viewed as a user charge that is based on the difference between the cost perceived by the user and the cost actually imposed on all users (including the user himself).

This section considers a simple urban highway system consisting of two routes connecting an origin (e.g., home) and a destination (e.g., the workplace). Note that there are no complementary routes in this model. The routes are assumed to be perfect substitutes, and all trips are made by private auto. The model includes two time periods, peak and off-peak, to describe the traveler's departure time choice. The study considers the problem of the morning commute; each traveler can travel either during the pre-peak (off-peak) period or during the peak period. The congestion toll is imposed on only one route, but the toll can be different in the pre-peak and peak periods.

Because the focus of the study is congestion, only short-run costs related to congestion are considered. The cost borne by an individual traveler consists of travel time cost and schedule-related cost. Travel time cost is caused by congestion in either the peak or pre-peak period, and is assumed to be a function of the traffic volume on the route in the period. Schedule-related cost is a penalty for a traveler who makes the trip in the pre-peak period, and is assumed to be exogenous in this study. Hence, an individual traveler can travel either in the peak period an incur higher travel costs and no schedule-related costs, or in the pre-peak period to avoid higher travel times but to bear the schedule-related cost. These two costs together constitute average cost, which is denoted by

$$c_{ir}(v_{ir}),\ i = 1,2;\ r = t,f, \tag{12}$$

where index i represents the time period (i=1 for peak and i=2 for pre-peak), index r represents the route (r=t for the toll route and r=f for the free route), and v_{ir} is traffic volume in period i on route r.

The cost of an additional unit of traffic volume, marginal cost, is

$$\begin{aligned} MC_{ir} &= d[v_{ir}c_{ir}(v_{ir})]/dv_{ir} \\ &= c_{ir}(v_{ir}) + v_{ir}c'_{ir}, \end{aligned} \tag{13}$$

where $c'_{ir}=dc_{ir}(v_{ir})/dv_{ir}$. The total cost consists of costs borne by all travelers (on all routes for all time periods), and is defined as

$$C = [v_{1t}c_{1t}(v_{1t}) + v_{1f}c_{1f}(v_{1f})] + [v_{2t}c_{2t}(v_{2t}) + v_{2f}c_{2f}(v_{2f})]. \quad (14)$$

It is assumed that the two periods are of equal duration.

The demand functions for the peak (i=1) and pre-peak (i=2) periods are given by $v_1=f_1(P_1,P_2)$ and $v_2=f_2(P_1,P_2)$, where v_i is the aggregate traffic volume for the period and p_i is the price of the trip for period i. It is assumed that own-price effects are negative and cross-price effects are positive. Income effects are assumed to be negligible. The inverse demand functions for each period can be derived from the demand functions, and are written

$$P_1 = P_1(v_1,v_2) \text{ and}$$

$$P_2 = P_2(v_1,v_2). \quad (15)$$

Given the inverse demand functions, the gross benefit for the system, denoted by B, can be expressed as the line integral of the sum of the two inverse demand functions. All of these features of the model are discussed in Chapter 8.

The second-best congestion pricing problem can thus be formulated as a constrained optimization problem. The problem is to maximize net benefit, or B-C, subject to pricing and traffic volume constraints in the two time periods written

$$P_1(v_1,v_2) = c_{1f}(v_{1f}) = c_{1t}(v_{1t}) + \tau_{1t}, \quad (16)$$

$$P_2(v_1,v_2) = c_{2f}(v_{2f}) = c_{2t}(v_{2t}) + \tau_{2t}, \text{ and} \quad (17)$$

$$v_1 = v_{1t} + v_{1f};\ v_2 = v_{2t} + v_{2f}. \quad (18)$$

Congestion tolls on the toll route are denoted by τ_{1t} and τ_{2t}. Equation (16) is the constraint on pricing of the free route in the peak period. In the peak period the equilibrium price of a trip on either route is equal to the average cost on the free route. Equation (17) is the similar condition for the pre-peak period, and equations (18) state that the total traffic volume in a period is the sum of the volumes on the tollway and the free route. The specification of exact cost and demand functions leads to optimal solutions for traffic volumes, average costs, and congestion tolls.

In order to evaluate the second-best congestion pricing scheme, it is necessary to study two other regimes for the system: the first-best problem in which optimal congestion tolls can be imposed on both routes in both time periods, and the no-toll problem in which congestions tolls cannot be imposed on either route. For the first-best problem, the pricing constraints do not exist. In this case net benefits (B-C) are maximized. The first-best tolls are equal to marginal congestion costs on each route in each time period (i.e., $\tau_{ir}=v_{ir}c'_{ir}$). For the no-toll problem no maximization is involved. Traffic volumes are determined by the equilibrium conditions

$$P_1(v_1,v_2) = c_{1f}(v_{1f}) = c_{1t}(v_{1t}) \text{ and}$$
$$P_2(v_1,v_2) = c_{2f}(v_{2f}) = c_{2t}(v_{2t}).$$

F. SIMULATION RESULTS

The average cost includes travel time and schedule-related costs:

$$c_{ir}(v_{ir}) = \alpha T_{ir} + \beta S_i, \; i = 1,2; \; r = t,f. \tag{19}$$

The values of α and β (cents/min.) are obtained from Small (1982), and are 11 and 6.5, respectively. The travel time cost includes vehicle operating costs and applies the FHWA function [Branston (1976)], which is

$$c_{ir} = T_r[1 + 0.15(v_{ir}/K_r)^4], \; i = 1,2; \; r = t,f, \tag{20}$$

where T_r is the uncongested travel time on route r and K_r is the level of capacity (vehicles per hour) on route r. Since K_r is less than the maximum flow on route r, traffic volume v_{ir} may exceed K_r. The value for K_t is assumed to be $0.5K_f$ because the tolled portion of SR-91 highway has one-half the capacity of the untolled portion. The schedule-related time (S_2) is assumed to be a constant equal to five minutes.

The demand functions for the peak and pre-peak periods are assumed to be linear:

$$v_1 = Q_1 - \beta_{11}P_1 + \beta_{12}P_2, \text{ and}$$

$$v_2 = Q_2 + \beta_{12}P_1 - \beta_{22}P_2. \tag{21}$$

Note that, as implied by the theory of demand, the cross-price effects are equal. For the base case simulation the values of Q_1 and Q_2 are set to produce a second-best toll in the peak period of \$0.25 per mile (to match the results in Chapter 7). The base-case values for the ß's are set to imply price elasticities of demand with no tolls of -.20 for the peak and -.39 for the pre-peak periods. The cross-price effects are set to imply cross-price elasticities of .15 for peak volume and .58 for pre-peak volume if no tolls are being charged. As we show below, alterations in these demand parameters has no effect on the basic nature of the results.

The results of the base case simulation are shown in Table 10-1. As stated above, the demand parameters were set to yield a peak period second-best toll of 24.79 cents per mile. The pre-peak toll in second best was not constrained to be zero or greater, and turned out to be -.91 cents. In other words, the pre-peak users of the toll lanes receive a payment of .91 cents per mile. Note that total traffic volume (peak plus pre-peak) is only 0.3% lower in the second-best case compared to the no-toll case. Also note that the split of traffic volume between the peak and pre-peak periods in the second-best case is very close to the split with no

Table 10-1

Simulation Results: Base Case[a]

Case	Tolls (cents/mi.)		Traffic Volumes		
	Peak	Pre-peak	Total	Peak (%)	Pre-peak (%)
No toll	0.00	0.00	100.00%	71.52	28.48
Second best	24.79	-0.91	99.67%	70.57	29.43
First best	103.22	13.53	94.18%	62.43	37.57

[a]Base case assumes highway capacity of the tolled lanes equal to one-half of the untolled lanes. Demand conditions are described in the body of the chapter.

tolls. In contrast, the first-best tolls of 103.22 cents per mile for the peak and 13.53 cents for pre-peak lead to a decline in total traffic volume of 5.82% and a sizable shift of that volume to the pre-peak period. Finally, the optimal second-best tolls generate only 9.3% of the welfare gain that is generated by the first-best tolls. This small relative welfare gain occurs because the optimal second-best tolls are small (compared to the first-best case) and cause very little alteration in behavior compared to the no-toll case.

Other simulations were run to test the sensitivity of the conclusions to changes in the demand parameters. In two cases the sensitivities of volumes to prices were increased (decreased) by one-third. Larger values for the ß's caused the first-best toll in the peak period to be somewhat lower (89.11 cents per mile), but had virtually no effect on the other results. The welfare gain in the second-best case is 11.2% of the gain in the first-best case. Similarly, smaller values for the ß's generated a higher peak period toll in the first-best case (125 cents per mile) and produced a relative welfare gain in the second-best case of only 6.9%. In two other cases the demand for trips during the peak period was increased (decreased) by 6.25% (i.e., Q_1 was changed by 6.25%). As one would expect, the increase in demand (decrease in demand) caused the peak period tolls to rise (fall), but the relative welfare gains in the second-best case changed very little. The welfare gain in the second-best case is 10.3% (8.3%) of the gain in the first-best case if peak period demand is increased (decreased). The authors have run many more simulations with different supply and demand parameters, and some of these other results are available upon request.

The simulation results in Table 10-1 can be compared briefly to the results obtained in other recent studies. Using a single-period model, in Chapter 7 we examined a case in which the toll route and the free route are of equal capacity. The first-best toll was found to be 3.77 times the optimal second-best toll (23.4 and 6.2 cents per mile). The relative welfare gain of the second-best optimum is 23%. These simulation results also showed that the relative welfare gain increases as the proportion of the highway system that is covered by the toll increases. Given that the results in Table 1 involve a toll that covers only 1/3 of highway capacity, it is not surprising that the relative welfare gain is lower.

Verhoef et al. (1996) also used a single-period model and examined a base case in which the toll route and free route are of equal capacity. The first-best toll was found to be 1.83 times the optimal second-best toll, and the relative welfare improvement in the second-best case is 27.3%. Verhoef et al. (1996) conducted an extensive examination of the profit-maximizing one-route toll, and found that this profit-maximizing toll is very nearly equal to the first-best toll on the tollway portion of the system. Verhoef et al. (1996) showed that, depending upon the particular combination of parameter values, a profit-maximizing one-route toll can cause welfare to increase or decrease relative to the no-toll case. In their base case the profit-maximizing one-route toll increased welfare by about 8% of the potential welfare gain.

Braid (1996) studied a dynamic bottleneck model with two routes; a tollway and a freeway. Assuming that total travel demand is inelastic, Braid (1996, p. 193) found that the relative welfare gain (RW) of the second-best toll schedule is

$$RW = 2\alpha/(2 + \alpha),$$

where α is the bottleneck capacity of the tollway relative to the capacity of the freeway. If $\alpha = .5$ (as in the SR-91 case), then RW = .4. The second-best toll schedule generates 40% of the potential welfare gain, a result that is in some contrast to the small relative welfare gain of 9% shown in Table 1. If $\alpha = 1$ (as in Chapter 7 and Verhoef et al. (1996)), RW = .67. This result is also in some contrast to the smaller relative welfare gains reported in Chapter 7 and by Verhoef et al. (1996) of 23% and 27%. Braid's toll schedule includes a negative toll before and after the "rush hour" to induce commuters to alter the times of their trips. Our results in Table 1 also include a small negative off-peak toll. However, other simulation results with our model (not reported) yield a small positive off-peak toll.

This brief comparison of our results using a two-period model with other simulation studies has shown that the conclusions reached using a one-period model are not altered appreciably. However, the addition of an off-peak period makes the model more realistic and, as a result, the findings are more convincing. Also, a second policy variable (the off-peak toll) is included. One-period models, of course, do not answer the question of the optimal off-peak toll. Some of the results obtained by Braid (1996) using a dynamic bottleneck model with two routes are rather different from the results of the one-period models and our two-period model. It would appear that a more detailed examination of the different simulation models may be needed, but is beyond the scope of this study.

G. CONCLUSIONS

The origins and operation of the SR-91 facility have been described in some detail. Clearly the SR-91 is an important test case for the economic viability for this strategy for alleviating traffic congestion. Construction of two additional lanes in the median of the highway has improved traffic flow dramatically, but it remains unclear as to whether the tolls on these lanes will generate adequate financial returns for the private company that holds the 35-year lease.

Our theoretical examination of efficient second-best pricing for such a facility shows that determination of efficient tolls is difficult. The two express lanes (in each direction) are substitutes for the original lanes of the highway, but the terminus of the facility is not the final destination for commuters. Commuters use additional free highways and arterials to reach their final destinations. As we demonstrated in Chapter 7, the existence of congested substitute (complementary) routes implies that the efficient second-best toll is less than (greater than) the first-best toll.

The simulation model for highway traffic developed in Chapters 8 and 9 is used to examine optimal second-best and first-best congestion tolls for the case in which there is no congestion on complementary routes. The crucial features of this model that only one-third of the lanes are subject to congestion tolls and that all lanes are otherwise identical. The simulations show that this constraint on congestion pricing implies that very little of the potential welfare gain from congestion pricing (only about 10%) can be captured. The actual relative welfare gain from the tolls that are imposed on SR-91 are even smaller to the extent that they depart from the second-best optimum.

The proponents of the SR-91 project can argue that the two additional lanes (in each direction) would not have been built without the ability to levy the congestion tolls, and that the benefits of these new lanes clearly exceed their costs. We agree. They may also argue that the public will accept tolls for access to new highway capacity, but that the public will not accept the imposition of congestion tolls on existing facilities. In the coming years as TEA-21 projects and other similar projects are implemented, we shall see if this notion of "value pricing" will provide an important part of urban transportation policy.

References

Braid, R., 1996, Peak-load pricing of a transportation route with an unpriced substitute, Journal of Urban Economics 40, 179-197.

Branston, D., 1990, Link capacity functions: A review, Transportation Research B 24, 209-228.

Reinhardt, W., 1995, 91 Express Lanes Opened, Public Works Financing 91, December, 1-6.

Rizzo, D., 1996, Highway value pricing on the SR91 express lanes, Traffic Technology International, April-May, 25-30.

Small, K., 1982, The scheduling of consumer activities: Work trips, American Economic Review 72, 467-479.

Sullivan, E. and J. El Harake, 1998, The CA Route 91 toll lanes - observed impacts and other observations, paper presented at the Transportation Research Board 77th Annual Meeting, Washington, D. C.

Verhoef, E., P. Nijkamp, and P. Rietveld, 1996, Second-best congestion pricing, the case of an unpriced alternative, Journal of Urban Economics 40, 279-302.

Appendix

Simulation Results for the Case of Profit Maximization

The case of the profit-maximizing toll road operator was presented theoretically in Chapter 8 (pp. 94-95). Simulation experiments were conducted that compare the profit-maximizing tolls and traffic volume with the no toll and first-best solutions. It is assumed that the toll covers one-third of road capacity, and that all lanes are perfect substitutes. The parameters for the base case were set to produce a profit-maximizing toll in the peak period of $0.22 per mile. Base case own price elasticities are -0.33 for the peak and -0.44 for the pre-peak periods. The cross-price effects are set to imply cross-price elasticities of 0.13 for peak volume and 0.49 for pre-peak volumes if no tolls are being charged.

The simulation results as reported in Liu and McDonald (1998) are as follows:

	No toll	First-Best Tolls	Profit-Maximizing Tolls
Tolls (cents/mile)			
Peak	0.00	31.56	22.49
Pre-peak	0.00	6.60	3.57
Traffic Volumes			
Total	100.00%	93.47%	97.66%
Peak	67.23	59.65	64.67
Pre-peak	32.77	40.35	35.33
Welfare Gain for Consumers	0.00%	100.00%	-84.60%

These simulation results show that the profit-maximizing tolls of $0.225 during the peak and $0.036 during the pre-peak periods are less than the first-best tolls and alter traffic volumes by smaller amounts than do the first-best tolls. As one would expect, monopoly pricing leads to a welfare loss by consumers (and a gain for the monopolist, of course).

PART IV

ROAD CAPACITY AND PRICING IN THE LONG RUN

11 ROAD CAPACITY WITH EFFICIENT TOLLS

A. INTRODUCTION

In the long run the capital input embodied in the streets and highways is variable. The era of highway building of the 1950s and 1960s reshaped urban areas. At this point the prospects for additions to the highway systems of most urban areas are few, but not zero. The emphasis in the previous chapters of this book is on the problem of traffic congestion and making more efficient use of existing highway systems. In this section of the book we presume that highway capacity is variable, and in this chapter we assume that efficient congestion tolls can be used on all parts of an urban highway system. We also assume that the demand for travel on the urban highways is known with certainty. Both of these assumptions are relaxed in subsequent chapters.

We begin with a problem that is easily studied in theoretical terms. We start with the usual short-run marginal and average cost curves that are depicted in Figure 6-2. To this set of cost curves we add the average fixed cost curve and the average total cost curve. This complete set of cost curves is shown in Figure 11-1. The new idea is average fixed cost; this is fixed cost divided by the volume of traffic. The fixed cost is the cost of the land and capital embodied in the highway for the time period that is being depicted (i.e., one hour). What is the cost of the land and capital embodied in the highway? Suppose that the highway cost $100 million and that the rate of interest is 6%. This means that the annual cost of the land and capital is $6 million. There are 8760 hours in a year, so the cost of land and capital for one hour in this example is $685. We have ignored the cost of maintenance to keep the highway functioning. The fixed cost per hour should include the annual maintenance cost divided by 8760. Also, if the highway depreciates over time, the hourly cost of capital should include a small amount to cover the eventual replacement of the facility. All of these ideas are built into the average fixed cost curve in Figure 11-1. The average total cost is simply the sum of average fixed cost and average variable cost.

Now consider the efficient congestion toll that should be imposed in Figure 11-1. Given demand curve DD, that toll is amount tt', as before. An interesting comparison to make is between the congestion toll and average fixed cost. As depicted in Figure 11-1, the congestion toll tt' exceeds the average fixed

Figure 11-1

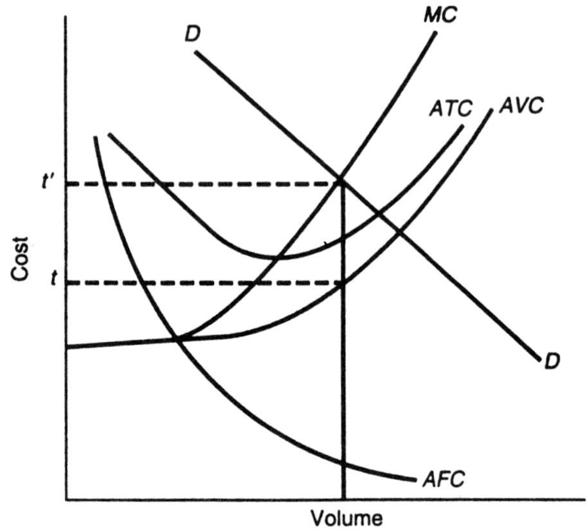

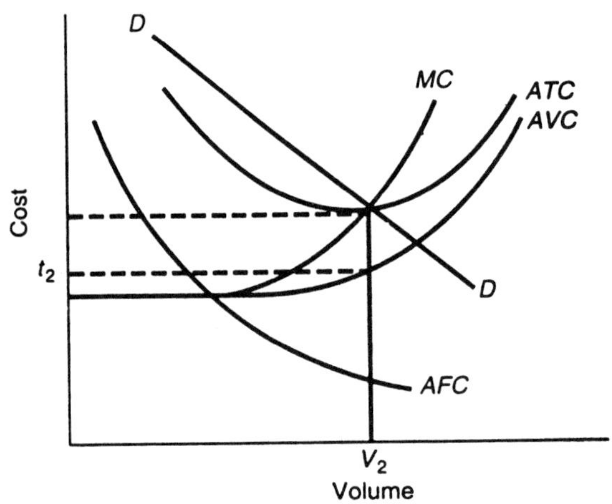

Figure 11-2

Figure 11-3

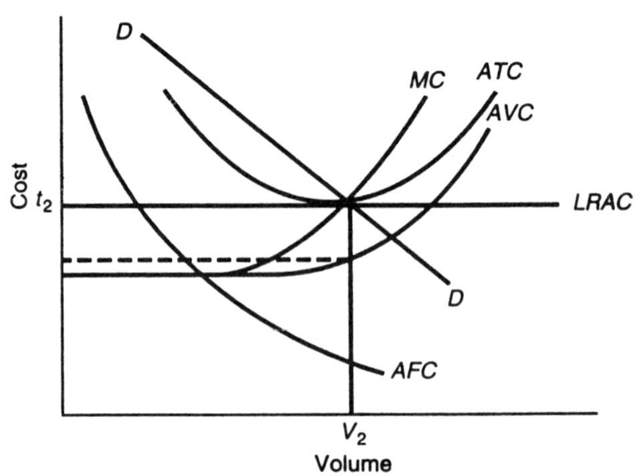

cost because the toll is larger than the vertical difference between average total cost and average variable cost. In other words, the toll revenue collected over the time period exceeds the cost of the land and capital embedded in the highway. What is the significance of this outcome?

Suppose that the demand curve DD is the demand curve for every time period. (A model with peak-period demand is examined below.) Given this assumption, toll revenues in excess of fixed costs are being collected in every time period. This would appear to signal that the highway should be expanded. An expansion of the highway is shown in Figure 11-2. This expansion is carefully designed so that the congestion toll revenue that is collected in each time period is just equal to average fixed cost. This means that the price that each commuter pays (average variable cost plus toll) is exactly equal to the average total cost of each trip. In Figure 11-2 this happens at traffic volume V_2, where the congestion toll of t_2 just equals average fixed cost. Note that the expanded highway has been designed so that traffic volume coincides with the minimum average total cost that is possible for that facility. We see that efficient use of this particular highway involves setting a congestion toll equal to average fixed cost.

Figure 11-2 depicts a nice result for efficiency in the short run, but suppose that the facility that was built is also the highway that provides for the minimum average cost in the long run at traffic volume V_2. In other words, suppose that the long-run average cost curve passes through the minimum point of the short-run average cost curve. This can happen only if the long-run average cost curve is tangent to the short-run average total cost curve at volume V_2 and is therefore a horizontal line. Figure 11-3 depicts this situation. A horizontal long-run average cost curve means that the production of traffic volume is subject to constant long-run marginal cost. Figure 11-3 therefore depicts a situation in which the price paid by commuters is equal to the long-run marginal cost as well as short-run marginal cost. Therefore we have shown that, if the production of traffic volume is subject to constant marginal and average cost in the long run, the efficient highway facility in the long run will be the one where the collection of congestion tolls just equals the cost of the land and capital embodied in the highway. The commuters just pay for their highway through the congestion toll.

B. LONG-RUN EFFICIENCY WITH PEAK-PERIOD DEMAND

The more realistic case to consider is the case of peak-period demand. The short run was examined extensively in Chapters 7, 8, and 9. Following Mohring and Harwitz (1962), this section extends the analysis of a single route to the long run. The model assumes that there are two periods; a period of peak demand and a period of lesser demand. For simplicity assume that the two time periods are of equal length, and that this length is one unit of time. A basic point is that the amount of land and capital embodied in the highway is the same in both periods. Given this condition, what conditions characterize efficiency in the long run?

This question can be investigated by using a long-run version of the model in Chapter 8. Recall the optimization problem in Chapter 8 to maximize net benefits, or

$$\max W = B - C \; = \tag{1}$$

$$\int_{(0,0)}^{(v_1,v_2)} P_1(w_1, w_2)dw_1 + P_2(w_1, w_2)dw_2$$

$$- [t_1d_1 - t_2d_2] - rK - \lambda_1[v_1 - F(d_1,K)] - \lambda_2[v_2 - F(d_2,K)],$$

where v_i is traffic volume in period i (1 = peak and 2 = off peak), t_i is the value of a unit of traffic density in period i, K is the capital embodied in the highway (with rental cost of r per unit), and $F(d_i,K)$ is the production function for traffic volume in period i (with d_i as traffic density). The issues at hand are the optimal amount of capital to build into the highway and the congestion tolls to charge in the two periods. Note that, if the capital input and the production functions are included in the equation for net benefits, then the other input - traffic density - must be included as well.

Maximization of W with respect to traffic volume in the two periods and capital (K) produces:

$$\partial W/\partial v_1 = P_1 - \lambda_1 = 0,$$

$$\partial W/\partial v_2 = P_2 - \lambda_2 = 0, \text{ and}$$

$$\partial W/\partial K = - r + \lambda_1 F_2(d_1,K) + \lambda_2 F_2(d_2,K),$$

where SMC is short-run marginal cost and F_2 is the marginal product of capital (K). These conditions mean that

$$r = (P_1)F_2(d_1,K) + (P_2)F_2(d_2,K); \tag{2}$$

the marginal cost of capital equals its marginal benefit over the two periods.

We now make use of the assumption that $F(d_i,K)$ is subject to constant returns to scale (CRS). With CRS we have

$$v_i = d_i(\partial v_i/\partial d_i) + KF_2(d_i,K),$$

so that

$$t_id_i + r_iK = P_iv_i,$$

where r_i is the price charged per unit of capital in period i. The setting of the price of capital in each period equal to the value of its marginal product in each period is written

$$r_i = P_iF_2(d_i,K),$$

so this pricing scheme will satisfy equation (2) above.

What are the efficient congestion tolls in the two time periods? We know that the efficient first-best toll in the short run is

$$\text{Toll(sr)} = v_i(dc_i/dv_i),$$

where c_i is average cost (as in the previous chapters). In the long run and short-run and the long-run tolls are equal, or

$$\text{Toll(sr)} = \text{Toll (lr)} = \text{MB - LRAC} = \text{LRMC - LRAC},$$

where MB is marginal benefit, LRMC is long-run marginal cost, and LRAC is long-run average cost. We also know that (again, given CRS),

$$P_iv_i = t_id_i + r_iK,$$

so that

$$P_i - t_id_i/v_i = r_iK/v_i = P_iF_2(d_i,K)K/v_i.$$

Because traffic volume equals traffic density times average speed (V = DS), the ratio of traffic density to traffic volume is the inverse of average speed (D/V = 1/S). The inverse of speed times the cost of a unit of traffic density (t_i) is the average variable cost of traffic volume; i.e.,

$$t_id_i/v_i = c_i. \tag{3}$$

Therefore the efficient toll can be written

$$\text{Toll} = P_i - c_i - r_iK/v_i. \tag{4}$$

The total tolls collected over the two periods are

$$v_1(\text{Toll}_1) + v_2(\text{Toll}_2) = r_1K + r_2K = rK.$$

The tolls just cover the cost of capital. The model in this section (with constant returns to scale in the production of traffic volume) produces the result that, with the long-run efficient amount of capital, the time-varying congestion tolls exactly cover the cost of that capital.

C. LONG-RUN MODELS IN SUBSEQUENT CHAPTERS

The long-run models discussed in Chapters 12 to 17 are characterized by the fact that road capacity is treated as a variable quantity. However, these partial equilibrium models do not take explicit account of any long-run effects of road capacity and location on alternative land-use decisions. This limitation is reflected in the fact that demand for road use is taken as a given, rather than emerging endogenously as a result of residential or employment location decisions. The benefits of road capacity are treated as an increasing function of road use and captured entirely by the road users themselves. The only externality considered is the congestion cost imposed on other actual or potential road users.

Certain recurring themes are emphasized throughout the chapters:

1. The nature of the "no-toll" (second-best) optimum;
2. The possibility and character of hypercongestion;
3. The relative size of first-best and second-best capacity;
4. The relationship between various formulations of congestions models; and
5. The relative size of social losses arising from second-best policies.

The origins of these problems is found especially in the work of Herbert Mohring (1970, 1974). Hau (1998) provides a thorough review of recent literature.

Chapter 12 examines the single-road model using the standard formulation of traffic congestion in which traffic flow is used to measure the output and consumption of road use (as in this chapter). Chapter 13 analyzes the case of two roads which are imperfect substitutes. Chapter 14 is a model with a single route and hypercongestion. Chapter 15 employs the Else (1981) model of demand for density in a two-period setting. A simple model of road capacity with uncertain demand is introduced in Chapter 16. Chapter 17, the last chapter in this part of the book, presents a simple bottleneck model with spatial dimensions appended that demonstrates essentially similar results to those in Chapter 12.

References

Else, P., 1981, A reformulation of the theory of optimal congestion taxes, Journal of Transport Economics and Policy XV, 217-232.

Hau, T., 1998, Congestion pricing and road investment, in K. Button and E. Verhoef, eds., Road Pricing, Traffic Congestion, and the Environment, Cheltenham, England: Edward Elgar.

Mohring, H., 1970, The peak load problem with increasing returns and pricing constraints, American Economic Review, 60, 693-705.

Morhring, H., 1974, Pricing and transportation capacity, Paper presented at the Seventh Summer Meeting of the Transportation Research Board, Jacksonville, FL.

Mohring, H. and M. Harwitz, 1962, Highway benefits: An analytical framework, Evanston: Northwestern University Press.

12 THE COMPARISON OF OPTIMAL ROAD CAPACITIES: NO TOLL VERSUS THE OPTIMAL TOLL

A. INTRODUCTION

This chapter examines what might be considered the "standard" or "traditional" (long-run) economic model of road congestion that is analogous to the short-run model presented in Chapters 6 and 7. Some alternative formulations are considered in subsequent chapters. The standard model is based on the assumption of a single traffic flow of indefinite duration which is uniform and continuous over time and (one-dimensional) space. The exact relationship of the individual road user to this flow is rarely specified. Presumably the individual road user exhibits a demand for "travel," more specifically a single "trip" measurable in units of distance (say miles). The individual derives a certain benefit from the trip that can be expressed as a benefit per mile. The trip is taken if and only if the benefit per mile is at least equal to the user's cost per mile. Benefits are assumed to vary over a large group of potential road users creating an aggregate demand for road use. The composition of benefits or benefit distribution among users is assumed to remain constant over time and space. This allows the analysis to focus attention on a single point in time and space. Particular individual drivers are not identifiable by departure or arrival times or locations along the road.

The plan of the chapter is as follows. First the model is formulated and the necessary conditions for both "first-best" (an optimal toll) and "second-best" (no toll) circumstances are derived, and the nature of the second-best solution is discussed. This latter undertaking is a traditional exercise somewhat akin to the examination of the elephant by the three blind men. Every author purports to have been gifted with a special insight into the essential nature of this equilibrium, and this chapter respects that time-honored tradition by revealing the true secrets. Secondly, the chapter looks at the special polar extremes of zero and infinite price elasticity. This is also a traditional preliminary, offering initial intuition into the issue. The third step in the analysis derives sufficient conditions for the second-best capacity to exceed the first best capacity. Finally the second-best case is illustrated for specific functions of cost and demand which seemed particularly instructive. The analysis uses the production function approach to describe the technology of road trip production. Under this approach, the dual inputs of road capacity and user time (density) are related to the output of traffic flow.

Throughout the analysis, the dimension or units of measure of each variable or parameter is indicated by brackets [ ]. This "dimensional analysis" contributes clarity to the formulation, avoids misunderstandings, and provides some presumptive indication of the accuracy of involved derivations. Notation is introduced as the need arises.

B. THEORY OF SECOND-BEST CAPACITY

For the production function describing the technology of road trip production:

Q = Rate of trip production (flow) [vehicles/hour],

N = Rate of drivers' time consumption (density) [vehicles/mile], and

K = Road capacity [vehicles/hour].

The production function is specified as follows:

$$Q = f(N, K), \tag{1}$$

where

$\partial Q/\partial N = f_1$, [miles/hour], $f_1 \geq 0$ *or* $f_1 < 0$,

($f_1 < 0$ identifies backward-bending portion of average cost), and

$\partial Q/\partial K = f_2$, [unit free], $f_2 > 0$.

This second derivative is unit free as Q and K are both [vehicles/hour]. We also assume that

$\partial^2 Q/\partial N^2 = f_{11} < 0$, [miles^2/vehicle·hour],

$\partial^2 Q/\partial K^2 = f_{22} < 0$, [hours/vehicle], and

$\partial^2 Q/\partial N \partial K = f_{12} > 0$, [miles/vehicle].

The social welfare function (the assumed social objective function) is specified as follows:

$$W = \int_0^Q P(q)dq \quad - C_1N - C_2K. \tag{2}$$

The inverse demand curve is denoted by P [\$/vehicle·mile] = P(Q). The cost of drivers' time is denoted by C_1 [\$/vehicle·hour]. The cost of capacity is denoted by C_2 [\$/vehicle·mile]. As a consequence, W is expressed as [\$/mile·hour]. To obtain the total dollar benefits of road use, first specify the road length [miles] and duration of flow considered [hours] and multiply the product by W.

To obtain the optimal second-best capacity for no toll, maximize (2) subject to the constraint that price equals average variable cost: i.e.,

$$\text{Max } W = \int_0^Q P(q)dq - C_1N - C_2K - \mu[Q - f(N, K)] - \lambda[PQ - C_1N]. \tag{3}$$

The constraint that price equals average cost has been written $PQ = C_1N$ to facilitate subsequent interpretation of the conditions for second-best optimum. The first order conditions are:

$$\partial W/\partial K = - C_2 + \mu f_2 = 0 \text{ or } \mu = C_2 / f_{2,} \tag{4}$$

$$\partial W/\partial N = C_1 + \mu f_1 + \lambda C_1 \quad \text{or } \lambda = 1 - C_2 f_1 / C_1 f_{2,} \text{ and} \tag{5}$$

$$\partial W/\partial Q = P - \lambda P\,(1 - 1/e) - \mu = 0 \quad \text{or} \quad Pf_2\,[1 - \lambda(1 - 1/e)\,] = C_{2,} \tag{6}$$

where $e = - P/P'Q$ denotes the price elasticity of demand. The first-best solution without the price constraint is well known:

$$P = C_1 / f_1 = C_2 / f_2 \quad \text{or} \quad C_2\, f_1 / C_1\, f_2 = 1. \tag{7}$$

It is important to clearly identify the components of equation (6). The marginal benefit *per unit of flow* is P. The increase (or decrease) of total drivers' time per unit of flow is $P(1 - 1/e)$, which can be seen because, from the constraint,

$$d(PQ)/dQ = P(1 - 1/e) = d(C_1N)dQ.$$

This increase (or decrease) in total driving time per unit of flow occurs *as flow is increased in the second best regime by increasing capacity*. Depending on price elasticity, total driving time increases (elasticity > 1) or decreases (elasticity < 1) as flow increases. This fact confers a special significance on unitary elasticity as the dividing line between increasing and decreasing density. It also raises the essentially empirical question of whether price elasticity really can be elastic over most ranges of traffic flow. The equivalent question is whether increased capacity can *actually increase* traffic density. Switching from a mud path to a modern highway could certainly be expected to increase density, but can an additional widening of an existing highway by a single lane increase density on a well-traveled road?

Substituting from (5) for λ, equation (6) may be written as:

$$[P - P(1-1/e)]f_2 + Pf_2(C_2f_1/C_1f_2)(1-1/e) = C_2. \tag{8}$$

Substituting $P = C_1N/Q$ for the third P in (8) and eliminating C_2 from the left-hand side of (8) gives:

$$[P - P(1-1/e)]\, f_2/\, [1 - \alpha(1-1/e)] = C_2, \tag{9}$$

where α [dimension free] is defined as:

$$\alpha = f_1N/Q < 1. \tag{10}$$

In conventional production theory, this might represent "labor's share of output," but here a better interpretation is that α is the ratio of average variable cost to short-run marginal variable cost:

$$\alpha = (C_1N/Q) / (C_1/f_1). \tag{11}$$

This explains why the definition in (10) states that α is less than positive 1. α would be negative on the "backward-bending" portion of the average cost curve. The term $f_2 / [1- \alpha(1-1/e]$ represents the equilibrium increase in Q brought about by a unit increase in K (dQ/dK) in the second-best regime. This can derived directly by noting that at all equilibrium points both the production function and the price constraint hold so that (from equations 2 and 3 above):

$$dQ/dK = f_1dN/dK + f_2\text{ , and} \tag{12}$$

$$P(1-1/e)dQ/dK = C_1dN/dK. \tag{13}$$

Substituting $P = C_1N/Q$

$$dN/dK = [(1-1/e)N/Q]\; dQ/dK, \tag{14}$$

and

$$dQ/dK = f_2 / [1 - \alpha(1- 1/e)]. \tag{15}$$

Essentially the first-order condition as given in (9) can be interpreted as:

(Marginal benefit per Q - Marginal cost of time per Q) x dQ/dK = C_2

Note that the marginal cost of time maybe either positive or negative depending on whether the price elasticity is greater or less than one. This, as previously mentioned, is the pivotal role played by the price elasticity in the second-best regime for which there is no counterpart in the first-best analysis. There are several characterizations of the second-best solutions in terms of elasticity which may add some clarity. The marginal rate of increase in benefits with respect to traffic flow as shown in (9) above is P/e or equivalently -P′Q. This expression represents the rate of change in "consumers' surplus," i.e. the change in the excess of the area under the inverse demand curve over the total variable cost.

Accordingly the elasticity e = P/-P′Q is the ratio of the first-best marginal benefit per Q to the second-best marginal benefit per Q at any Q (but in general for different values of K for each regime). The larger the second-best benefit relative to the first-best, the more inelastic is the demand for a given Q. But little can be said on the basis of price elasticity alone about the relative sizes of the optimal capacities.

In the extreme case where demand is totally inelastic, the level of flow (Q) is fixed for both regimes. Increasing capacity then has identical effects for both the first and second-best cases. Increasing capacity decreases the average variable cost for the fixed flow by the same amount in either case. Consequently, the optimal capacities are the same. On the other extreme, if demand is perfectly elastic, (the inverse demand curve is a horizontal line), then the second-best capacity is smaller if any first-best capacity at all is warranted, (and such may be the case for the first-best regime). Here in the first-best case, marginal cost pricing (imposition of a toll), carves out a net benefit to offset and possibly exceed capacity costs. But in the second-best case, there is no consumers' surplus to justify any capacity costs. Therefore, the second-best capacity for "infinite elasticity" is zero. These results may have some limited generality in the sense that for any demand elasticity approaching infinite, it is always difficult to justify any second-best capacity, while the two optimal capacities always converge as elasticity goes to zero. The trouble is that there is a lot of ground between zero and infinity, where these two polar extremes offer little guidance as to the relative magnitude of the optimal capacities.

A direct comparison of the relative size of the two optimal capacities can be made by connecting the first-order conditions of the two regimes. To review, at the first-best optimal point:

$$Pf_2 = C_2 \tag{16}$$

At the second-best optimal point:

$$Pf_2 /[e\{1 - \alpha(1 - 1/e)\}] = C_2 \tag{17}$$

Let K* denote the first-best optimal capacity and K** denote the second-best capacity. Consider the following mental experiment: Start at the first-best capacity K*, (with the requisite toll in place), and then holding capacity fixed, remove the toll, and allow N to increase to a "second-best" equilibrium point To try to keep things clear, picture the three-dimensional space with axes for measuring Q, N, and K. Call the triple (K*, N*,Q*) = x*, and (K**,N**,Q**) = x**. These are the first and second-best optimal points respectively. The equilibrium point (K*, N_2, Q_2) attained in the mental experiment is denoted x_2. If by some stroke of good fortune (17) holds at this new equilibrium point x_2, then K** = K*. Note that the left-hand side of (17) is the marginal benefit of capacity for all values of K in the second-best regime, not just at the optimal point.

Accordingly, if the marginal (second-best) benefit of capacity *exceeds* C_2 at the point x_2, K** > K*. This conclusion makes three implicit assumptions:

1. The possibility of multiple maxima can be safely ignored;
2. Sooner or later, the marginal benefit of capacity must fall and cut the assumed constant cost of capacity from above (meeting the second-order condition); and
3. The *average benefit* exceeds the marginal benefit at the optimal point (insuring that zero capacity is not the best choice).

Two conditions are *sufficient* to insure that the second-best marginal benefit exceeds the marginal cost, C_2:

1. Elasticity at x_2 is less than 1; and
2. Pf_2 at x_2 exceeds Pf_2 at x*.

The elasticity condition can be explained as follows. Under all circumstances,

$$\alpha < 1. \tag{18}$$

If e < 1, then it follows that:

$$(1 - 1/e) < 0. \tag{19}$$

Therefore multiplying (18) by (19) reverses the direction of the inequality:

$$\alpha(1 - 1/e) > 1 - 1/e\,. \tag{20}$$

Or

$$1/e > 1 - \alpha(1 - 1/e), \tag{21}$$

or

$$1 > e\,[\,1 - \alpha(1 - 1/e)\,]. \tag{22}$$

In other words if e at x_2 is less than 1, the denominator of the second-best marginal benefit in (17) is less than 1 at this point also.

The second sufficient condition can be expressed in a much more informative manner. In the previously described "mental experiment," both $P = P(f(N,K))$ and $f_2(N,K)$ are functions of N since K is held fixed. Define Z and η as follows:

$$Ln(P^*) = Ln(Z) - \eta\, Ln(N^*) \text{ and}$$

$$Ln(P_2) = Ln(Z) - \eta Ln(N_2),$$

so that

$$\eta = -[Ln(P_2) - Ln(P^*)] / [Ln(N_2) - Ln(N^*). \quad (23)$$

In similar fashion define θ so that

$$\theta = [Ln\{f_2(N_2)\} - Ln\{f_2(N^*)\}] / [Ln(N_2) - Ln(N^*)]. \quad (24)$$

The notation P_2 and N_2 refer to the values at the point x_2.

A sufficient condition for the second-best marginal benefit at x_2 to exceed the first-best at x^*, may be written:

$$1 + \theta - \eta / e_2 [1 - \alpha_2 (1 - 1/e_2)] > 1, \quad (25)$$

or

$$\theta > (e_2 - 1)(1 - \alpha) + \eta. \quad (26)$$

In (25), $1 + \theta - \eta$ is the ratio of $Pf_2(x_2)$ to $Pf_2(x^*)$. The elasticities η and θ have the following interpretations. Divide the interval $[N^*, N_2]$ into m sub-intervals such that for each interval, $Ln N_{i+1} - Ln N_i$ is a constant say $Ln M_0$.

Let:

$$D_1 = [(Ln P_1 - Ln P^*) + \ldots(Ln P_{i+1} - Ln P_i) \ldots(Ln P_m - Ln P_{m-1})]$$

and

$$D_2 = [(Ln N_1 - Ln N^*) + \ldots(Ln N_{i+1} - Ln N_i)\ldots(Ln N_m - Ln N_{m-1})].$$

Then from (23)

$$\eta = -D_1 / D_2 = -D_1 / m\, Ln M_0 \quad (27)$$

It follows that η also may be written as:

$$\eta = -(1/m) \sum [\text{Ln}(P_{i+1}) - \text{Ln}(P_i)] / \text{Ln}\, M_0 . \tag{28}$$

In other words, as $m \to \infty$, η approaches the *average of the point elasticities* of P with respect to N over the interval $[N^*, N_2]$. The individual point elasticities may be negative (on the backward-bending portion of the average cost curve) as well as positive. The same reasoning interprets θ as the average of the point elasticities of f_2 with respect to N over the same interval. The point elasticities for f_2 on the other hand are all positive ($f_{12} > 0$).

The point elasticity of P with respect to N is:

$$-(dP/dN)(N/P) = -(P'f_1)(N/P) \tag{29}$$

$$= -(P'Q/P)(f_1N/Q) \tag{30}$$

$$= \alpha(1/e). \tag{31}$$

The point elasticity of f_2 with respect to N (with K constant) is defined as

$$(df_2 / dN)(N/f_2) = f_{12}N/f_2 > 0. \tag{32}$$

To provide some intuition as to the nature of this elasticity, for a linear homogeneous production function, the better-known *elasticity of substitution* is related as follows:

$$(df_2 / dN)(N/f_2) = f_{12}N/f_2 = (f_1N/Q)/ (f_1f_2/f_{12}Q) = \alpha/\sigma. \tag{33}$$

Accordingly, the sufficient condition in (26) may be restated as:

$$\theta\{\alpha/\sigma\} > (e_2 - 1)(1 - \alpha_2) + \eta\{\alpha/e\}. \tag{34}$$

The notations $\theta\{\alpha/\sigma\}$ and $\eta\{\alpha/e\}$ are intended to denote the fact that θ and η are averages of the point elasticities enclosed in the brackets. The first term on the right hand side of (34) is always negative if $e_2 < 1$. Therefore, the price elasticity condition by itself gives (34) a good chance of holding. The condition (34) will hold for $e_2 < 1$ unless η is positive (not on the backward-bending portion of the cost curve) and exceeds θ by enough to offset the first term. Since α appears in the numerator of both η and θ, this can happen only for sufficiently large σ. Note σ as used here is defined as:

$$\sigma = f_1f_2/f_{12}Q,$$

which is the elasticity of substitution for a linear homogenous production, but not in general. The reciprocal $1/\sigma$ is however always the elasticity of the marginal product of capacity (f_2) with respect to flow (Q), with K fixed and N variable.

This is the critical cost-side factor in the second-best analysis. If $1/\sigma$ is large, the additional density resulting from elimination of any toll makes the beneficial effect of added capacity large. If σ is large, it is possible that first-best capacity is larger then second-best. But it seems probable that a small value of σ is a characteristic of traffic congestion.

C. EXAMPLES

There are several additional points which are best illustrated by specific examples. The first example raises the question of multiple equilibria. For a fixed capacity, average variable cost may equal price at more than one level of traffic flow. The essential case is shown in Figure 12-1. Possible equilibria occur at points labeled A, B, and C. Two occur on the backward-bending portion of the average cost curve (at A and B), while C lies on the upward-sloping portion just below capacity flow. The short-run average cost curves shown correspond to the first-best optimal capacity for the parameters illustrated. For a slightly smaller capacity, all three points would lie on the backward-sloping portion. At an even smaller capacity, there would be only one intersection with the demand curve at a point like A. At point A the demand curve cuts the cost curve from below while at B it cuts from above. Which of these equilibrium points is likely to occur, and which if any are stable is an open question.

Point A occurs at much higher density than point C, but at much lower flow. If it is assumed that each road user, (the hypothesized rational decision maker in establishing the equilibrium), makes one trip during each "commuting" period, then *more not fewer* users make trips at point C than at point A. The higher density at A means more users are using the road at each moment in time. But over the commuting period, more individual users complete their trip at point C. The higher velocity at point C more than compensates for the fact that there are fewer cars on the road at each moment. Regular road users will tend to distribute their travel evenly over the entire commuting period, with individual users traveling at different times. This smoothing out of travel demand over the commuting period is an essential assumption of the standard congestion model. The relevant point is that equilibria like A do not arise because *additional* road users who are not being accommodated at a point like C start using the road.

In the region where both average cost and traffic flows are increasing, the mechanism bringing about the equilibrium might seem clear, but once the backward-bending portion of the curve comes into consideration, there is no such mechanism evident. An equilibrium like point A arises when (relatively) few road users all try to use the road at the same time. This produces high density and low flow which then persists throughout the commuting period. But apart from equalizing costs, there is no mechanism in the standard model which accounts for the particular way in which demand is smoothed over the commuting period. Points like A are every bit as reasonable as points like C. If potential road users *expect* an equilibrium like A, it will tend to be self-fulfilling. The wisdom of

Figure 12.1 Short-Run Equilibria

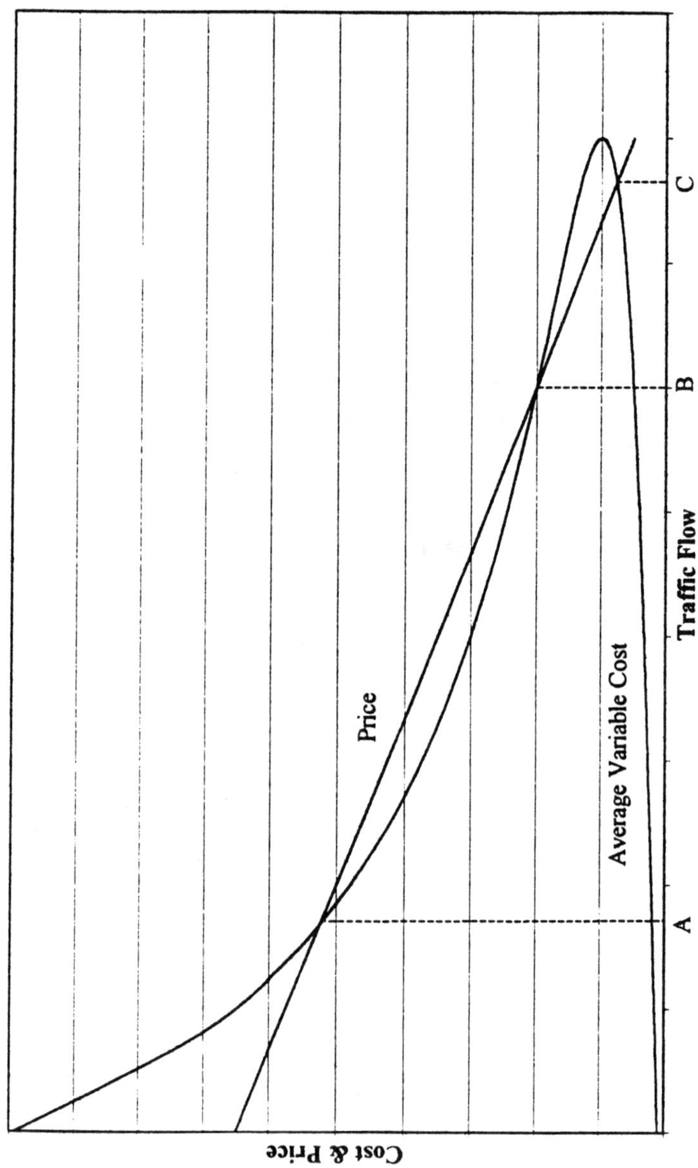

encouraging commuters to leave early for work in inclement weather may be misguided. Obviously, points like C are vastly superior to points like A (the capacity cost is the same but the "consumers' surplus is much greater at C). For this reason, only points like C are candidates for optimal outcomes (which as noted above can be located on the backward-bending portion of the average cost curve). In any event, the inability of the standard traffic congestion theory to specify which of several equilibria will arise is hardly unique in economics.

The model presented in Figure 12-1 is based on a linear demand function of the form:

$$P = A - bQ. \tag{36}$$

The production function is:

$$Q = [\, 2sNK - s^2N^2]^{1/2}\,. \tag{37}$$

For simplicity, the dimensional constant s [miles/hour] was normalized to equal 1. This function has maximum flow at Q = K = N. The relevant derivatives are as follows:

$$\partial Q/\partial N = f_1 = (K - N)/Q \text{ and} \tag{38}$$

$$\partial Q/\partial K = f_2 = N/Q. \tag{39}$$

From the first order conditions,

$$P = C_1/f_1 = C_2/f_2 \tag{40}$$

it follows that

$$K^* = [\, (C_1 + C_2)/C_2]N^*\,. \tag{41}$$

Substituting (41) into the production function:

$$Q^* = [2(C_1 + C_2)/\, C_2 - 1\,]^{1/2}N^*\,. \tag{42}$$

Then:

$$P^* = C_2 \,/\, f_2 = C_2\, Q/N, \tag{43}$$

or:

$$P^* = (2C_1C_2 + C_2^{\,2}\,)^{½}\,. \tag{44}$$

From P* all other variables are easily calculated:

$$Q^* = (A - P^*)/b \qquad \text{(from the demand curve)}, \tag{45}$$

$$N^* = C_2\, Q^*/P^* \qquad \text{(from equation (43))}, \tag{46}$$

and

$$K^* = [\,(C_1 + C_2)/C_2]N^* \qquad \text{(equation (41))}. \tag{47}$$

The parameter values used in Figure 12-1 are as follows:

$A = 600$
$b = .19$
$C_1 = 66.67$
$C_2 = 75$

The values of course are relative and have no absolute significance. The first-best outcomes for these parameter values (again relative) are:

$P^* = 125$
$Q^* = 2500$
$N^* = 1500$
$K^* = 2833$

The second-best outcomes are fairly typical for inelastic demand:

$P^{**} = 43$
$Q^{**} = 2933$
$N^{**} = 1837$
$K^{**} = 3260$

The second-best capacity is 15% above the first-best, while the second-best flow and density are 17% and 22% above their first-best counterparts respectively. The second-best price is only 34% of the first-best price. The price elasticity drops from .26 at first-best to .08 at second-best.

The second example demonstrates conditions for the optimal second-best capacity to have an equilibrium point in the "uneconomic region" of production. See Chapter 14 for a more complete discussion of this model. Example 2 will utilize the same production function as example 1, but will substitute a constant elasticity demand curve for the linear demand of example 1:

$$P = AQ^{-b}\,. \tag{48}$$

To simplify the exposition and permit closed-form solutions, let b = 1 (unitary elasticity). For this case N is constant:

$$N^{**} = A/C_1 . \tag{49}$$

The second-best first-order condition simplifies to:

$$Pf_2 = A^2/C_1Q^2 = C_2 , \tag{50}$$

or:

$$Q^{**} = A / (C_1C_2)^{1/2} . \tag{51}$$

Then from the production function:

$$K = (Q^2 + N^2) / 2N, \tag{52}$$

or

$$K^{**} = A\ (1/C_1 + 1/C_2) / 2 = A(C_1 + C_2)/2C_1C_2 . \tag{53}$$

This solution lies on the backward-bending portion of the average variable cost curve if, from (38):

$$f_1 = (K - N) / Q < 0 . \tag{54}$$

From (49) and (53) it is obvious that (54) holds when

$$A/C_1 > A/(1/C_1 + 1/C_2)/2 \qquad \text{or } C_2 > C_1 . \tag{55}$$

For sufficiently costly capacity, the second-best optimal point lies on the backward-bending portion of the average variable cost curve. This case is shown in Exhibit 12-2, which shows, if nothing else, that in the benefit/capacity plane, this type of outcome is not distinguished in any respect.

The first-best solution for this case is derived as in (40) to (44)

$$P^* = (2C_1C_2 + C_2^2)^{1/2} . \tag{56}$$

For this demand curve:

$$Q^* = A/(2C_1C_2 + C_2^2)^{1/2} \tag{57}$$

From $P = C_2/f_2$:

$$N^* = C_2Q/P = A/(2C_1 + C_2). \tag{58}$$

Figure 12.2 Second Best Optimal Point in "Uneconomic Region of Production"

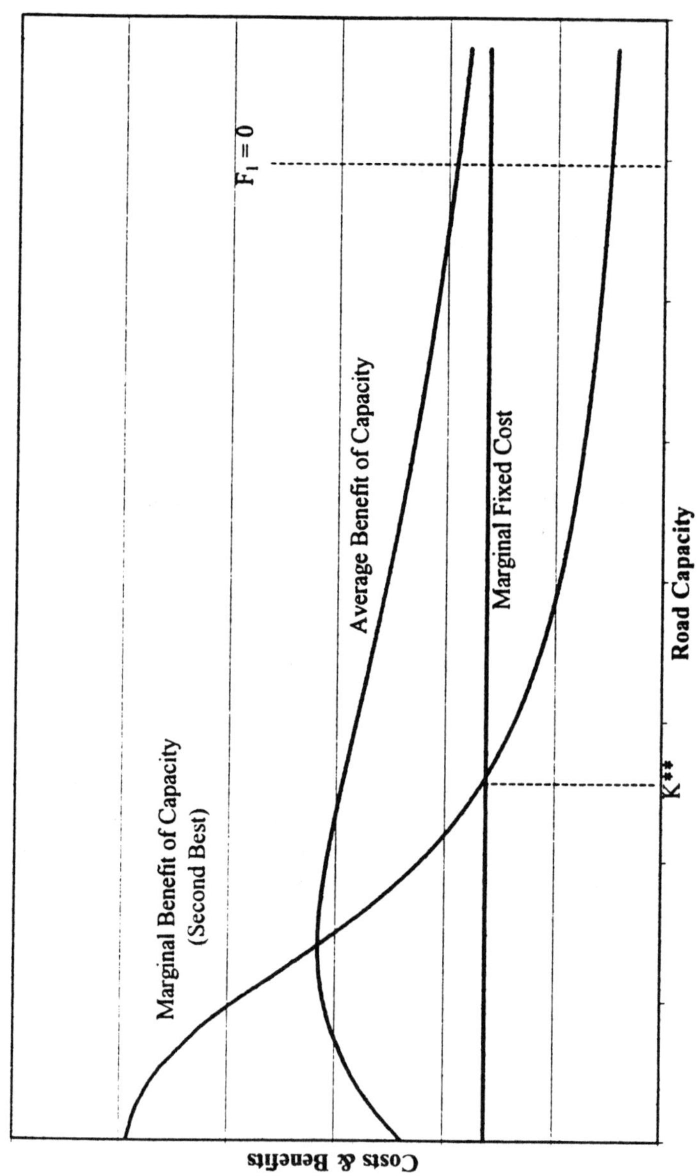

From the production function:

$$K^* = (Q^2 + N^2) / 2N = A(C_1 + C_2)/(2C_1C_2 + C_2^2). \tag{59}$$

The direct comparison between (53) and (59) indicates $K^* < K^{**}$ if

$$(C_1 + C_2)/(2C_1C_2 + C_2^2) < (C_1 + C_2)/2C_1C_2 \,. \tag{60}$$

Obviously, (61) holds for any $C_2 > 0$. Thus $K^* < K^{**}$ in this example ($e = 1$) for all cost parameters. For this production function:

$$\sigma = f_1f_2 / f_{12}Q = (1 - N/K) < 1. \tag{61}$$

For the following parameter values:

$A = 4.0 \times 10^5$
$C_1 = 90$
$C_2 = 110$

The second-best outcomes are:

$P^{**} = 99$
$Q^{**} = 4020$
$N^{**} = 4444$
$K^{**} = 4040$

The first-best outcomes are:

$P^* = 179$
$Q^* = 2240$
$N^* = 1379$
$K^* = 2508$

The final example is a case for which the second-best capacity is *smaller*. As previously noted, this arises only for cases in which the elasticity of substitution is larger than may be expected for normal congested traffic flow. The production function illustrated in this example is a simple CES function:

$$Q = (N^{1/2} + K^{1/2})^2 \,. \tag{62}$$

All dimensional or "scale" parameters have been normalized to 1. The elasticity of substitution is 2. Although the function does not exhibit any maximum flow for a fixed capacity, it is a generalization of the Cobb-Douglas production function, which in the context of traffic congestion models is known as a Vickrey-type cost function and commonly used in analytical models. The appearance of the short-run marginal and average variable costs curves is shown in Figure 12-3. The derivatives have a simple form:

$$\partial Q/\partial N = f_1 = 1 + (K/N)^{1/2} \tag{63}$$

and

$$\partial Q/\partial K = f_2 = 1 + (N/K)^{1/2} . \tag{64}$$

The first-order conditions for the first-best case simplify to:

$$P = C_1/f_1 = C_2/f_2 , \tag{65}$$

or

$$(K/N)^{1/2} = (C_1/C_2) \tag{66}$$

and

$$P^* = C_1C_2 / (C_1 + C_2). \tag{67}$$

Assuming a constant elasticity demand function:

$$P = AQ^{-b} , \tag{68}$$

we have the solutions

$$Q^* = (A/P^*)^{1/b} , \tag{69}$$

$$N^* = [C_2/ (C_1 + C_2)]^2 Q^*, \tag{70}$$

and

$$K^* = [C_1/ (C_1 + C_2)]^2 Q^*. \tag{71}$$

The model was evaluated at the following values:

$A = 10^6$
$b = 1.25$ (Note the price elasticity is .8 < 1)
$C_1 = 105$
$C_2 = 95$

The first and second-best outcomes are as follows:

Figure 12.3 Smaller Second-Best Capacity

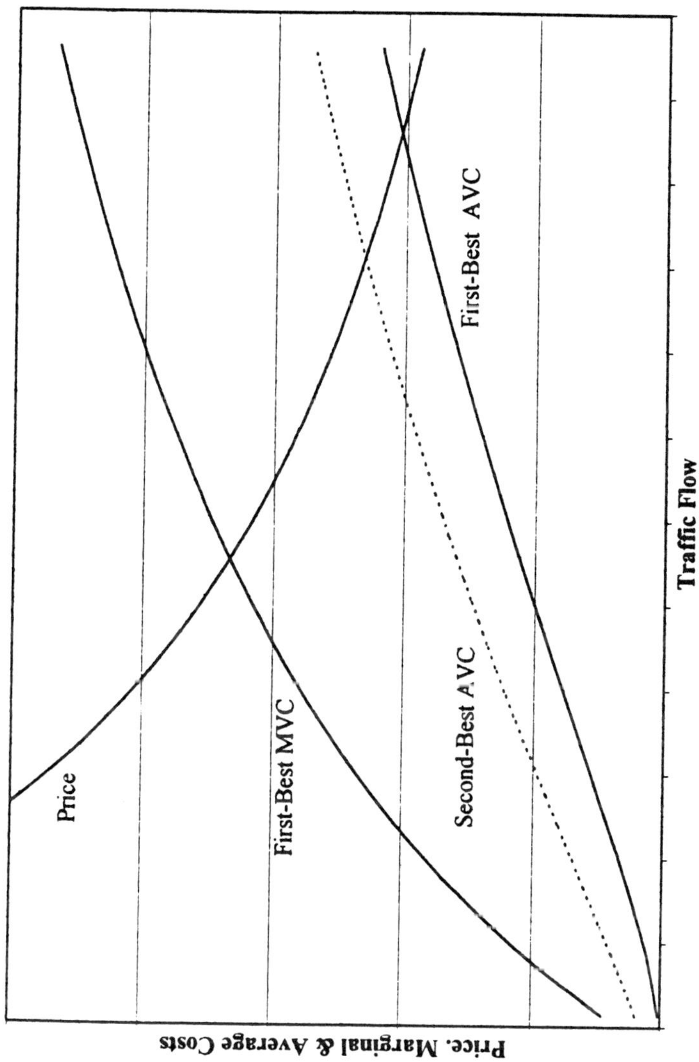

P* = 50	P** = 36
Q* = 2765	Q** = 3600
N* = 624	N** = 1230
K* = 762	K** = 622

The first and second-best outcomes are shown in Figure 12-3. The fact that the second-best capacity is smaller is reflected in the fact that for any given Q the average variable cost for the second-best capacity is higher.

D. SUMMARY

This chapter has presented an analysis of "second-best" capacity for a single road that is subject to traffic congestion, but cannot have a toll imposed.. Sufficient conditions are given for the second-best capacity to be larger than first-best capacity (with an efficient toll). Second-best capacity is larger if demand is inelastic and if the elasticity of substitution of drivers' time for road capital is small. In general the second-best capacity can be larger or smaller than first-best capacity, and examples are provided of both possibilities.

13 THE LONG-RUN TWO-ROAD MODEL OF TRAFFIC CONGESTION

A. INTRODUCTION

This model extends the standard long-run model of congestion presented in Chapter 12 to two roads, and extends the short-run model in Chapter 7 (one toll road and one free road) to the long run. In this chapter we examine the case in which we seek the optimal long-run capacities for a toll road and a free road. One result is immediately obvious. If the toll road and the free road are perfect substitutes, then only the toll road should be built. The optimal capacity of the free road is zero. In this chapter we assume that the toll road and the free road are less-than-perfect substitutes, and obtain results regarding the optimal levels of capacity for the two roads. It turns out that the optimal capacity of the free road can be zero even if the two roads are not perfect substitutes. However, a second-best optimum with one toll road and one free road can involve building both roads at some level of capacity.

B. THEORY OF SECOND-BEST CAPACITY WITH TWO ROADS

For the second-best comparison of interest, Road X is a free road with no toll imposed. Road Y is a toll road for which any desired toll may be imposed. The model posits a known social benefit function dependent jointly on the rates of travel consumption on the two roads:

$$B = B(Q_x, Q_y), \tag{1}$$

where Q_x and Q_y denote the rates of travel on each road. The benefit function is assumed to have the following derivatives:

$$\partial B/\partial Q_x = P_x > 0$$

and

$$\partial B/\partial Q_y = P_y > 0.$$

The use of the notation P for the first partial derivatives identifies the assumed equality between these derivatives and the respective inverse demand curves. One example is the linear demand model:

$$P_x = A_1 - b_1Q_x - b_3Q_y \qquad A_1, b_1 > b_3 > 0 \tag{2}$$

and

$$P_y = A_2 - b_2Q_y - b_3Q_x \qquad A_2, b_2 > b_3 > 0. \tag{3}$$

Equations (2) and (3) can be solved for the quantities in terms of the prices. Let

$$D = b_1b_2 - b_3^2 > 0. \tag{4}$$

The solutions for traffic flow are

$$Q_x = [(b_2A_1 - b_3A_2) - b_2P_x + b_3P_y]/D \tag{5}$$

and

$$Q_y = [(b_1A_2 - b_3A_1) - b_1P_y + b_3P_x\,]/D. \tag{6}$$

As this linear model demonstrates $\partial P_x / \partial Q_y < 0$ for the function $P_x = P(Q_x, Q_y)$ implies $\partial Q_y / \partial P_x > 0$ for the function $Q_y = Q(P_y, P_x)$, so that the assumption that $b_3 > 0$ identifies X and Y as substitutes, i.e., an increase in the price of X increases the consumption of Y. The following analysis may be extended to cover complements by changing this assumption.

Two "inverse" elasticities will be defined for the inverse demand system:

$$\varepsilon_1 = -(\partial P_x / \partial Q_x)(Q_x / P_x\,) > 0 \tag{7}$$

$$\varepsilon_3 = -(\partial P_y / \partial Q_x\,)(Q_x / P_y) > 0 \tag{8}$$

The technology of the roads is represented by two production functions of a similar nature to the standard congestion model presented in earlier chapters:

$$Q_x = f\,(\,N_x\,,\,K_x\,) \tag{9}$$

and

$$Q_y = g\,(\,N_y\,,\,K_y\,) \tag{10}$$

As usual it is assumed that:

$$f_1 = \partial Q_x / \partial N_x \quad \text{(may be positive or negative)}, \tag{11}$$

$$f_2 = \partial Q_x / \partial K_x \; > 0, \tag{12}$$

and

$$f_{12} = \partial^2 Q_x / \partial N_x \, \partial K_x > 0. \tag{13}$$

N represents drivers' aggregate rate of time consumption (density) on a given road and K denotes the road capacity. The subscripts x and y identify the road. The derivatives of g are similar to f as to sign, but the technology of the roads may differ.

The problem is to maximize W, the excess of benefits over costs:

$$W = B - C_1 N_x - C_2 K_x - C_1 N_y - C_2 K_y \,. \tag{14}$$

The C's represent the respective unit costs of the two resources. Different cost parameters could be assigned for the two roads but this refinement contributes very little to the theoretical analysis. This maximization is subject to two constraints for the first-best case. One additional constraint is required for the second-best case. These first-best constraints and their assigned multipliers represent the technology of travel production:

$$\mu \, [\, Q_x - f\,(\, N_x \,,\, K_x \,)] \tag{15}$$

and

$$\pi [\, Q_y - g\,(\, N_y \,,\, K_y \,)]. \tag{16}$$

And, in addition, for the second-best case, the price must equal average cost on the free road:

$$\lambda [\, P_x Q_x - C_1 N_x \,]. \tag{17}$$

The first-order conditions for the first-best case are:

$$P_x = \mu = C_1/f_1 = C_2/f_2 \tag{18}$$

and

$$P_y = \pi = C_1/g_1 = C_2/g_2 \,. \tag{19}$$

The marginal-cost pricing of the first-best case makes the two-road case hardly distinguishable from the one road case. The equality of the short-run marginal cost and the long-run marginal cost determines the first-best relationship between density and capacity. This relationship between N and K can be converted into a first-best relationship between Q and either N or K via the production function. Additionally, if the production function is linear homogenous, the equality of short-run and long-run marginal costs determines the marginal cost itself (π or μ) and therefore optimal price independently of the inverse demand functions. This follows from the fact that the marginal products (e.g. f_1 and f_2) are each functions of a single variable (N/K), which can be eliminated between the two first-order conditions to yield the value of the multiplier (marginal cost) in terms of the parameters. The optimal values of the individual Q's must be disentangled from the demand functions, and then utilized to determine N and K via the previously established relationships.

For the second-best case, the first-order conditions in somewhat greater detail are:

$$\partial W/\partial Q_x = P_x - \mu - \lambda P_x (1 - \varepsilon_1) = 0, \quad (20)$$

$$\partial W/\partial Q_y = P_y - \pi + \lambda \varepsilon_3 P_y = 0, \quad (21)$$

$$\partial W/\partial N_x = -C_1 + \mu f_1 + \lambda C_1 = 0, \quad (22)$$

$$\partial W/\partial K_x = -C_2 + \mu f_2 = 0, \quad (23)$$

$$\partial W/\partial N_y = -C_1 + \pi g_1 = 0, \quad (24)$$

and

$$\partial W/\partial K_y = -C_2 + \pi g_2 = 0. \quad (25)$$

The first observation about the second-best case concerns the density-capacity ratio on the toll road. From (25) and (26), it is evident that the first-best relationship still holds on the toll road:

$$C_1/g_1 = C_2/g_2 . \quad (26)$$

If the production function is a linear homogeneous function, this implies that the marginal cost on the toll road (π) is even the same as the first-best case. Of course, this does not mean that density and capacity or road use is the same as the first best case. It does mean that if the second-best flow is greater than the first-best then the second-best capacity on the toll road is larger.

Next consider the price on the toll road:

$$P_y = \pi/(1 + \lambda \varepsilon_3). \quad (27)$$

The price on the toll road is lower than the first-best price if λ is positive. From (22) and (23):

$$\lambda = 1 - (C_2/f_2)/(C_1/f_1). \tag{28}$$

In the first-best case, the ratio of the marginal fixed cost (C_2/f_2) to the marginal variable cost (C_1/f_1) is 1 and the λ would be 0. It might seem an obvious conclusion that under second-best conditions, where density is not restrained by a toll, the ratio would be less than one and perhaps even negative (i.e. λ is positive). This is certainly true if no toll is imposed at the first-best capacity. It is true that if demand is "inelastic" (i.e. $\varepsilon_1 > 1$), it is possible that the capacity might in theory be expanded until density is so "scarce" that $\lambda < 1$. From equation (20):

$$P_x [\ 1 - \lambda(1 - \varepsilon_1)\ ] = C_2/f_2\ . \tag{29}$$

If demand is assumed to be inelastic, $(1 - \varepsilon_1) < 0$, so that:

$$[1 - \lambda(1 - \varepsilon_1)] < 0 \text{ if } \lambda < 0. \tag{30}$$

But this would imply that (for average variable cost = AVC)

$$P_x = AVC > C_2/f_2 > C_1/f_1\ , \tag{31}$$

which is obviously a contradiction. Accordingly λ must be positive at any optimal point.

Perhaps a direct interpretation of λ would be helpful. The constraint for the multiplier may be written as:

$$-\lambda[\ P_xQ_x - T - C_1N], \tag{32}$$

where T is total toll revenue, which for the no toll case is zero. Then

$$\partial W/\partial T - \lambda. \tag{33}$$

Then λ is the marginal benefit of increases in the toll revenue which is clearly positive for the no toll case. Equation (29) can be written as:

$$P_x\ f_2[\ 1 - \lambda(1 - \varepsilon_1)\ ] - C_2, \tag{34}$$

which is analogous to the equation of the one road case analyzed in the previous chapter. Equation (34) holds for both the first-best case where λ is zero as well. The same reasoning may be applied to test whether the second-best marginal benefit exceeds the marginal cost of capacity at the first-best level of capacity, and a similar elasticity condition derived for the second-best capacity to exceed first-best.

There are certain differences. For one thing (34) is written in terms of the elasticity of price with respect to quantity, rather than in terms of ordinary price elasticity of demand. In a sense, $\varepsilon_1 > 1$, describes an "inelastic" demand system, but it depends on all three demand elasticities :

$$e_1 = -(\partial Q_x/\partial P_x)(P_x/Q_x) > 0, \tag{35}$$

$$e_2 = -(\partial Q_y/\partial P_y)(P_y/Q_y) > 0, \tag{36}$$

and

$$e_3 = -(\partial Q_x/\partial P_y)(P_y/Q_x) > 0, \tag{37}$$

and is not the simple reciprocal of the regular price elasticity. Instead

$$\varepsilon_1 = 1/(e_1 - e_3^2/e_2), \tag{38}$$

which is somewhat greater than the reciprocal. In other words, if $e_1 < 1$, then $\varepsilon_1 > 1$, but ε_1 is quite likely > 1 even if $e_1 > 1$. Considering this factor alone, it seems highly likely that $(1 - \varepsilon_1) < 0$ so that the term $[\,1 - \lambda(1 - \varepsilon_1)]$ is greater than 1 at the equilibrium reached from the first-best capacity by removing the toll.

The second factor distinguishing the two road case is that there are additional variables influencing P_x in the transition from the first-best point to the new equilibrium point. In particular, Q_y changes (assuming optimal adjustments in N_y and K_y) in response to the decrease in the toll on road X.. This change causes P_x to decrease. While it may seem unlikely that this decrease is enough to make the marginal benefit of capacity decrease overall, it does make the possibility of a "corner" solution to the original maximum problem more likely. If the cross-price effect is significant, the possibility of shutting down the free road (providing zero capacity in the long run) becomes a more attractive alternative. This is illustrated by the following numerical example.

C. EXAMPLES

Figure 13-1 presents the optimal capacities for a two road system with identical linear demands in which only one road is tolled. With no cross-price effect, the optimal capacity of the free road exceeds the tolled road (as might be expected) to accommodate the heavier traffic flow. As the "cross" coefficient in the linear demand functions increase, the roads become better substitutes. Both optimal capacities fall in response, as total benefits are less for any given positive levels of road use. However, the optimal capacity of the tolled road falls slightly *faster* than the un-tolled alternative. But at some point (depending upon the cost structure),

Figure 13-1

Optimal Second-Best Capacities

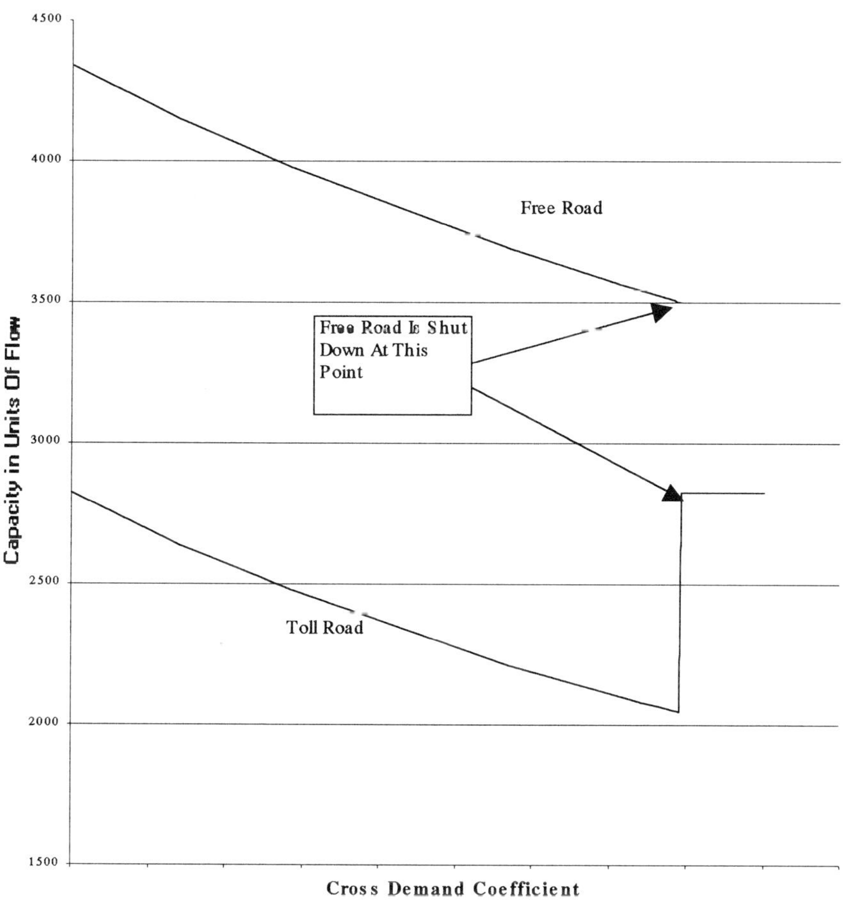

the benefits of the second-best two road system fall below the benefits of a single first-best road. At this point, the optimal capacity for the un-tolled road jumps discontinuously to zero. This shift occurs even before the roads become perfect substitutes, but it is obviously true for the case of perfect substitutes. Accordingly, a smaller second-best capacity for the free road (i.e., smaller than the first-best capacity) is more likely than in the one road case, in the sense that it would not require assumptions as extreme.

This raises the question of whether this analysis can shed some light on what percentage of potential social gains can be achieved by a partial tolling scheme. The analysis is long-run in the sense that the capacities of all roads including un-tolled roads can be varied to accommodate the tolling regime. Accordingly, the first question presented is how to measure the portion of the road system subject to tolls. This is simple enough if road capacities are fixed, but if capacity depends on the tolling scheme, it is not clear what portion of the system should be said to be tolled. For example, if the optimal second-best capacity of the un-tolled road is zero, is 100% of capacity tolled? If so then the first-best solution yielding positive capacities for both routes would have the same percentage but a higher social welfare unless the roads were perfect substitutes. Suppose the inverse demand functions for the two roads are identical and only cases where the optimal second-best un-tolled capacity is positive are considered. What are the effects on the portion of potential gains realized of:

1. Variations in $\partial P_x / \partial Q_y = \partial P_y / \partial Q_x$; and
2. Variations in the relative price of capacity.

The following numerical illustration assumes two roads, X and Y, each of which has a linear demand function:

$$P_x = A_x - b_x Q_x - b_{xy} Q_y , \tag{39}$$

and

$$P_y = A_y - b_y Q_y - b_{xy} Q_x . \tag{40}$$

The calculations assume $A_x = A_y = 400$, $b_x = b_y = .05$. Road trips are produced on each road by a linear homogeneous production function :

$$Q = f(N, K), \tag{41}$$

with Q attaining a maximum for fixed K_0 at $Q = K_0$. The marginal product of capacity is:

$$\partial Q / \partial K = N/Q = 1/V. \tag{42}$$

In other words, the marginal product of capacity is inversely proportional to the velocity (V) on the road. For this case, the optimal capacities were calculated for three tolling regimes:

1. No toll on either road;
2. Only one road tolled; and
3. Both roads tolled.

The calculations were done for a "low" unit capacity cost and a "high" unit capacity cost which was twice the lower cost. The potential gain from tolling is defined by the difference in social welfare between case 3 and case 1. The difference between case 2 and case 1 is the portion of the potential gain recouped by second-best tolling. This can be expressed as a percentage of the potential gain. Arguably, since the roads are identical as to demand, the percentage of potential gain recovered could be said to be attributable to tolling 50% of the system.

The results are shown in Figure 13-2. If the demands are independent, ($b_{xy} = 0$), second-best pricing recovers exactly 50% of the losses due to no toll. This result seems almost obvious. As b_{xy} increases, the percentage of recovery decreases in a *linear* fashion. Interestingly, the same linear function applies to both high and low cost capacity. But relative capacity cost does influence, not only the absolute amount of optimal capacity, but also the *relative* amount of second-best capacity (as a percentage of first-best capacity).

Figure 13-3 shows the relative second-best capacity (for the free road) as a function of the cross demand parameter for both high-cost and low-cost capacity. For both cost parameters, the relative second-best capacity increases at a non-linear (decreasing) rate. Somewhat paradoxically, the high-cost capacity is significantly greater than the low-cost capacity. In absolute terms, of course, the high-cost capacities for all tolling regimes are less than the corresponding low-cost capacities.

In summary, the benefits of a second-best tolling scheme in the long-run depend heavily on the degree to which un-tolled roads are a substitute for the tolled roads. In the long-run imposing tolls on roads which have good substitutes is not very effective. Additionally, any measurement of the percentage of the system subject to tolls based on the relative capacities (tolled to un-tolled) presents certain logical difficulties.

Figure 13-2

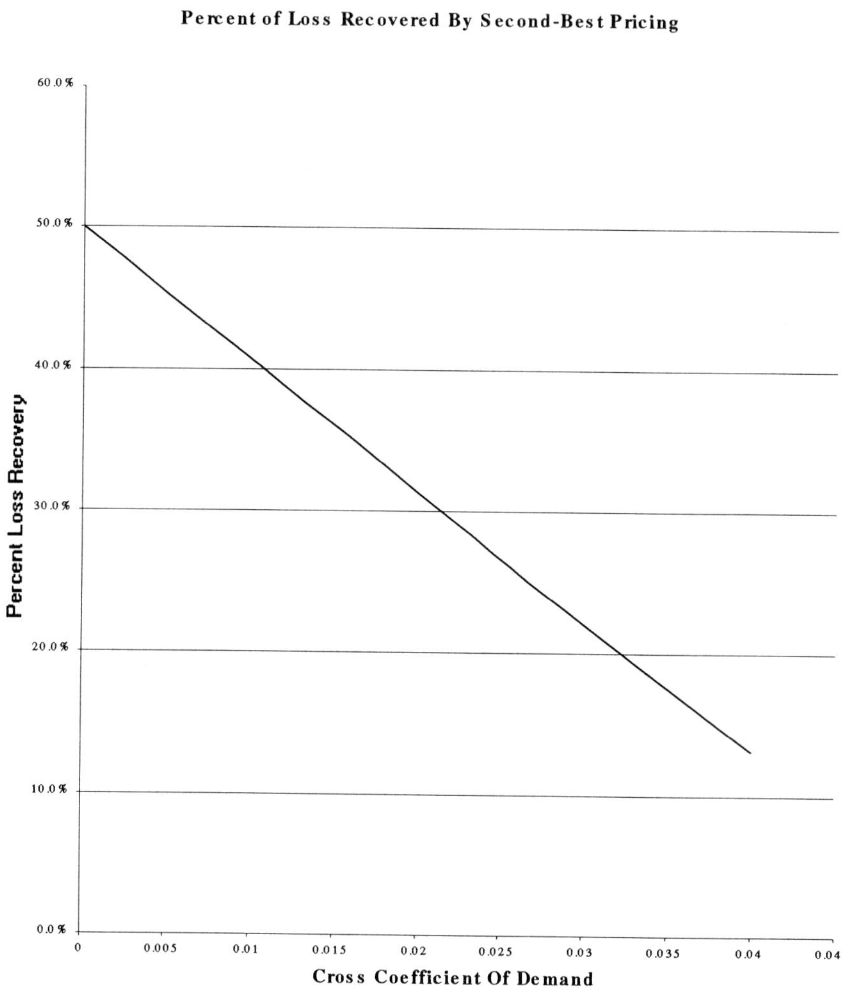
Percent of Loss Recovered By Second-Best Pricing
Percent Loss Recovery
60.0%
50.0%
40.0%
30.0%
20.0%
10.0%
0.0%
0
0.005
0.01
0.015
0.02
0.025
0.03
0.035
0.04
0.045
Cross Coefficient Of Demand

Figure 13-3

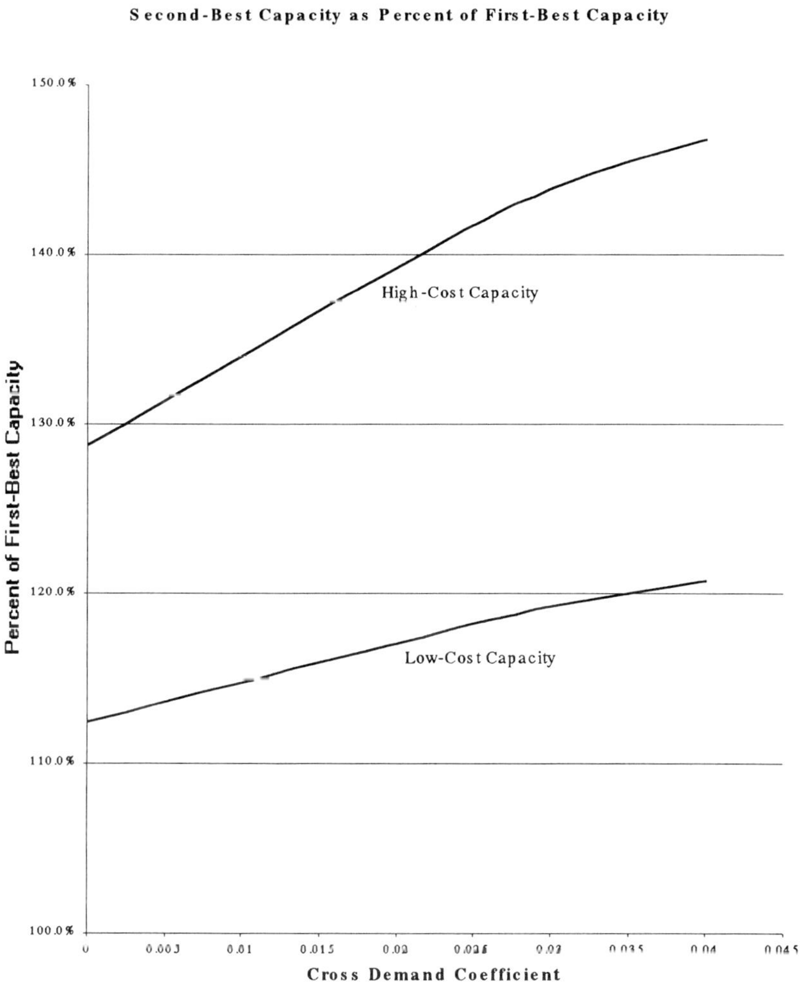
Second-Best Capacity as Percent of First-Best Capacity
Percent of First-Best Capacity
150.0%
140.0%
130.0%
120.0%
110.0%
100.0%
High-Cost Capacity
Low-Cost Capacity
0
0.01
0.015
0.035
0.04
0.045
Cross Demand Coefficient

14 OPTIMAL ROAD CAPACITY WITH HYPERCONGESTION IN THE ABSENCE OF TOLLS

A. INTRODUCTION

In most urban areas, peak traffic volumes exceed the hypercongestion level at which traffic flow begins to decline in response to increases in density. It is an interesting and important question whether this situation reflects a chronic underinvestment in road capacity or whether outcomes of this nature may be socially optimal given the absence of congestion tolls. Previous analyses of optimal second-best capacity have either avoided the question or explicitly assumed that an optimal equilibrium point will not occur on the backward-bending portion of the average variable cost curve. See Wilson (1983), for example. This assumption may also arise implicitly where average variable cost is taken as a primitive concept and treated in the analysis as a strictly increasing function of road use.

In the formulation we use in this book, highway travel is viewed as a production process in which the output of road trips is produced by inputs consisting of total drivers' travel time and road capacity. Treating the production function as the primitive concept facilitates the simultaneous analysis of the regions both above and below the point at which maximum flow occurs. Our analysis characterizes the circumstances where the optimal equilibrium traffic density exceeds density at the hypercongestion point. The nature of the fundamental result has intuitive appeal; optimal equilibrium traffic density exceeds hypercongestion density if the cost of road capacity is relatively high and/or if travel demand is price elastic.

The plan of the chapter is to discuss the basic model used in Section B, and Section C characterizes the traffic flow equilibria of that model. Section D presents the first-order conditions for social welfare maximization in the second-best case of no congestion toll, and Section E discusses the second-order conditions. The chapter concludes with a numerical example that makes use of a particular functional form for the traffic flow production function.

B. THE BASIC MODEL

The model employs the standard simplification of an idealized road on which there occurs a uniform continuous flow of vehicles. The basic notation is as follows.

L_o = fixed length of the road and distance of one trip.

T_o = fixed duration of the period of analysis.

F = rate of traffic flow.

D = traffic density and drivers' time input for T_o.

K = capital input embodied in the road.

Assuming that L_o and T_o are normalized to equal one by choosing appropriate units of measure for time and distance, F equals the number of trips per period and D also is numerically equal to the total travel time (variable input) per period. These assumptions are the same as those made in the previous chapter. The unit of measurement for the capital input is arbitrary; we shall assume that road capital is measured in the same units as the capacity of the road, which is the maximum traffic flow for a given road facility. For example, empirical evidence in Chapter 6 indicates that maximum flow is about 1900 vehicles per lane per hour. A highway with two lanes (in one direction) thus embodies a capacity of 3800 vehicles per hour and 3800 units of capital.

We assume that the production function

$$F = f(D, K) \tag{1}$$

is homogeneous of degree one. This is equivalent to the standard assumption that speed (F/D) depends only on the ratio of density to road capacity because speed is the average product of the variable input (D) and the ratio of density to road capacity (D/K) is the input ratio. We assume the production function has the following properties:

f_1 (marginal product of density),

f_2 (marginal product of road capacity) > 0,

$f_{12} > 0$,

$\alpha_1 = f_1 D/F$, and

$\alpha_2 = f_2 K/F > 0$.

The sign of f_1 is positive at densities below the bottleneck point and negative at densities above the bottleneck point. Of course, α_1 has the same sign as f_1. The sign of f_2 states that additions of capital increase flow at any given density. The sign of f_{12} indicates that the marginal product of capacity is greater at higher traffic densities. Linear homogeneity implies that $\alpha_1 + \alpha_2 = 1$.

The cost equation for this process is given by

$$TC = D + cK, \tag{2}$$

where c is the cost of capital relative to the cost of time. It is assumed that the per-unit value of travel time and the per-unit cost of capital are given constants, and the per-unit value of travel time has been normalized to equal one. Thus the relative cost of capital, c, is measured in the same units as the density-road capacity ratio. Recall that density is measured in vehicles per mile and in hours of labor per unit of time. The price of a unit of this labor has been normalized to equal one.

The (inverse) aggregate demand for road use is given by

$$P = P(F) = \beta/F^{1/e}. \tag{3}$$

We define price elasticity (e) as a positive number, so

$$1/e = -P'(F)F/P. \tag{4}$$

Under second-best conditions with no toll imposed, the price of a trip under equilibrium equals the average variable cost (the inverse of speed), or

$$P = D/F. \tag{5}$$

In this circumstance, the constant elasticity demand function has an interesting implication. From Eq. (5), "total revenue" (P times F) is simply equal to D, which from Eq. (3) is $\beta F^{(e-1)/e}$. Thus D is a constant if e = 1, the case of unitary demand elasticity. This finding suggests that one method for determining demand elasticity for a particular highway would be to study traffic density before and after some improvement is introduced that lowers P on that highway.

Next consider the stability of a consumer equilibrium arising for any given K. The average variable cost curve may be regarded as a supply function indicating the traffic flow which the road accommodates at each price (average variable cost). The standard Walrasian stability condition requires that demand intersect the average variable cost below the hypercongestion point or that it cut the backward-bending segment from below. For a general discussion, see Hicks (1939, Ch. 5) or Samuelson (1983, p. 263). In effect the stability condition proposed states that if at an equilibrium point the price is perturbed upward (downward), then at the new (disequilibrium) price, demand is less (more) than the flow accommodated by the road, causing price to return to the equilibrium level. In terms of slopes of the inverse demand curve and the average variable cost curve, this condition may be written as

$$1 - P(1 - 1/e)f_1 > 0. \tag{6}$$

This result follows because the Walrasian stability condition is that

$$(dF/dP) - f_1(dD/dP) < 0.$$

Substitution for dF/dP and dD/dP, and recalling that D=PF, produces

$$(1/P') - f_1(F + P/P') < 0.$$

Multiplication by P' (which is less than zero) and use of the definition of 1/e produces Eq. (6). Equivalently, using P=D/F and $\alpha_1 + \alpha_2 = 1$,

$$\alpha_2(1 - 1/e) + 1/e > 0. \tag{7}$$

For notational convenience, let

$$\tau = [\alpha_2(1 - 1/e) + 1/e]^{-1}.$$

C. EQUILIBRIUM VARIATION IN FLOW AND DENSITY

Both the equilibrium condition of Eq. (5) and the production function hold in any equilibrium, so that

$$dF/dK = f_1 dD/dK + f_2 \tag{8}$$

and

$$P(1 - 1/e)dF/dK = dD/dK, \tag{9}$$

where dF/dK and dD/dK represent the equilibrium variation in F and D as K is varied. Solving for dF/dK we have

$$dF/dK = f_2[1 - P(1 - 1/e)f_1]^{-1} = \tau f_2 > 0 \tag{10}$$

or

$$dF/dK = f_2[\alpha_2(1 - 1/e) + 1/e]^{-1} = \tau f_2 > 0. \tag{11}$$

The sign follows directly from Eqs. (7) and (8). Solving for dD/dK produces

$$dD/dK = P(1 - 1/e)\tau f_2. \tag{12}$$

The sign of dD/dK is positive (negative) if the price elasticity of demand is greater (less) than one, i. e., total travel time increases with capacity if demand is elastic (e>1), but decreases if demand is inelastic (e<1).

It is useful to define two related elasticities. The first is:

$$\mu = (dF/dK)K/F = \alpha_2[\alpha_2(1 - 1/e) + 1/e]^{-1} = \alpha_2\tau. \tag{13}$$

Note that at a bottleneck point $f_1 = 0$, so that $\alpha_1 = 0$. And since $\alpha_1 + \alpha_2 = 1$, $\mu = 1$. Above the bottleneck $\mu > 1$, and below the bottleneck $\mu < 1$. The second related elasticity is:

$$\Theta = (dD/dK)K/D = \tau\alpha_2(1 - 1/e) < 1. \tag{14}$$

Note that Θ is negative for $e < 1$ and positive for $e > 1$. As e approaches (positive) infinity, Θ approaches +1.

D. THE FIRST-ORDER CONDITION

Capital is chosen to maximize the objective function

$$W = \int P(F)dF - D - cK. \tag{15}$$

This formulation adopts the standard measure of gross social benefits of road use as used by Mohring (1970), for example. The first-order condition is given by

$$dW/dK = P(F)dF/dK - dD/dK - c = 0. \tag{16}$$

Substituting for dD/dK from Eq. (9) gives

$$PdF/dK - [P(1 - 1/e)]dF/dK = (P/e)dF/dK = c. \tag{17}$$

The left-hand side of Eq. (17) may be considered the marginal benefit of road capital. As one would expect, the marginal unit of capital generates additional traffic flow valued at PdF/dK <u>and</u> reduces the variable cost of producing traffic flow by dD/dK. What is slightly different from the usual analysis is the fact that the reductions in variable cost accrue directly in the form of time savings to the consumers of the trips (the vehicle drivers). The net benefit of road capital to the vehicle drivers consists of the excess of the area under the inverse demand curve over the cost of the total travel time. The latter is the average variable cost (price) multiplied by the number of road trips. Hence the net benefit (before subtracting the cost of added capital) is equal to the consumers' surplus of the drivers.

The marginal benefit of capital is the rate of change of consumers' surplus per unit increase in F, (P/e), multiplied by the "second-best marginal product," dF/dK. Substituting for dF/dK from Eq. (11) gives

$$(P/e)\tau f_2 = c. \tag{18}$$

Using P = D/F and the definition on μ in Eq. (13), the optimal density-capital ratio is given by

$$D^*/K^* = ec/\mu. \tag{19}$$

Because $\mu > 1$ above the hypercongestion point and $\mu < 1$ below this point, it follows immediately that the optimal equilibrium implies hypercongestion if

$$D^*/K^* < ec$$

and below the hypercongestion point if

$$D^*/K^* > ec.$$

If effect, outcomes above the hypercongestion point are associated with high capital costs and/or a travel demand which is price elastic.

E. THE SECOND-ORDER CONDITION

It seems probable that concern over satisfaction of the second-order condition in the region above the hypercongestion point accounts to a large extent for the customary assumption that the optimal outcome lies below this point. Nevertheless, there is no inherent difficulty in meeting the second-order condition in this region. It is only necessary that the marginal benefit be declining at the critical point. This may occur either because the rate of change of consumers' surplus is decreasing as flow increases or because the "second-best marginal product," dF/dK, is declining (or both).

The marginal benefit of capacity may be written as

$$MB_k = - P'(F)FdF/dK. \tag{20}$$

Differentiating Eq. (20), we obtain the second-order condition. It may be written compactly as

$$r(P) + r(F)/\mu > 1, \tag{21}$$

where

$$r(P) = -P''(F)F/P'(F)$$

and

$$r(F) = -[(d^2F/dK^2)K]/(dF/dK).$$

The function r( ) is a standardized measure of curvature which is independent of the units of measurement.

In addition to the properties of the production function discussed above, the assumption that the demand function has constant elasticity is <u>sufficient</u> to insure that the second-order condition is always satisfied. Using this assumption,

$$r(P) + r(F)/\mu = 1 + \tau/e + [\tau/e^2\alpha_2][Df_{12}/f_2] > 1. \quad (22)$$

Note that Df_{12}/f_2 is the elasticity of f_2 with respect to D. This derivation is somewhat involved and is omitted. It can be obtained from the authors upon request. We give instead a short proof for the region above hypercongestion only.

The marginal benefit may be written as in Eq. (19) as

$$MB_k = (D/K)\mu/e. \quad (23)$$

From this we can derive

$$d(D/K)/dK = -D(1 - \Theta)/K^2. \quad (24)$$

The equilibrium density-capacity ratio is decreasing as K increases since $\Theta < +1$. From Eq. (13)

$$\mu = \alpha_2\tau. \quad (25)$$

From this

$$d\mu/d\alpha_2 = \tau^2/e > 0 \quad (26)$$

and

$$d\alpha_2/dK = f_{22}(1 - \Theta)K/F + f_2(1 - \mu)/F. \quad (27)$$

Since $\mu > +1$ for all points above the hypercongestion point, both terms of Eq. (27) are negative in this region. It follows from Eqs. (26) and (27) that

$$d\mu/dK < 0. \quad (28)$$

Eqs. (24) and (28) show that the marginal benefit of capacity is decreasing in the region above the hypercongestion point.

F. A NUMERICAL EXAMPLE

The theory of the preceding sections may be illustrated by an example. This example is intended only to show how the model can be used. The numerical values used in the example are drawn from the literature, but no policy conclusions are intended. Assume that the production function is given by

$$F = [2bKD - b^2D^2]^{1/2}. \tag{29}$$

This is a particular version of a well-known production function introduced to the economics literature by Allen (1938, p. 315). The function is defined for densities in the range from 0 to 2K/b. We continue to assume that capacity is measured in the same units as flow, i. e. capacity is measured as the maximum flow. For example, empirical evidence indicates that maximum flow is about 1900 vehicles per lane per hour. The density associated with this flow is 80 vehicles per mile, and the speed at the bottleneck is thus 23.75 miles per hour.

The first derivatives of the production function are

$$f_1 = [bK - b^2D]/F \tag{30}$$

and

$$f_2 = bD/F. \tag{31}$$

At the point at which hypercongestion begins $f_1 = 0$, so that for any given capacity (i.e., maximum flow) K_o, the density D_o is given by

$$D_o = (1/b)K_o. \tag{32}$$

Similarly, by substitution, the maximum flow F_o is

$$F_o = K_o. \tag{33}$$

Note that the parameter b may be interpreted as the speed (F/D) at the hypercongestion point.

Recall from Eq. (18) that the first-order condition is

$$(P/e)\tau f_2 = c.$$

Substituting for f_2 from Eq. (31) and τ from above, and recalling that P = D/F, leads to

$$c = (bD^2/eF^2)[\alpha_2(1 - 1/e) + 1/e]^{-1}. \tag{34}$$

Substitution for F from Eq. (29) implies that

$$c = (D/e)[K(1 - 1/e) + (1/e)(2K - bD)]^{-1}. \tag{35}$$

Manipulation of this equation produces

$$D^*/K^* = (1+e)c/(1+cb). \tag{36}$$

This result corresponds to the more general expression for the optimal density-capacity ratio in Eq. (19).

Equation (32) shows that, if the optimal density-capacity ratio is at the bottleneck point, $D^*/K^* = 1/b$. From Section D, and Eq. (36), this means that the optimal density-capacity ratio is at the hypercongestion point if

$$ec = 1/b. \tag{37}$$

The data on urban highway costs provided by Keeler and Small (1977) can be used to provide a numerical example for this condition. Recall b is the speed at the bottleneck point, which is approximately 24 mph. Thus, $1/b = .0417$ hours per mile.

The work of Keeler and Small (1977) can be used to derive some alternative values for c. They found that the annual cost of an urban-central city expressway in 1972 was approximately $118,000 per lane mile (using a 6% real discount rate). The annual costs of suburban and rural freeways in 1972 were about $34,000 and $32,000 per lane mile. The annual cost of a lane-mile of urban-central city expressway of $118,000 translates into $323 per lane-mile per day. To simplify the analysis further, we assume that the marginal unit of capacity has a nonzero benefit only during the peak demand period. This may not be literally true, of course; our assumption is that the marginal product of capacity is negligible during off-peak periods. We therefore charge the cost of the marginal unit of capacity to the peak demand period. Assuming the peak demand period is three hours in duration five days per week, the marginal capacity cost translates into $151 per lane mile per hour of peak demand. Dividing this cost by 1900 vehicles per hour (the traffic flow per lane mile at capacity) yields a value of c of .080 dollars per unit of traffic flow at capacity.

The study in Chapter 5 of rush-hour commuters in 1972 found that the value of reductions in commuting time was approximately $2.00 per hour. Thus c measured in terms of time per unit of traffic flow is .040 hours per mile. This particular set of figures indicates that the optimum capacity implies peak traffic volume approximately at the hypercongestion point if e is about equal to 1.0. The lower cost of capacity in suburban and rural areas would imply that a higher demand elasticity is associated in these areas with an optimal outcome that is at the hypercongestion point.

G. CONCLUSION

We have shown that as a theoretical matter the optimal capacity may lead to an equilibrium point on the backward-bending portion of the average variable cost curve under the second-best conditions of no toll. Whether this occurs in actual practice is an empirical matter. A numerical example based on capacity costs and value of commuting time in 1972 suggests that the optimal outcome might have been approximately at the hypercongestion point for urban-central city freeways if demand is of unitary elasticity.

The basic result of the chapter is contained in Section D, which states that the optimal capacity depends on the cost of capacity relative to drivers' time and the price elasticity of demand. However, the determination of whether an existing density-capacity ratio is optimal requires, in addition to the information on price elasticity of demand and the relative cost of capacity, an estimate of the equilibrium flow elasticity with respect to capacity. At any point near the hypercongestion point, the marginal product of drivers' time is close to zero, so that if demand is not very elastic, the elasticity of flow with respect to capacity is approximately equal to one in this region. Thus a rule of thumb is that the density-capacity ratio is close to being optimal anywhere in the vicinity of the hypercongestion point if it is approximately equal to the relative cost of capacity multiplied by the price elasticity of demand. It is clear that the price elasticity of demand is a crucial parameter, and further research should be devoted to determining demand elasticities under a variety of circumstances.

References

Allen, R. G. D., 1938, Mathematical Analysis for Economists, New York: St.Martin's Press.

Hicks, J. R., 1946, Value and Capital, 2nd ed., Oxford: Oxford University Press.

Keeler, T. and K. Small, 1977, Optimal peak-load pricing, investment and service levels on urban expressways, Journal of Political Economy 85, 1-25.

Mohring, H., 1970, The peak load problem with increasing returns and pricing constraints, American Economic Review 60, 693-705.

Samuelson, P., 1983, Foundations of Economic Analysis, enlarged edition, Cambridge: Harvard University Press.

Wilson, J., 1983, Optimal road capacity in the presence of unpriced congestion, Journal of Urban Economics 13, 337-357.

15 A MODEL OF DEMAND FOR TRAFFIC DENSITY

A. INTRODUCTION

An alternative model of urban traffic congestion of this type was first proposed by Else (1981). In the conventional model, the traffic flow continues for a fixed time interval. The traditional analysis focuses on the aggregate amount of travel (e.g.vehicle-miles) occurring within this fixed time interval. An individual road user may complete his entire "trip" in a fraction of the period or he may complete only a fraction of his trip within the whole period. The uniformity of the traffic flow does not assume a fixed identity of road users at all points of time during the interval. "Atomic" individual users may enter or exit the flow at any time. The model ignores any significance of arrival or departure times during the fixed interval. All time spent in travel is valued uniformly over the interval, which is consistent with a no-toll equilibrium with uniform density and flow over time. Obviously this model does not capture all aspects of reality attendant to urban traffic congestion.

There are alternative formulations of the problem which capture certain other relevant features of periodic traffic congestion while perhaps ignoring some of those which are well-modeled in the conventional theory. In the present model, based on the model proposed by Else (1981), all individual road users travel simultaneously, making "trips" of the same length. Conceptually the road may be thought of as a closed loop. Users enter the system simultaneously at evenly spaced entry points around the loop. Flow begins at a fixed time and *continues until the trip is completed.* (Alternatively, the flow can end at a fixed endpoint with the starting point adjusting to accommodate the trip's duration). Thus in this model, the time during which the flow is "active" varies. It is implicitly assumed that all flows of whatever time duration are contained within a larger fixed time interval. In this sense the flow is intermittent - there is an assumed "quiet" period within the larger fixed period when no flow occurs. This larger fixed time period will be referred to as a "day." Variable time periods of active road use are measured in "hours."

B. THE ELSE MODEL: FIRST BEST AND SECOND BEST

Density, N, is conventionally measured in terms of vehicles per unit length of road, say [vehicles/mile]. If the length of the road loop is specified as L_0 [miles], then the total number of vehicles participating in the traffic flow is NL_0. If the length of the "trip" is L_1 road loops, then the total vehicle-miles driven our NL_0L_1. Since both L_0 and L_1 remain fixed throughout the analysis, the length of L_0 can be defined as "one loop" and the length of L_1 can be defined as "1 trip," both without any loss of generality. Accordingly N then represents not only the density, but is also equal to the number of trips taken during the period of analysis. The dimension (units) of this new N is [trips] or [vehicles], a cardinal number.

Any individual road user derives a certain benefit from a trip. There are many potential users and the benefits of a trip vary among this group. Each individual demand is a demand for travel, i.e., the "trip." The trip is taken if the trip's benefit equals or exceeds its cost. Obviously the individual cannot complete a road trip without entering the road, thereby increasing density. To call this a "demand for density" may be a semantic stretch not particularly calculated to stimulate clarity of thought. Nevertheless it is clear that in this model the aggregate inverse demand curve can be written:

$$P\ [\$/\text{trip}] = P(N)\ ,\ \ P' < 0. \tag{1}$$

The price elasticity of demand is defined as:

$$e = -\ P/P'N.$$

In effect, one might properly speak of the aggregate demand for density, with the tacit understanding that this is simply a numerical equivalence which is an artifact of the particular model under discussion. The model in Evans (1992) also uses this formulation.

The technology of the road can be stated in "conventional" terms:

$$Q\ [\text{vehicles /hour}] = f\,(N, K), \tag{2}$$

where Q is instantaneous traffic flow or volume, and N, as previously defined is density. K representing capacity is also measured as [vehicles] or [trips] per hour. N is the variable trips actually taken during the period of analysis, while K is the maximum number of trips possible on a given road in a fixed time period. As usual,

$$\partial Q/\partial N = f_1\ \ [\text{trips per hour}],\ \text{and}$$

$$\partial Q/\partial K = f_2\ \ > 0,\ [\text{no units}].$$

Note that for distance fixed at 1, the reciprocal of time, [trips per hour] represents units of velocity or "speed" of the traffic flow. The individual cost of travel time is C_1 [$/vehicle hour]. The cost of capacity is C_2 [$ per vehicle/hour].

Consider a simple numerical example that is similar to the one used above in Chapter 2. Suppose that the road is a circular track of one lane and one mile in circumference. There are 50 vehicles on the track (N), and they travel at a speed of 30 mph. A "trip" is defined as 60 miles, which takes two hours. Therefore, during the two-hour period, 50 trips are demanded (equal to the number of vehicles). The road produces 1500 miles of travel per hour (Q), which is 50 times 30 mph.

The objective function is formulated as follows:

$$W = \int_0^N P(x)dx - C_1N^2 / Q - C_2K. \qquad (3)$$

This formulation of the variable cost makes use of the identity:

$$Q = NV.$$

where V [trips/ hour] denotes the velocity or speed. The time required for one trip is 1/ V or N/Q, and the time cost of each individual trip ("average variable cost") is C_1N/Q. Multiplying by N (the number of trips) gives the total variable cost. W is measured in [$].

The first order conditions are:

$$\partial W/\partial N = P - 2C_1N/Q + C_1(N^2/Q^2)f_1 = 0, \text{ and} \qquad (4)$$

$$\partial W/\partial K = C_1(N^2/Q^2)f_2 - C_2 = 0. \qquad (5)$$

Substituting (5) into (4) gives:

$$P = C_2(2Q/N - f_1)/f_2. \qquad (6)$$

By observation it is clear that (6) may easily hold for an $f_1 < 0$. The fact that a first-best optimum can arise in a region where Q is decreasing (in response to increases in N) was perhaps the most surprising result shown by Else (1981). But obviously in an economic sense the relevant "flow" per day is N and by definition this is less than the capacity per day. This in no way detracts from the important insight derived from Else's contribution. The economic flow need not coincide with an instantaneous rate of flow as used in engineering road technology.

The second-best problem is a constrained optimization:

$$W = \int_0^N P(x)dx - C_1N^2/Q - C_2K - \lambda(PN - C_1N^2 / Q). \qquad (7)$$

Note that the constraint, that price equal average variable cost, has been stated in the form: price times quantity equals total variable cost, to simplify the derivation.

The first order conditions are:

$$P - \lambda P(1\text{-}1/e) - (1\text{-}\lambda)2C_1N/Q + (1\text{-}\lambda)C_1\,(N^2/Q^2)\,f_1 = 0, \text{ and} \tag{8}$$

$$(1 - \lambda)C_1(N^2/Q^2)\,f_2 - C_2 = 0. \tag{9}$$

Note that equation (9) holds for the first-best case, as well, since λ equals 0 for the first-best case and equation (9) simplifies to (5) for that special case.

The next focus of analysis is the determination of the conditions under which the second-best capacity exceeds the first-best. The approach is similar to that of the previous chapter for the conventional model. Suppose capacity is set at the first-best level, and the toll is removed. A new equilibrium arises. The question is whether the marginal benefit of added capacity (under the no-toll regime) exceeds the marginal cost of capacity at that new equilibrium. In the plane of costs and benefits on the Y-axis and N on the X-axis, the first-best point and the new equilibrium point are separated by a finite interval. If these two points are connected by a line of constant elasticity, this elasticity can be interpreted as an average of the actual point elasticities. For a further discussion, see the previous chapter. The first step is to solve equation (8) for $(1 - \lambda)$. Define the elasticity of Q with respect to N as:

$$\alpha = f_1N/Q. \tag{10}$$

Using the constraint that price equals average variable cost ($P = C_1N/Q$), equation (8) can be written as:

$$P(1 - \lambda) + \lambda P/e - (1 - \lambda)\,P\,(2 - \alpha) = 0. \tag{11}$$

Or, dividing by P:

$$\lambda/e = (1 - \lambda)\,(1 - \alpha) \tag{12}$$

Solving for λ:

$$\lambda = e(1 - \alpha)\,/\,[1 + e(1 - \alpha)], \tag{13}$$

or

$$(1 - \lambda) = 1/\,[1 + e(1 - \alpha)]. \tag{14}$$

Returning to equation (5), the net marginal benefit of capacity, (after deducting variable costs, but before marginal cost of capacity), at the first-best point is:

$$MBC = C_1(N/Q)^2 f_2 . \tag{15}$$

The elasticity of MBC along the constant elasticity curve to the new equilibrium is the average of the following point elasticities:

$$(dMBC/dN)(N/MBC) = 2(1-\alpha) + f_{12}N/f_2 . \tag{16}$$

Combining (16) with (14) leads to the following conclusion: the marginal benefit of added capacity under the no toll regime exceeds the marginal cost of capacity at the first-best capacity level if:

$$2(1 - \bar{\alpha}) + \bar{\rho} > 1 + e_2 (1 - \alpha_2). \tag{17}$$

where $\bar{\alpha}$ and $\bar{\rho} = f_{12}N/Q$ are the average elasticities along the path to the new equilibrium point, and e_2 and α_2 are the values of the elasticities at the new equilibrium point. Clearly α is decreasing as N increases for any fixed capacity so that $\alpha_2 < \bar{\alpha}$. Equation (17) may be written as :

$$(1 - \bar{\alpha}) + \bar{\rho} > \bar{\alpha} + e_2 (1 - \alpha_2). \tag{18}$$

Note that, by definition, $\bar{\rho} > \bar{\alpha}$ if

$$f_{12}N/f_2 > f_1N/Q, \tag{19}$$

which is equivalent to

$$\sigma = f_1 f_2 / f_{12} Q < 1. \tag{20}$$

Accordingly, sufficient conditions for a larger second-best (no toll) capacity are:
1. Inelastic demand: $e_2 < (1 - \bar{\alpha})/(1 - \alpha_2) < 1$; and
2. Inelastic factor substitution: $\sigma < 1$.

In this respect the alternative formulation exhibits little difference from the traditional model. Under either model, the second-best capacity is larger under the conditions normally assumed to apply.

The major difficulty with this alternative model lies in the fact that the analysis of the duration of the flow for the period considered does not take into account the cost effect on following or leading traffic flows in other periods. This can easily be seen in a two period model. Assume the model depicts an evening commuting period in which workers return home after work. There is a choice of two periods in which to return to home. In the first period, (the "peak" period), workers leave immediately at the end of the workday (a fixed time). The second period begins immediately after the peak period ends. In the first period, the average private cost is:

$$AVC_1 = C_1N_1/Q_1 \, . \tag{21}$$

In the second period, the average variable cost includes a waiting cost which depends on the duration of the delay before the second period begins:

$$AVC_2 = C_1N_2 /Q_2 + WN_1/ Q_1 \, . \tag{22}$$

W is the waiting cost per unit of time incurred by the second period travelers. The total cost for both commuting periods would be:

$$TVC = C_1N_1^2/Q_1 + WN_1N_2/Q_1 + C_1N_2^2/Q_2 \, . \tag{23}$$

The marginal variable cost of peak period travel is:

$$MC_1 = (2 - \alpha)C_1N_1/Q_1 + (1 - \alpha)WN_2/Q_1 \, . \tag{24}$$

The marginal variable cost in the later period is:

$$MC_2 = (2 - \alpha)C_1N_2/Q_2 + WN_1/Q_1 \, . \tag{25}$$

In both periods, the marginal cost includes an element which increases as the trips in the other period increases. But the delay cost imposed on second-period travelers by peak travelers is not a part of the private cost of the peak period. Taking into consideration an additional period, the alternative formulation begins to strongly resemble the traditional formulation.

In Chapter 9, a traditional type of two period model was analyzed with the following two period demand structure:

$$N_1 = 7{,}500 - 21P_1 + 15P_2, \text{ and} \tag{26}$$

$$N_2 = 4{,}000 + 15P_1 - 25P_2. \tag{27}$$

To this demand structure, we add cost functions based on the production function:

$$Q = (2KN - N^2)^{.5} \tag{28}$$

which is discussed in the previous chapter.

The cost parameters for driving time, waiting time, and capacity were assigned to approximate the first-best flows obtained in the base case of Chapter 9, as follows:

	Peak Period	Off-Peak
Travel Rates		
Chapter 9	6,439	3,900
Present Model	6,396	3,903
Travel Prices		
Chapter 9	93.4	60.0
Present Model	96.8	61.9

The No-toll outcomes for the same cost parameters are as follows:

	Peak Period	Off-Peak
Travel Rates		
Chapter 9	7,405	3,289
Present Model	7,124	3,720
Travel Prices		
Chapter 9	43.4	54.5
Present Model	45.4	38.4

In the model in Chapter 9, the no toll off-peak price exceeds the peak price, whereas in this alternative model, the opposite is true. The factors which influence the relative prices of the two periods can be seen in Figure 15-1. In this two dimensional rendering, the off-peak period is represented by the dotted lines, while the solid lines represent the peak period. Each set of lines is drawn with the values of the other period fixed at their equilibrium values. In general the greater the difference in the demand functions for each period, the more likely it is that the price of the peak period (the greater demand) would exceed the off-peak price. The demand functions reflected in the comparison above between this model and the Chapter 9 model were identical however. Additionally, the greater amount by which the average cost of the off-peak period (which includes a waiting cost) exceeds the peak average price (which does not include any waiting cost), the more likely the off-peak price would exceed the peak price. The inter-period disparity in average cost in this model is much greater than the inter-period marginal cost disparity because the peak period marginal cost fully reflects the waiting cost imposed by peak commuters on off-peak travel. In the Chapter 9 model, delay cost is fixed and does not affect peak-period marginal cost. For these reasons it is quite surprising that the models differ as to relative inter-period price in the direction observed. Apparently this is attributable to greater curvature of the average cost function in this model. In any event, this two-period refinement of the model presented above, behaves in a quite similar manner to the more conventional model, and seems useful in modeling a variable delay cost which is dependent on the duration of the peak period.

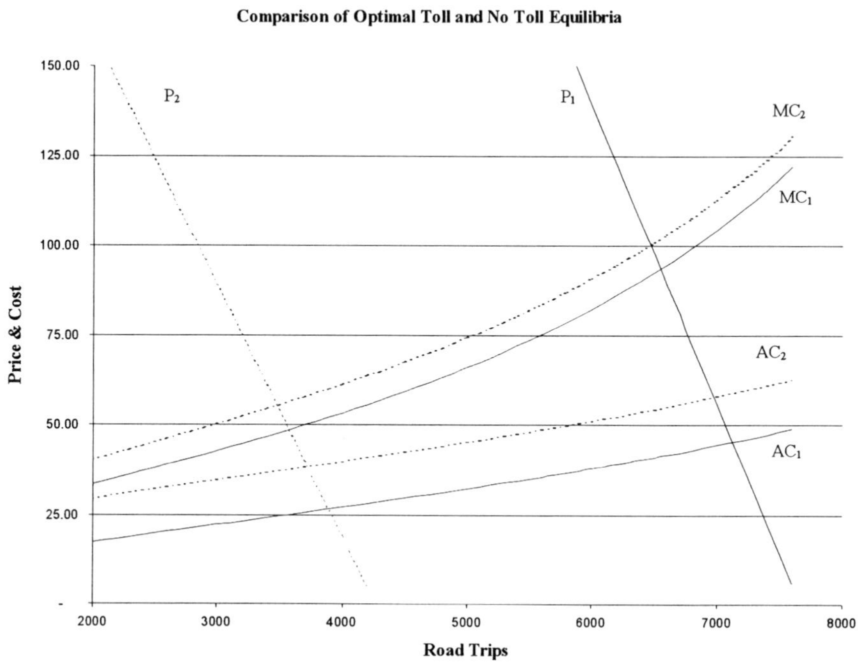
Comparison of Optimal Toll and No Toll Equilibria
Price & Cost
Road Trips
P2
P1
MC2
MC1
AC2
AC1
150.00
125.00
100.00
75.00
50.00
25.00
-
2000
3000
4000
5000
6000
7000
8000

Figure 15-1

References

Else, P., 1981, A reformulation of the theory of optimal congestion taxes, Journal of Transport Economics and Policy XV, 217-232.

Evans, A., 1992, Road congestion: The diagrammatic analysis, Journal of Political Economy 100, 211-217.

APPENDIX: A LONG-RUN, TWO-ROAD MODEL

A. INTRODUCTION

This is a two period model of traffic congestion based on the type of model is discussed in Chapter 15. Each road is pictured as a closed loop on which travel occurs. Travelers enter the road simultaneously at the start of each period at points uniformly distributed around the loop. The periods are called the "peak" period and the "off-peak" period. The model assumes that the morning commute from home to work is the focus of the analysis. In this setting the off-peak period occurs first and is identified as period 1. The peak period begins immediately after period 1ends, and is denoted as period 2. Period 2 ends exactly at the time when work begins. Commuters learn by experience when to leave to arrive exactly on time. Similarly, the off-peak commuters know by experience when to leave to avoid the peak traffic flow. They arrive at work exactly when the peak flow begins and have to wait at work before their workday begins. The duration of each flow is endogenous. The early commuters pay a waiting cost that is proportional to the duration of the peak-period. Each road has unit length of 1 "loop". Each trip has identical unit distance of one "trip". There is no required relationship between 1 trip and 1 loop, but since it involves no real loss of generality , the model assumes they are equal. There are also two roads available for the trip. The roads are not perfect substitutes. However, on any particular road, there is perfect substitution between time periods. The basis for this assumption is discussed below. The remainder of this chapter is divided into two sections. In the first section, the theoretical problem is posed and "solved" by deriving first order conditions for the various distinct tolling regimes. In the following section ,an example is constructed and numerical solutions are derived for a particular cost and demand structure.

B. THE MODEL

In an attempt to make the analysis reasonably comprehensible, a fairly large amount of specialized notation will be introduced. To begin with, the gross benefits of road use are posited directly and denoted:

$$B = B(N_1, N_2)$$

as a function of the total usage on each road, N_1 and N_2. On either road, there is a perfect substitution between time periods as to benefits. This seems to be a reasonable assumption. Each road transports an individual from one specific point to another specific point. In terms of pure geographic displacement, the time of use is immaterial. Clearly, there are contexts in which time of travel does affect the benefits of travel. For a shopping trip, for example, one may find the variety of open stores depends upon the timing of the trip. But the situation modeled is the commuting trip from home to work (or from work to home). The long-run benefit has to do with enabling an individual to work and live at particular different locations. As long as both peak and off-peak periods are contained comfortably (with some slack) within a larger basic "commuting" period, it seems reasonable to assume perfect substitution. Exactly the same travel is accomplished regardless of when the trip is taken. Moreover, to a certain extent, the division between costs and benefits is always somewhat arbitrary. The present model incorporates two types of cost differences between time periods and this fact tends to offset the assumption of perfect substitution between periods. Accordingly,

$$N_1 = N_{11} + N_{12}$$

and

$$N_2 = N_{21} + N_{22}$$

Therefore:

$$\partial B/\partial N_{11} = \partial B/\partial N_{12} = P_1,$$

$$\partial B/\partial N_{21} = \partial B/\partial N_{22} = P_2,$$

$$\partial P_1/\partial N_{11} = \partial P_1/\partial N_{12} = P_{11} < 0,$$

$$\partial P_1/\partial N_{21} = \partial P_1/\partial N_{22} = P_{12} < 0,$$

$$\partial P_2/\partial N_{21} = \partial P_2/\partial N_{22} = P_{22} < 0, \text{ and}$$

$$\partial P_2/\partial N_{11} = \partial P_2/\partial N_{12} = P_{21} = P_{12} < 0.$$

For N, the first subscript indicates the road (1= Y and 2 = X)and the second indicates the period (1 = off-peak and 2 = peak). For the price derivative with respect to road use, the double subscript identifies first that it is a partial derivative, and secondly, the first subscript identifies the road to which the price applies and the second identifies the road on which the use occurs.

Turning now to the notation for the cost side, the technology of the roads are described by a production function:

$$Q = Q(N, K)$$

For the long-run, it may as well be assumed that the technology is the same for both roads, but the cost of capacity may be different. In the following analysis N and K will be considered the variables and differentiation will be carried out with respect to these two variables directly as though the production function was transparent. The total cost for road 1(Y) is:

$$TC_1 = C_{11}N_{11}^2/Q_{11} + WN_{11}N_{12}/Q_{12} + C_{12}N_{12}^2/Q_{12} + C_{k1}K_1$$

To review the notation, C_{11} is the cost of driving time on road 1 in the off-peak period measured as [$/hour]. C_{12} is the corresponding cost on road 1 for the peak period. W is the waiting cost for early arrival at work. It is assumed this is the same regardless of which road got the commuter there. But note the possibly different driving time costs in the two periods is retained, as is the possibility of different capacity costs C_k on each road. Note the capacity of the roads does not vary between periods. For the trip of unit length, the duration equals 1/V(velocity) = N/Q, and the number of trips is N. For further discussion, see Chapter 15 on alternative demand formulations. To avoid the peak period, the off-peak traveler must pay the waiting cost for the duration of the peak period.

TC_2 is similarly defined for road 2(X). Two different names are retained for each road to more accurately reflect commuting conditions in City of Chicago, as well as to establish a connection to the Cartesian plane used below to explain the benefit distribution. The average variable cost (the private cost) for each period is:

$$AC_{11} = C_{11}N_{11}/Q_{11} + WN_{12}/Q_{12}$$

$$AC_{12} = C_{12}N_{12}/Q_{12}$$

Define the elasticity of flow Q with respect to N as:

$$\eta_{11} = -(\partial Q_{11}/\partial N_{11})(N_{11}/Q_{11})$$

Note this elasticity as defined is negative for the region where Q is increasing in N and positive for the region where Q is decreasing in N. With this definition, the marginal costs for each period are:

$$MC_{11} = (2 + \eta_{11})\, C_{11}N_{11}/Q_{11} + WN_{12}/Q_{12}$$

$$MC_{12} = (2 + \eta_{12})\, C_{12}N_{12}/Q_{12} + (1 + \eta_{12})\, WN_{11}/Q_{12}$$

Next consider the possible constraints for each road and period for which no toll is in effect. These restrictions constrain the prevailing price on each such road to equal the average variable cost. The four constraints are:

$$Z_{11} = \lambda_{11}(P_1N_{11} - C_{11}N_{11}^2/Q_{11} - WN_{11}N_{12}/Q_{12}),$$

$$Z_{12} = \lambda_{12}(P_1N_{12} - C_{12}N_{12}^2/Q_{12}),$$

$$Z_{21} = \lambda_{21}(P_2N_{21} - C_{21}N_{21}^2/Q_{21} - WN_{21}N_{22}/Q_{22}), \text{ and}$$

$$Z_{22} = \lambda_{22}(P_2N_{22} - C_{22}N_{22}^2/Q_{22}).$$

The simplest procedure is to include all four constraints and apply the results of the maximization to all tolling regimes simultaneously by setting the Lagrange multiplier for unconstrained roads or periods equal to zero.

The maximization problem may be stated as maximize W (net social welfare) defined as follows:

$$W = B - TC_1 - TC_2 - Z_{11} - Z_{12} - Z_{21} - Z_{22}$$

The constraints were written after multiplying through by the road trips N for each period on each road to simplify the exposition. When finding the partial derivatives of W with respect to N_{11}, the result involves all four constraints as a result of the inclusion of either P_1 or P_2 in each constraint The same is true for the other N's as well. In each case the derivative contains four terms of the following nature:

$$\text{for } N_{11}{:}\ \zeta_{11} = -\lambda_{11}P_{11}N_{11} - \lambda_{12}P_{11}N_{12} - \lambda_{21}P_{21}N_{21} - \lambda_{22}P_{21}N_{22}$$

$$\text{for } N_{12}{:}\ \zeta_{12} = -\lambda_{11}P_{11}N_{11} - \lambda_{12}P_{11}N_{12} - \lambda_{21}P_{21}N_{21} - \lambda_{22}P_{21}N_{22}$$

$$\text{for } N_{21}{:}\ \zeta_{21} = -\lambda_{11}P_{12}N_{11} - \lambda_{12}P_{12}N_{12} - \lambda_{21}P_{22}N_{21} - \lambda_{22}P_{22}N_{22}$$

$$\text{for } N_{22}{:}\ \zeta_{22} = -\lambda_{11}P_{12}N_{11} - \lambda_{12}P_{12}N_{12} - \lambda_{21}P_{22}N_{21} - \lambda_{22}P_{22}N_{22}$$

Notice that the ζ_{11} and ζ_{12} (on Road 1) are equal as are ζ_{21} and ζ_{22} (on Road 2), since each road is a perfect substitute between time periods. The marginal benefit of an increase in use of one road with the use of the other road held constant requires a decrease in both prices. This marginal benefit equals the change in consumers' surplus brought about the price changes (i.e. the rate of price change multiplied by quantity). The marginal benefit thus described is net of variable costs. The ζ's can be considered weighted sums of these net benefits from each road-period with weights being the Lagrange multipliers.

The effects of capacity are exhibited through the reduction of variable costs on each road. The partial derivative of total variable cost with respect to capacity is negative and represents a cost reduction or benefit. The marginal benefits of capacity (with road use constant) in each period for road 1 are:

$$MBC_{11} = C_{11}(N_{11}/Q_{11})^2(\partial Q_{11}/\partial K_1) + W(N_{11}N_{12}/Q_{12}^2)\,(\partial Q_{12}/\partial K_1)$$

$$MBC_{12} = C_{12}(N_{12}^2/Q_{12}^2)(\partial Q_{12}/\partial K_1)$$

And similarly for Road 2 (X) and K_2.

Finally, with this extensive preparation, the first-order conditions for a maximum can be presented:

$$P_1 - AC_{11} + \zeta_{11}/(1 - \lambda_{11}) = MC_{11} - AC_{11}$$

$$P_1 - AC_{12} + \zeta_{12}/(1 - \lambda_{12}) = MC_{12} - AC_{12}$$

$$P_2 - AC_{21} + \zeta_{21}/(1 - \lambda_{21}) = MC_{22} - AC_{22}$$

$$P_2 - AC_{22} + \zeta_{22}/(1 - \lambda_{22}) = MC_{22} - AC_{22}$$

$$(1 - \lambda_{11})MBC_{11} + (1 - \lambda_{12})MBC_{12} = C_{k1}$$

$$(1 - \lambda_{21})MBC_{21} + (1 - \lambda_{22})MBC_{22} = C_{k2}$$

The conditions hold for all tolling regimes, although the interpretations vary. The final two conditions relating to the capacities are illustrated in Figure A15-1.

In the absence of constraints, (first-best pricing on both roads in both periods), the λ's are all equal to zero and the optimal outcome arises at a point "like" A in Figure A15-1 where the marginal benefit equals marginal capacity cost. If one or both periods are priced at average cost, then MBC exceeds the marginal cost C_k. A portion of the marginal benefit, indicated by the Lagrange multipliers, is set aside, as it were, to offset the marginal externalities caused by increasing capacity. (The N's increase as K increases which is not reflected in MBC as defined). The equilibrium would be at a point "like" B. Incidentally, all of the λ's are dimension-free fractions between 0 and 1. Figure A15-1 is interesting because on the basis of graphs of this nature, it is sometimes asserted that the second-best capacity, if not strictly speaking smaller than the first-best, is at least smaller than the first-best capacity would be if the first-best road use equaled the actual optimal second-best road-use. In other words, the second-best capacity is smaller than it would be if it were larger.

The first four conditions describe the optimal outcomes on the four road-period combinations. If all road-period combinations have an optimal toll, price exceeds the average cost, the toll (P - AC) on the left hand side equals the marginal externality (MC - AC) on the right. All ζ's are zero for this case. If a given road-period combination is optimally priced but some of the others are not, price again, in general, differs from average cost, but this time some ζ's are

Figure A15-1
Marginal Benefit of Capacity

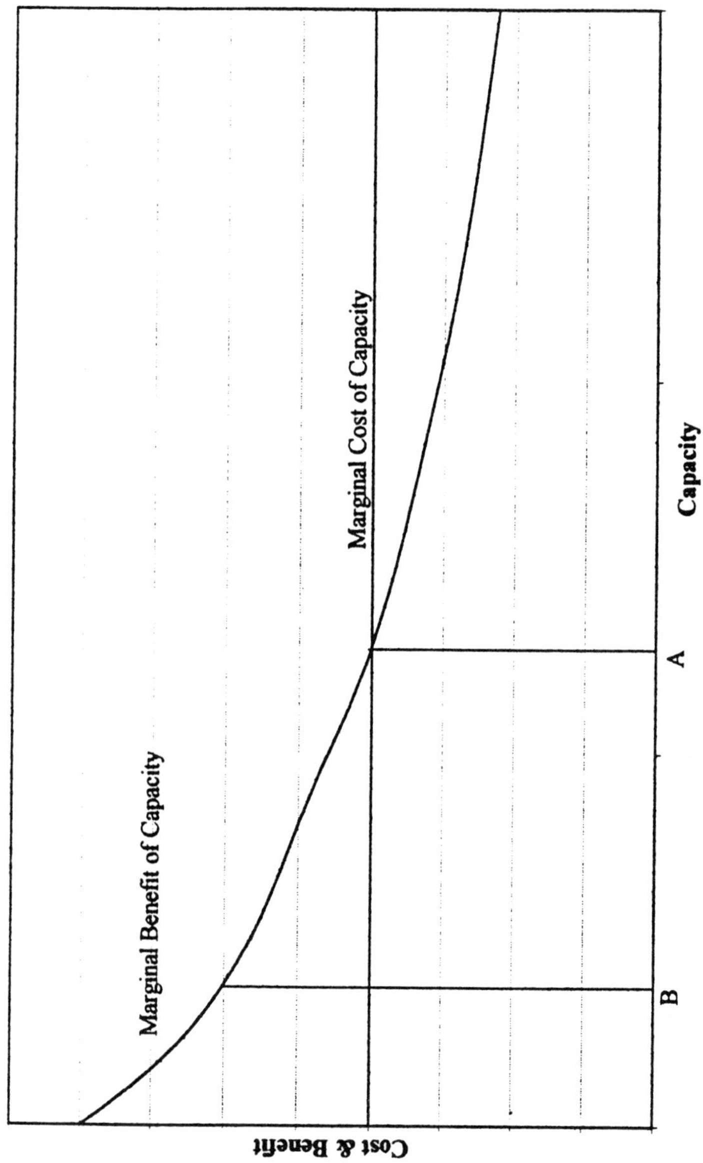

positive (the ζ's can only be zero or positive), so that the toll (P - AC) in this case is set below the marginal externality by the sum of the positive ζ's. (It may even be negative - a subsidy). If price equals average cost (no toll), then on that road/period combination, the marginal consumers' surplus represented by the ζ's offsets the marginal externalities on the right-hand side. Some additional features can be illustrated by the numerical example.

A particular two-road benefit structure is derived as follows. There are U individual potential road users or commuters. Each potential road user Ui is characterized by an ordered pair of real numbers : (x_i, y_i) where x_i denotes the gross benefits of a trip on road X, and y_i denotes the benefits of a trip on road Y. Each potential user takes either 0 or 1 trip during the entire commuting period, and if 1, chooses the period. As one specific example, suppose the individual potential users are *uniformly distributed over a square region* of the plane as shown in Figure A15-2.

This symmetric treatment of benefits or demand for each road avoids the possibly confounding effects of demand differences on the effects of alternative tolling regimes. On the other hand, it also limits the generality of the model. The model could accommodate (tolerate), in principle, any distribution over the plane. However, a priori, it is difficult to suggest any more appealing distribution. The side of the square in Figure A15-2 is length A. Given a set of prices for using each road, an individual user will not travel if his benefits lie inside the rectangle with sides of P_x and P_y. Elsewhere the user will choose road X if $(x_j - P_x) > (y_j - P_y)$ and choose road Y if $(x_j - P_x) \leq (y_j - P_y)$. Each set of prices (P_x, P_y) uniquely determines the total trips on each road. To see this, note if both prices increase (decrease) then the total number of trips overall decreases (increases) so both N_x and N_y cannot be the same. On the other hand if P_x, for example, increases, while P_y decreases (or stays the same), then N_x will decrease while N_y will increase. This one to one correspondence between a price pair and quantity pair means the gross benefits could be expressed either as function of prices or as a function of quantities. The latter formulation is assumed in the model treated above. Note particularly that given the formulation in terms of quantities, the marginal benefit of a change in one quantity say N_x *with the other quantity held constant* will equal the price on that road P_x. To see this, notice that to increase N_x requires an decrease in P_x and also a decrease in P_y in order hold N_y constant. The increase in benefit from the marginal Road X user at point U_1 who was previously staying home is P_x. But what about the former Y user at point U_2 who *shifts* to X? He is replaced as a Road Y warrior by the guy at point U_3 who was not previously playing the game. So the net change is + P_y for the guy at U_3, - $[P_y + (B_y - P_y)]$ for the Y shifter at U_2, who then picks up $P_x + (B_x - P_x)$ as an X user. Since Mr. U_2 was right on the margin previously, $(B_y - P_y) = (B_x - P_x)$. Consequently, the net increase is P_x per additional user on X. The definition of B_y and B_x should be self-evident.

Given the assumption of uniformly distributed users, the aggregate demand for trips by each route is proportional to and can be ascertained by computing the areas shown in Figure A15-2. The relevant shapes depend on

Figure A15-2
Demand for Travel on Two Roads

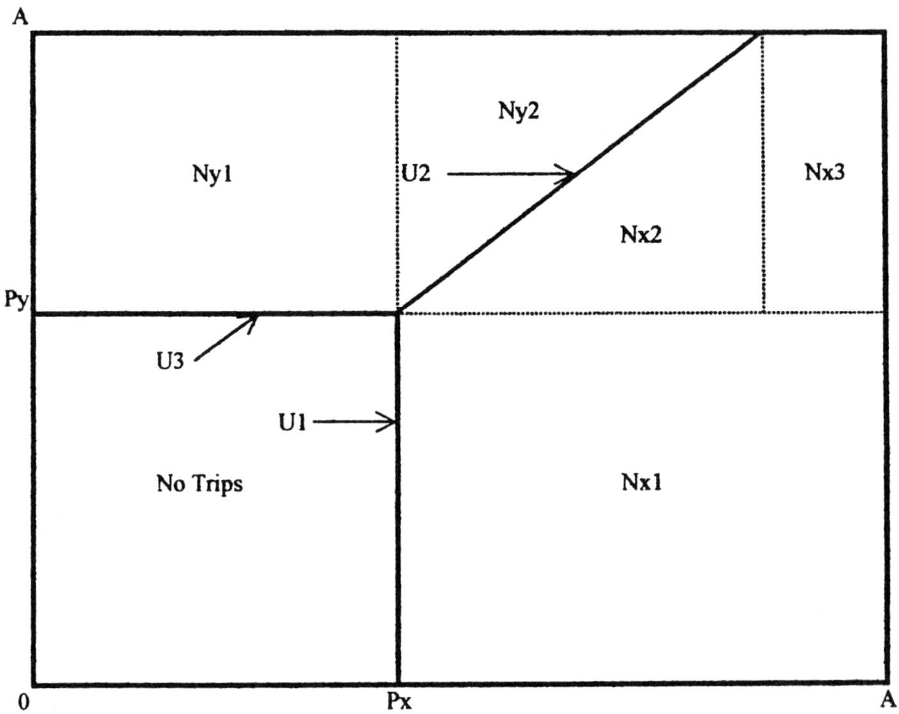

which price is the higher price. The figure shows the case where P_y exceeds P_x. The diagonal dividing line is at a 45^0 angle from the point (P_x, P_y). The areas denoted by N_{x1}, N_{x2}, and N_3 choose road X, while the areas denoted N_{y1}, and N_{y2} choose Y. For $P_x > P_y$ there arises a different but analogous allocation of trips. The functions describing the allocations between roads on either side of equal prices converge at the point of equality, and the combined function is continuous and differentiable at the point $P_x = P_y$. The aggregate demand functions are as follows:

$$N_x = A^2/2 + A(P_y - P_x) - P_y^2/2 \qquad \text{For } P_y > P_x$$

$$= A^2/2 + A(P_y - P_x) + P_x^2/2 - P_xP_y \qquad \text{For } P_x > P_y$$

$$N_y = A^2/2 - A(P_y - P_x) + P_y^2/2 - P_xP_y \qquad \text{For } P_y > P_x$$

$$= A^2/2 - A(P_y - P_x) - P_x^2/2 \qquad \text{For } P_x > P_y$$

It might be noted that the integrability condition

$$\partial N_x/\partial P_y = \partial N_y/\partial P_x$$

is satisfied . See Chapter 7 for a discussion. The gross benefits can be similarly ascertained in terms of the P's by multiplying the areas by the average benefit in that area. This works well enough for the rectangular areas where each benefit has the same number of adherents so that the average benefit is evident. For the triangular areas, integration can be considered as a last resort.

For example, the gross benefits of the triangular region N_{y2} in Figure 2 would be:

$$B(N_{y2}) = \int_0^{A - Py} (P_y + x)x \, dx = [(A - P_y)^2/2][P_y + 2/3(A - P_y)]$$

where it is now evident that $P_y + 2/3(A - P_y)$ is the average price. Let:

$$P_{max} = \text{Max} (P_x, P_y)$$

$$P_{diff} = \text{Abs} (P_x - P_y)$$

Then the total gross benefits are as follows:

$$B_{x1} = P_y (A - P_x)(A + P_x)/2$$

$$B_{y1} = P_x (A - P_y)(A + P_y)/2$$

$$B_{x2} = (P_x + (A - P_{max})/1.5)(A - P_{max})^2/2$$

$$B_{y2} = (P_y + (A - P_{max})/1.5)(A - P_{max})^2/2$$

$$B_3 = P_{diff}\,(A - P_{max})(A - P_{diff} / 2)$$

$$B = B_{x1} + B_{y1} + B_{x2} + B_{y2} + B_3$$

C. NUMERICAL EXAMPLE

The production function chosen is the same function used for illustration in several earlier chapters:

$$Q = (2sKN - s^2 N^2)^{1/2}$$

K and Q have the same dimension: [vehicles / time]. But N is a density measured as [vehicles / distance] where the unit of distance has been normalized to equal 1 (the unit of distance is one uniform trip). This assumption concerning the measurement of distance in computing the density allows the number of trips to be equal numerically to the density. Accordingly the dimensional constant, s, has the dimension of a velocity [distance / time]. The distance has already been fixed, so s can be eliminated from the function by assuming a time unit, such that s = 1. Hereafter s will be suppressed with this understanding. The production function is a linear homogeneous production function. Q is maximized for a given K when N = K = Q. For purposes of calculation, the demand parameter A is set equal to 1 so that road usage is computed a percent of possible road usage (A^2 = 100%).

The cost parameters illustrated are as follows:

Cost of driving time			
	Road 1		
		Off- peak	= .15
		Peak	= .11
	Road 2		
		Off-peak	= .15
		Peak	= .11
Cost of waiting time			= .065
Cost of Capacity			
	Road 1		= .30
	Road 2		= .30

Table A15-1 presents the results of the numerical illustration. Four tolling regimes are shown:

1. The first column reports the results for a first-best regime in which optimal tolls are imposed on both roads in both periods.

2. Column two reports results where one road has no tolls and the other has the best possible tolls under the circumstances in both periods.

3. Column three illustrates the case where optimal tolls (under the circumstances) are imposed on both roads, but only during the peak period.

4. Finally, the last column reports results for the case where no tolls are imposed on either road in either period.

The table reports in percentage form five types of comparisons:

1. The effect of the tolling regime on road use in total, by roads, and by periods for each road.
2. The relative social welfare or loss attributed to each regime.
3. Relative trip times in each period on each road.
4. The optimal capacity for each regime for both roads.
5. The relative level of tolls for each tolled alternative.

Qualitatively, the results are quite similar to the short run effects reported in Chapter 9. Road use in total is not greatly affected for the somewhat price inelastic demand system considered. The total reduction in road trips under the first-best tolling regime is only 7% of the no toll usage. The reduction is only 2% when only peak periods are tolled. If one road remains free while the other is tolled, usage is virtually unchanged. The effect between periods however is dramatic. First-best tolls more than double usage in the off-peak period, and reduce trips in the peak period to 64% of the no toll usage. Where the tolls are restricted to one road, there is an even greater effect on the off-peak usage of the tolled alternative. However, the usage of the untolled alternative is nearly identical to no toll usage in both periods. Tolling only the peak periods on both roads , pushes even more traffic into the off-peak period than first-best tolls, but reduces the peak use by a smaller amount than first-best tolls.

The trip time comparisons are equally revealing. In a no toll situation, the capacity cost was set so that off-peak commuting time is only 30% of peak time. This may reflect the extremes of probable deviation. If the off-peak speed is 70 miles per hour, the corresponding peak speed is 21 miles per hour. The speed of 21 arises well into the region of the model where flow is decreasing with increasing density. For first-best tolls, the equivalent average speeds would be 36 in the off-peak period and 28 in the peak period. These are very close to the speeds attained with tolls imposed only during the peak period. With only one road operating under a toll regime, the speeds on the free road are about the same as the no toll case and the speeds on the toll road approximate the first-best speeds.

The first-best off-peak toll is about 58% of the peak toll. While this is an appreciable difference, the off-peak seems a bit excessive. With only peak periods tolled, the toll falls to only 44% of the first-best peak toll. Even more interesting is the fact that with only one road tolled, the peak period toll falls to only 23% and the off-peak period receives a substantial subsidy.

Table A15-1
Summary of Numerical Results

Long Run Two-period Two Road Model	Tolling Regime			
	First-best	One road	Peak only	No tolls
		Both times	Both roads	
Road use:				
Percent of use under no tolls regime				
Total both roads	93%	100%	98%	100%
Road 1 - total	93%	100%	98%	100%
Road 2 - total	93%	100%	98%	100%
Road 1 off-peak period	213%	102%	230%	100%
Road 1 peak period	64%	99%	67%	100%
Road 2 - off-peak period	213%	230%	230%	100%
Road 2 - peak period	64%	69%	67%	100%
Social Welfare				
% of first best obtained	100%	95%	99%	91%
% of loss recouped by tolls	100%	43%	91%	0%
Trip Times as % no-tolls peak-period time				
Road 1 off-peak period	59%	31%	61%	30%
Road 1 peak period	75%	102%	75%	100%
Road 2 - off-peak period	59%	59%	61%	30%
Road 2 - peak period	75%	75%	75%	100%
Road Capacity - percent of first-best				
Road 1	100%	122%	104%	124%
Road 2	100%	108%	104%	124%
Tolls - percent of first-best peak tolls				
Peak period	100%	23%	44%	0%
Off - peak period	58%	-19%	0%	0%

In terms of social welfare, it is evident that there is very little to be gained by extending tolls from the peak periods to off-peak periods, but this could probably have been anticipated in advance. Tolling only one road loses more than half the possible benefits from full marginal cost pricing.

The optimal capacities, not surprisingly, are highest for the no toll scenario. Capacities for the peak-period-only toll regime are only slightly (4%) above first-best levels, but if only one road is tolled the free road capacity is nearly at no-toll levels, while the tolled road is still 8% above first-best levels. There is one area in which the implications of this model differ significantly from the short-run models of Chapters 7-10. In the short-run models in which the roads are assumed to be perfect substitutes, capacity was taken as given and it was observed that a much greater portion of potential gains are realized when a larger portion of the system's capacity is tolled, i.e. the road with a larger capacity is tolled. Actually if only one road is to be tolled, the optimal capacity ratio is in the opposite direction. The capacity of the free road should be much larger than the tolled road.

16 DEMAND UNCERTAINTY, OPTIMAL CAPACITY, AND CONGESTION TOLLS

A. INTRODUCTION

This chapter presents an analytical treatment of the effect of uncertain demand on optimal highway capacity and congestion tolls. A similar problem has been studied by DeVany and Saving (1980), but their analysis assumes that highways are supplied by firms in a competitive market. Traffic has a stochastic arrival rate which depends upon the price of travel. The firms maximize expected profits but do not experience any change in capital, monitoring, or maintenance costs due to variations in the rate of road use. Under these assumptions, the "optimal" capacity and "optimal" toll are identical to those for the case of nonstochastic demand. In our model, expected social welfare is maximized so that the fluctuating cost of traffic delay is taken into account and uncertainty does affect the optimal solution. Our conclusions are consistent with those of Kraus (1982). Using numerical methods he estimated the differences in optimal capacities and tolls for several cases. He found that the optimal capacity under demand uncertainty consistently exceeded the capacity appropriate for conditions of certainty, while the optimal toll for uncertainty could be either larger or smaller depending on the parameters of the problem.

In an analysis that assumes certainty it is appropriate to treat all decisions as though they were made simultaneously. Uncertainty introduces an additional dimension. Even in the context of a single period model, there is an implied chronological sequence of decisions. With the passage of time the uncertainty changes. This may be taken into account by altering the information set assumed to be available to the various agents at the time of each decision. The planner chooses the road capacity first and subsequently sets tolls on the basis of his expectations concerning the benefits of road travel and the future decisions of potential road users. These expectations are reflected in his assumptions concerning the uncertain future toll revenue and the portion of capacity cost to be financed from taxes. Consumers maximize expected utility wit certain knowledge of their own benefit from a road trip but with uncertain knowledge of the price of a trip and the future level of taxes. These latter parameters also enter consumer calculations as expectations. After travel occurs, toll revenue is determined and taxes are adjusted to balance the government's budget. Finally, on the basis of the realization of the price of travel and taxes, consumers balance their individual budgets by adjusting their residual consumption.

B. OPTIMAL CAPACITY AND TOLLS WITH CERTAINTY

In this section we give a brief treatment of the conventional analysis under certainty in order to introduce our notation and set up a basis for comparison. Let the aggregate demand for road trips be given by

$$M = N[1 - F(P)], \tag{1}$$

where M denotes road trips, N is a positive integer, P is the price of a trip, and F(P) varies from 0 to 1 for relevant prices. The demand curve is negatively sloped as

$$dF/dP = g(P) > 0 \qquad \text{for } 0 < F(P) < 1. \tag{2}$$

The user's private cost of a trip is given by

$$P + T + A(M,K), \tag{3}$$

where T is the toll, K denotes road capacity, and A( ) is the average variable cost function. Average cost is an increasing function of M (traffic volume) and a decreasing function of K (road capacity). Road capacity is publicly supplied at a social cost of cK that is financed by toll revenue and head taxes.

The planner chooses K and P (via the toll T) to maximize

$$W = \int_0^{M^*} P dM - A(M,K)M - cK, \tag{4}$$

where the limits of integration run from 0 to M*. It is well known that the indicated measure of gross benefits (area under the inverse demand curve) assumes the existence of an outside good with constant marginal utility. Consequently the standard analysis given here, and also the analysis for uncertainty given below, neglect any income effects. The first-order conditions for a maximum are given by

$$\partial W/\partial P = Pg(P) - A(M,K)g(P) - (\partial A/\partial M)g(P)M = 0. \tag{5}$$

Or

$$P^* = A(M,K) + M(\partial A/\partial M); \tag{6}$$

$$T^* = M(\partial A/\partial M). \tag{7}$$

And

$$\partial W/\partial K = -M\partial A/\partial K - c = 0. \tag{8}$$

Or

$$M\partial A/\partial K = c. \tag{9}$$

Equation (7) states that the optimal toll equals the excess of marginal social cost over average variable cost. Equation (9) states that the marginal benefit of capacity (reduction of variable travel costs) equals the marginal cost of capacity, c. For an explicit solution in terms of the optimal level of road use , we consider the following specific average cost function:

$$A = A_0 + aM^2/K^2; \tag{10}$$

$$\partial A/\partial K = -2aM^2/K^3; \text{ and} \tag{11}$$

$$\partial A/\partial M = 2aM/K^2. \tag{12}$$

Then the optimal capacity is

$$K^* = (2a/c)^{1/3}M. \tag{13}$$

For any capacity the optimal toll is

$$T^* = 2a(M/K)^2. \tag{14}$$

For the optimal capacity,

$$T^* = 2a(c/2a)^{2/3}. \tag{15}$$

C. OPTIMAL CAPACITY AND TOLLS WITH UNCERTAIN DEMAND

We assume that there are N potential road users with identical tastes and incomes. The representative utility function is of the form

$$U = X + h(m). \tag{16}$$

X is a composite consumption good with constant marginal utility. The number of trips taken by the individual (on a given day) is denoted by m and is restricted to the values 0 or 1. The benefit of a trip in terms of utility is given by the function h(m), where h(0) = 0 and g(1) = B, a nonnegative random number. It is assumed that there is a set of N independent and identically distributed random variables B with one corresponding to each individual. Assume that B has a density function f(B) an a distribution function F(B). Each individual knows the realization of his own B = b prior to deciding whether to make a trip on any given day. He does not know the realization of any other B and consequently regards the price of travel as uncertain. His budget constraint is given by

$$X + Pm = D, \tag{17}$$

where D denotes disposable income after tax. The individual maximizes expected utility, i.e., he chooses the maximum of

$$E(D) - E(P) + b \text{ or}$$

$$E(D),$$

where E( ) indicates expectation. Note that E(D) is an expectation also by reason of the uncertainty of future taxes. He travels if b > E(P).

The highway planner constructs his expectation of individual utility in the following manner. The ex ante probability of any individual taking a trip given that the expected price of a trip is E(P) is

$$\prod = 1 - \int_0^{E(P)} g(B)dB = 1 - F[E(P]. \tag{18}$$

The limits of integration run from 0 to E(P). The total expected number of trips is given by

$$E(M) = \prod N = N\{1 - F[E(P)]\}. \tag{19}$$

This may be regarded as the expected aggregate demand curve. Note that M is a random variable with a binomial distribution and variance

$$Var(M) = N\prod(1-\prod) = E(M)[1 - E(M)/N]. \tag{20}$$

The expected price is given by

$$E(P) = T + E(A(M,K)). \tag{21}$$

Equations (19) and (21) determine the equilibria E(P) and E(M) corresponding to each choice of T and K. The planner takes into account the effect of his decisions on the expected disposable income, so that from his viewpoint

$$E(D) = Y_0 - cK/N + TE(M)/N, \tag{22}$$

where Y_0 is the exogenous component of disposable income. Thus he views the expected utility of every potential user as

$$E(U) = Y_0 - cK/N - E(A(M,K))[1 - F(E(P))] + \int Bg(B)dB, \tag{23}$$

where the limits of integration run from E(P) to ∞. Note that we have substituted E(A) = E(P) - T in obtaining equation (23).

The planner maximizes equation (23) by choosing optimal K and E(P) via T. The first-order conditions are:

$$\begin{aligned}\partial E(U)/\partial E(P) &= E(A(M,K))f(E(P)) \\ &\quad + \partial E(A)/\partial E(M)[1 - F(E(P))]Nf(E(P)) - E(P)f(E(P)) \\ &= 0.\end{aligned} \tag{24}$$

Or

$$P = A(M,K) + E(M)\partial E(A)/\partial E(M); \tag{25}$$

$$T = E(M)\partial E(A)/\partial E(M) \tag{26}$$

and

$$\partial E(U)/\partial K = - c/N - [1 - F(E(P))]\partial E(A)/\partial K. \tag{27}$$

Or, using E(M)/N = 1 - F(E(P)),

$$- E(M)\partial E(A)/\partial K = c. \tag{28}$$

The form and interpretation of the optimal decision rules for uncertainty and identical to those for the certainty case. The only difference arises from the distinction between the expected average cost and its certainty counterpart. However, this distinction is sufficient to alter the characteristics of an optimal solution. This outcome may be illustrated by the specific cost function considered in Section B, where

$$A = A_0 + aM^2/K^2. \tag{29}$$

The expectation is given by

$$E(A) = A_0 + a(E(M))^2/K^2 + aE(M)(1 - E(M)/N)/K^2. \quad (30)$$

The corresponding marginal terms are

$$\partial E(A)/\partial E(M) = 2aE(M)/K^2 + aE(M)(1 - 2E(M)/N)/K^2 \quad (31)$$

and

$$-\partial E(A)/\partial K = 2a[E(M)]^2/K^3 + 2aE(M)(1 - E(M)/N)/K^3, \quad (32)$$

so that,

$$T^* = 2a[E(M)/K]^2 + aE(M)(1 - E(M)/N)/K^2 \quad (33)$$

and

$$K^* = (2a/c)^{1/3}\{[E(M)]^3 + [E(M)]^2(1 - E(M)/N)\}^{1/3}. \quad (34)$$

Under certainty the optimal capacity is directly proportional to the optimal level of road use. Under uncertainty the optimal capacity is larger relative to the mean level of road use. Under certainty the optimal toll is directly proportional to the square of the volume-capacity ratio. This ratio is a common measure of the level of congestion. Under uncertainty the optimal toll may be either larger or smaller relative to the mean level of observed congestion. The direction of the change depends on the effect of the toll on the variance of road use. This explained by the fact that the effective price under uncertainty depends positively on the variance, which therefore in itself operates somewhat like a toll in limiting road use to socially optimal levels. Increases in the toll decrease E(M). In $E(M) < N/2$, then increasing the toll decreases the variance and the required toll is larger. If $E(M) > N/2$, then increasing the toll increases the variance and the required toll is smaller. These results hold for any positive random variable M for any average variable cost function of the form

$$A = A_0 + aM^r/K^r, \; r > 1.$$

If the rth moment exists and $M > 0$, then

$$E[M^r] > [E(M)]^r \text{ for any real } r > 1.$$

Or equivalently,

$$E[M^r] = [E(M)]^r + v(r,M),$$

where v is some positive function depending on r and M. For a proof see Gnedenko (1962, p. 228). It follows immediately that optimal capacity under uncertainty is always larger relative to the mean level of road use and that the toll is larger (smaller) relative to the mean volume-capacity ratio if $\partial v/\partial E(M) > 0$ ($\partial v/\partial E(M) < 0$).

This chapter has shown that, under the case of risk-neutral commuters, the optimal capacity under conditions of demand uncertainty is larger relative to the mean level of road use than the efficient capacity under conditions of certainty. The first-best optimal toll may be either larger or smaller with uncertain demand depending upon the effect of the toll on the variance of equilibrium road use.

References

DeVany, A. and T. Saving, 1980, Competition and highway pricing for stochastic traffic, Journal of Business, 53, 45-60.

Gnedenko, G., 1962, The Theory of Probability, New York: Chelsea.

Kraus, M., 1982, Highway pricing and capacity choice under uncertainty, Journal of Urban Economics, 12, 122-128.

Appendix
Example of Uncertain Demand

This appendix illustrates the effect of uncertain demand on the optimal toll and capacity for a single congested road. The intention is to compare the *uncertainty* case with an *certain* case which is in some sense analogous. To avoid any misunderstanding, those parameters and relationships which are assumed to be invariant between the certain and uncertain cases need to be set out. Similarly the assumed distinctions need to be articulated. In this model a linear demand schedule is utilized for both cases. In the uncertain case, the expected road use is a linear function of the expected price. This entails two parameters for the slope (N) and intercept (A) respectively. For the certainty case, the same linear demand function is assumed with parameters of equal value. The average cost function in both cases is a simple power function of the volume of road use and the road capacity. This is a two parameter formulation, where one parameter (C_0) is the "congestion-free" cost per unit of volume and the other (C_1) is the congestion cost parameter. Both parameters are the same in the two cases. The final parameter (C_2), the cost per unit of capacity, is also the same in both cases. Variables corresponding to the certainty case will be indicated by upper case letters, to distinguish them from the comparable variables in the uncertainty case which are

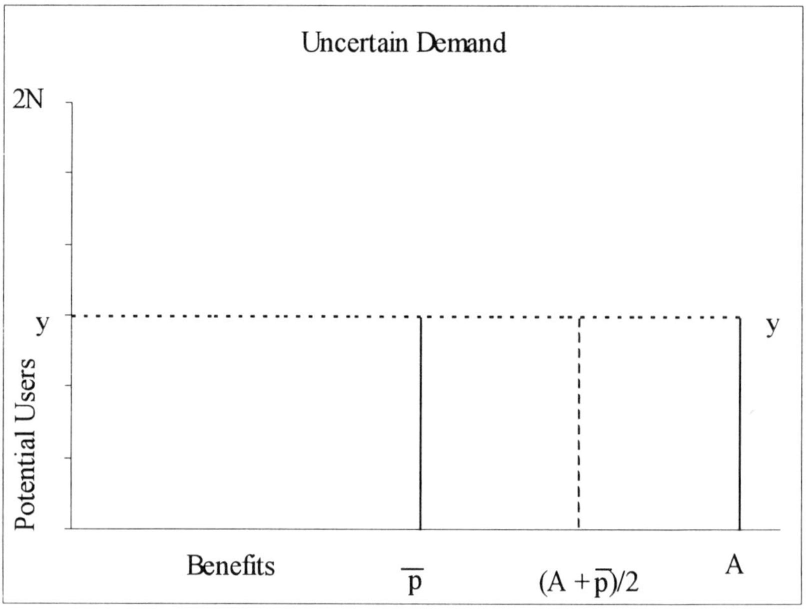

Figure A16.1

identified by lower case letters. M (m) denotes volume of road use, K (k) is road capacity, P (p) is price, and T (t) is the toll. Expected values are indicated by an overscore. The assumed nature of the uncertain demand is presented in Figure

A16.1. The benefit of a single road trip is measured along the X-axis. The maximum benefit is A. Corresponding to each benefit level along the X-axis from 0 to A, is a certain number of potential road users, denoted "y" and measured along the Y-axis. For simplicity, it is assumed that the number of users at each benefit level is the same. It is also assumed that y is a random variable with a uniform distribution over the range 0 to 2N. The expectations of various powers of the random variable y can be calculated as follows. For this uniform distribution, the density function is the constant 1/2N.

$$E(y) = (1/2N) \int_0^{2N} y \, dy = N \qquad (1)$$

$$E(y^2) = (1/2N) \int_0^{2N} y^2 \, dy = 4N^2/3 \qquad (2)$$

$$E(y^3) = (1/2N) \int_0^{2N} y^3 \, dy = 2N^3 \qquad (3)$$

For any expected price $\bar{p}$, the quantity of road use demanded is given by:

$$m = (A - \bar{p})y \qquad (4)$$

The rationale for this formulation is as follows. Assuming risk-neutral individuals, any potential road user will travel if the benefit equals or exceeds his expectation of price. It is assumed that all users have the same expectation of price based on full information about A and the *distribution* of y. The analogous certainty case is represented by the demand curve:

$$M = (A - P)N \qquad (5)$$

where N is the expected value of y. The aggregate benefit is calculated by multiplying the number of trips m by the average benefit $(A + \bar{p})/2$:

$$b = (A^2 - \bar{p}^2)y/2 \qquad (6)$$

It is evident from (4) and (6) that both m and b are also random variables with a uniform distribution. The average variable cost is specified as:

$$avc = C_0 + C_1 m^2/k^2 \qquad (7)$$

From (2) the expected equilibrium price is defined as:

$$\bar{p} = t + C_0 + (4/3)C_1\bar{m}^2/k^2 \qquad (8)$$

The aggregate net benefit of road travel is given by:

$$w = (A^2 - \bar{p}^2)y / 2 - C_0 m - C_1 m^3/k^2 - C_2 k \tag{9}$$

The *expected* net benefit from (3) is given by:

$$\bar{w} = (A^2 - \bar{p}^2)\bar{y} / 2 - C_0 \bar{m} - 2 C_1 \bar{m}^3/k^2 - C_2 k \tag{10}$$

Next note from (4) that:

$$d\bar{m}/d\bar{p} = -\bar{y} = N \tag{11}$$

One first order condition to maximize the expected net benefit is:

$$\partial \bar{w}/\partial \bar{p} = -N\bar{p} + N C_0 + N\, 6C_1 \bar{m}^2/k^2 = 0 \tag{12}$$

or

$$\bar{p} = C_0 + 6C_1 \bar{m}^2/k^2. \tag{13}$$

It follows from (8) that the optimal toll is given by:

$$t = 4.67\, C_1 \bar{m}^2/k^2 \tag{14}$$

The other first order condition is:

$$\partial \bar{w}/\partial k = -C_2 + 4\, C_1 \bar{m}^3/k^3 = 0, \tag{15}$$

or

$$k = (4C_1/C_2)^{.333}\, \bar{m} \tag{16}$$

and

$$\bar{m}^2/k^2 = (C_2/4C_1)^{.667} \tag{17}$$

Substituting (17) into (13) gives a closed-form solution for $\bar{p}^*$:

$$\bar{p}^* = C_0 + 2.38 C_1^{.333} C_2^{.667} \tag{18}$$

or

$$t^* = 1.85 C_1^{.333} C_2^{.667} \tag{19}$$

From the "expected" demand function , the solution for $\bar{m}$ is:

$$\bar{m}^* = (A - \bar{p}^*)N \tag{20}$$

Finally from (16):

$$k^* = (4C_1 / C_2)^{.333} \ \bar{m}^* \qquad (21)$$

Turning attention to the certainty case, the equilibrium price satisfies:

$$P = T + C_0 + C_1M^2/K^2 \qquad (22)$$

The net benefit W is given by:

$$W = (A^2 - P^2)N/2 - C_0M - C_1M^3/K^2 - C_2K \qquad (23)$$

We might remark here that the gross benefit can be shown to be equivalent to the area under the inverse demand function:

$$(A^2 - P^2)N/2 = \int_0^M P(M)dM \qquad (24)$$

Of course the same is also true for the expected benefit in the uncertainty case which equals the area under the *expected* inverse demand curve. The first order conditions are:

$$\partial W/\partial P = - NP + NC_0 + 3NC_1M^2/K^2 = 0 \qquad (25)$$

$$\partial W/\partial K = - C_2 + 2C_1M^3/K^3 = 0 \qquad (26)$$

Consequently,

$$P = C_0 + 3C_1M^2/K^2 \qquad (27)$$

$$(M/K)^2 = (C_2/2C_1)^{.667} \qquad (28)$$

and

$$K = (2C_1/C_2)^{.333}M \qquad (29)$$

Substituting from (28) into (27):

$$P^* = C_0 + 1.89C_1^{.333}C_2^{.667} \qquad (30)$$

$$T^* = 1.26\ C_1^{.333}C_2^{.667} \qquad (31)$$

From the demand function:

$$M^* = (A - P^*)N \qquad (32)$$

From (27):

$$K^* = (2C_1/C_2)^{.333}M^* \tag{33}$$

These solutions may be evaluated for appropriate values of the parameters. For example, assume:

$A = 2.00$
$C_0 = .40$
$C_1 = .15$
$C_2 = .50$
$N = 1000$

The optimal outcomes are shown in the following table and graph.

Variable	Certainty	Uncertainty
Price	1.03	1.20
Toll	.42	.62
AVC	.61	.58
Price Elasticity	1.07	1.49
Road Use	967	803
Road Capacity	816	964

The same information is shown graphically in the familiar short-run traffic diagram in Figure A16.2. The expected average variable cost (avc) under uncertainty lies below the certain average variable (AVC) throughout the entire range although graphically they appear very close. This arises because the "congestion cost" portion of average is lower under uncertainty due to less volume and greater road capacity. However the marginal variable cost (mc) under uncertainty is significantly greater at any level of road use despite the higher capacity. This accounts for the higher toll and lower mean level of road use. Generally speaking, the existence of uncertainty entails additional costs. In the present example, the uncertain demand reduces the overall social welfare that can be derived with optimal tolls and optimal capacity by approximately 15 percent.

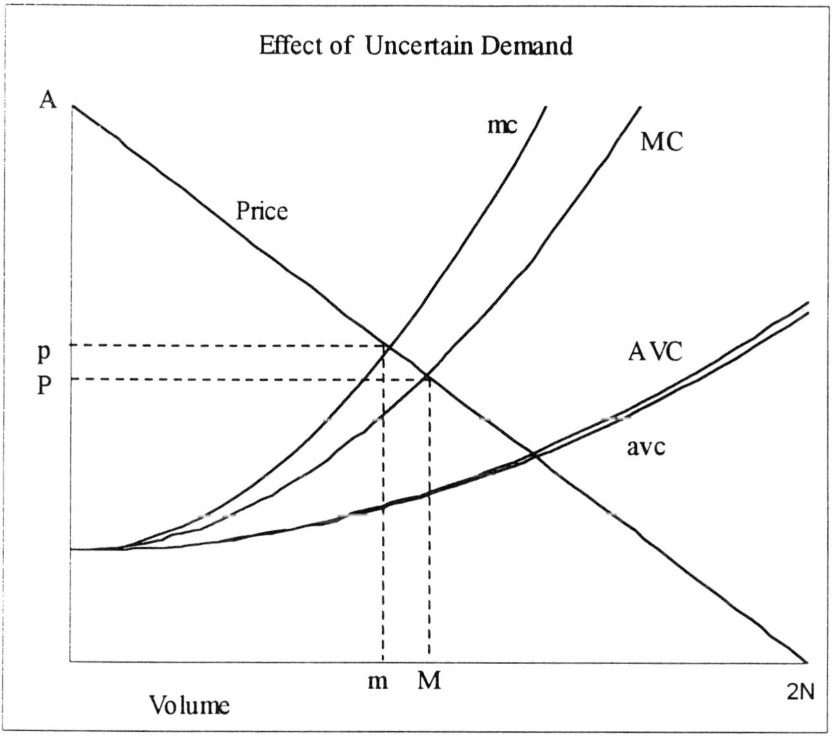

Figure A16.2
Optimal Outcomes for Certain (M) and Uncertain (m) Demand

17 OPTIMAL CAPACITY FOR A BOTTLENECK AND SUB-OPTIMAL CONGESTION TOLLS

A. INTRODUCTION

The effective capacity for a road segment leading to a bottleneck is the maximum flow accommodated by the bottleneck. In bottleneck models it is assumed that flow on a congested road through the bottleneck does not fall below capacity. This assumption is distinct from the hypercongestion model. Assuming this maximum flow can, in the long run, be varied at a cost, the question arises as to whether the optimal capacity for the unregulated case with no congestion tolls is larger or smaller than the first-best case of optimal road pricing. The model presented here shows that the relative size of the first- and second-best capacities depends in the bottleneck case on the same demand and cost elasticities that determine relative capacity size in the standard road congestion model. Inelastic demand is associated with larger second-best capacities. Elastic demand implies a smaller second-best capacity. This model seeks clarity and simplicity at the necessary expense of some loss of generality. Other treatments of various aspects of the bottleneck problem may be found in the series of papers by Arnott, de Palma, and Lindsey (1990a), (1990b), (1993a), (1993b), and (1997), and particularly Arnott, and Kraus (1995). The present model adopts the formulation and most of the notation of Mun (1994). Units of measure are indicated in brackets [ ]. Small (1992) provides an excellent textbook treatment of the bottleneck model.

B. DESCRIPTION OF THE BOTTLENECK

The model considers a road of length L [miles] starting at point α and ending at a bottleneck point ω. Traffic along the road is described at any point in terms of Q ("flow") ,[vehicles / hour] , N ("density") [vehicles / mile], and V ("speed") [miles / hour], where

$$Q = NV. \qquad (1)$$

In full generality, the variables Q, N, and V are "local" variables describing traffic at a particular point in time and space (along the road), although this model imposes certain uniformities over time and space as a special case. Such assumptions are indicated when made. Ignoring the bottleneck, the capacity of the road is Q_0 [vehicles/hour] occurring at the density N_0 . Q is a continuous function of density. For $N \leq N_0$, speed is assumed to be a constant V_1. For densities above N_0,, V is a decreasing function of N such that :

$$-(dV/dN)(N/V) \geq 1. \tag{2}$$

In other words Q is decreasing in N for $N \geq N_0$. The assumption that V is constant below capacity density is equivalent to assuming that the road is free of congestion below capacity apart from the effect of the bottleneck. This is contrary of course to standard congestion theory, and requires some explanation. In the first place, one could argue that this assumption is not particularly unrealistic .The curvature of the speed-density relationship tends to be small until the neighborhood of the capacity density is approached. Secondly, the assumption allows the model to focus exclusively on the bottleneck problem without the confounding influence of other types of congestion. Finally it should be pointed out that this assumption greatly simplifies the analysis whenever time-varying flows are considered.

The problem is that if the road has length and the flow rate at the entry point varies in the time domain, then the flow rate also must vary in space domain (along the road before the flow reaches the traffic jam in front of the terminal point). Otherwise faster following traffic would run over the slower traffic in front, or slower traffic would fall back from faster traffic in front thereby decreasing local density and presumably increasing speed. In this case, the length of the road itself becomes much more than a passive variable, since over a sufficiently long road, initial fluctuations in traffic flows tend to smooth out in an entropic fashion. This problem can be handled by structuring the model in terms of flow rates at the point of entry into the bottleneck queue with average velocity up to that point vaguely defined as some sort of increasing function of the flow rates of vehicles entering the queue at all prior times. Any gain in realism derived in this manner does not seem to justify the increased complexity and loss of clarity.

The outflow of vehicles at the bottleneck point ω is limited to Q_2. When Q exceeds Q_2 on the "open" portion of the road, a traffic jam or queue develops in front of the bottleneck. Within the jam the density N_2 exceeds N_0 , so that at the reduced velocity V_2 ($< V_1$) the traffic flow is reduced to the bottleneck outflow Q_2. The model contemplates two rates of flow on the road, Q_1 for traffic before the jam and Q_2 within the jam. The transition between rates is assumed to be instantaneous, occurring over an interval of zero length. The introduction of this point of discontinuity is again an abstraction from reality for simplicity sake but such a transition actually occurs over very short intervals of time and space. Since the arrival rate of vehicles at the jam is Q_1 and the departure rate is Q_2, the number of vehicles in the queue grows at the rate $Q_1 - Q_2$. Assuming $Q_0 > Q_1 > Q_2$, the number of vehicles in the queue at time t [hours] is $(Q_1 - Q_2)$ t. This assumes Q_1 is a constant rate of flow and that t is measured from time zero when the queue first arises. The length of the queue at time t is given by:

$$J \text{ [miles]} = (Q_1 - Q_2)t/N_2 . \qquad (3)$$

The notation "J" is for "jam". Note that $dJ/dN_1 = (t/N_2), V_1 > 0$.

C. THE BACKWARD-BENDING PORTION OF THE AC CURVE

In a comparable model, Mun (1994) identified the "cost" (actually travel time) of one trip from point α to point ω as:

$$AC \text{ [hours]} = (L - J)/V_1 + J/V_2 \qquad (4)$$

This is the "average trip cost" for vehicles arriving at the queue (jam) at time t. The trip is divided into two parts - the journey over the "open" road (L – J) at a speed of V_1 and the passage through the traffic jam J at the slower speed V_2. Since in this model (and similarly in Mun's model), $dAC/dQ_1 = (V_1 - V_2)(dJ/dQ_1)/V_1V_2 > 0$, it might be thought that there is no "backward-bending" portion of the average cost curve. This is an erroneous interpretation even if the entire length of the road is viewed as a single production process producing trips with the variable input of drivers' time and the fixed input of road capacity. The problem is that the contemplated "trip" for which the above cost is measured is produced over an *interval* of time during which many additional "partial trips" are produced and much additional travel time is consumed. At a point t in time, the rate at which road users' time is being consumed is:

$$C \text{ [vehicles]} = N_1 (L - J) + N_2 J. \qquad (5)$$

Note the dimension of C. This is the cardinal number of vehicles on the road and is not, properly speaking a "density", although it is true that if the density were uniform and the road length were taken as the unit of length, then C would be numerically equal to density expressed as [vehicles / road length]. The derivative of C with respect to N_1 is given by:

$$dC / dN_1 = (L - J) + (N_2 - N_1), dJ/dN_1 > 0. \qquad (6)$$

The rate at which road trips are being produced at the same point in time is:

$$M \text{ [vehicle·miles / hour]} = Q_1 (L - J) + Q_2 J. \qquad (7)$$

The derivative with respect to N_1 is:

$$dM/dN_1 = (L - J)\, dQ_1/dN_1 - (Q_1 - Q_2)dJ/dN_1 =$$

$$dM/dN_1 = V_1 (L - J) - V_1 (Q_1 - Q_2)t/N_2 =$$

$$dM/dN_1 = (L - 2J)V_1 . \tag{8}$$

Accordingly, the "marginal product" of users' time

$$dM/dC = (L - 2J)V_1/\{(L - J) + (N_2 - N_1)dJ/dN_1\} \tag{9}$$

is negative for $J > L/2$. This corresponds to the so-called backward-bending portion of the cost curves. This should not be too surprising as the length of road covered by J is by definition operating in the "uneconomic" region of production, while the "open road" $(L - J)$ is congestion free. Once the traffic jam covers more than half the road, the road as a whole is hypercongested.

D. A MODEL OF THE MORNING COMMUTING TRIP

The commuting period ends at a fixed time. The possibility of late arrivals at work at some incremental cost is an extension not considered. The starting time for commuting activity is variable, adapting to cost and demand conditions, but it is understood implicitly that all commuting activity takes place in a time interval that is contained within a time frame of reference called a "morning". In other words, there is always some slack time at the start of the morning before the commuting activity starts. At the start of the morning, the road is empty. Commuting activity begins at point α with a flow of Q_1 which remains *constant* until a point in time when the flow at point α returns instantaneously to zero. The commuting period continues thereafter until the road is cleared when the last vehicle reaches point ω. This occurs exactly at the fixed ending time (there is no provision for a safety margin in this model containing no uncertainty). The first vehicles of the morning commute reach point ω at the time L/V_1 [hours] after setting out. At this point in time the queue starts to build, and continues to grow for T [hours]. The time at this point is $L/V_1 + T$ after the start of the first flow. The length of the queue J at this point is $(Q_1 - Q_2)T/K_2$. The last vehicle in this maximal queue traveling at V_2 reaches point ω after another $(Q_1 - Q_2)\, T/Q_2$ [hours]. Accordingly, the duration of the entire commuting period is $L/V_1 + (Q_1/Q_2)T$ [hours]. The total number of trips completed during this period, X, is determined by the bottleneck exit rate at ω, Q_2 [vehicles / hour], and the period over which the "exiting" occurs $(Q_1/Q_2)T$ [hours], or:

$$X[\text{vehicles (or trips)}] = Q_1T. \tag{10}$$

This is an important identity which will later be used to change variables so as to replace T with X. Figure 17-1 shows the behavior of the traffic jam over time.

Potential road users have three alternative uses of time during the commuting period, as shown in Figure 17-2. Time at home produces the greatest utility, traveling time the least, and waiting time at work after arrival but before the start of work produces an intermediate amount. In this formulation travel time has a constant unit cost C_1 [\$/vehicle·hour] that exceeds the constant unit cost of waiting time C_2 [\$/vehicle·hour]. It goes without saying that more sophisticated and complex formulations can be entertained. The costs are not likely to be constant but probably vary with the amount of the time spent in the activity as well as the absolute time of occurrence. Even more problematical is the "representative commuter" assumption which treats all road users as having the same values of time. This is more or less a time-honored economic tradition although heterogeneity of preferences concerning uses and values of time, can and have been utilized in this context. Nevertheless, the simple structure used here is often employed and seems to capture the essential elements responsible for commuting behavior.

The traveling cost of a trip for a vehicle arriving at the traffic jam at a time t hours after the start of the queue follows from equation (4) as:

$$\text{ATC [\$/vehicle]} = C_1(L/V_1) + C_1\{(1 - v)(Q_1 - Q_2)/Q_2\}t \qquad (11)$$

where $v = 1 - V_2/V_1$. Note v is dimension-free.

A vehicle, arriving at queue at t hours after the queue began, arrives at ω after an additional J/V_2 hours or at $L/V_1 + (Q_1/Q_2)\,t$ after start of the commuting period. As previously noted, the entire commuting period ends at $L/V_1 + (Q_1/Q_2)$ T, so the waiting cost is:

$$\text{AWC [\$/vehicle]} = C_2(Q_1/Q_2)(T - t). \qquad (12)$$

So the average trip cost, AC [\$/vehicle] is:

$$AC = C_1(L/V_1) + C_1\{(1 - v)(Q_1 - Q_2)/Q_2\}t + C_2(Q_1/Q_2)(T - t). \qquad (13)$$

E. DEMAND FOR TRIPS

The aggregate (inverse) demand function for trips seems very straightforward, but since it has been very controversial e.g. Else (1981), Evans (1992), it may be worthwhile to present the development in elementary detail. The model assumes a large number of potential road users. This allows a continuous representation of a discrete demand schedule. Each potential user chooses either one or zero road trips. Each individual would derive a certain benefit from a trip taken that is completely separate and distinct from whatever the cost of the trip may be. The benefits vary among users, no two benefits are exactly equal, and all can be

Figure 17.1 Behavior of Traffic Jam Over Time

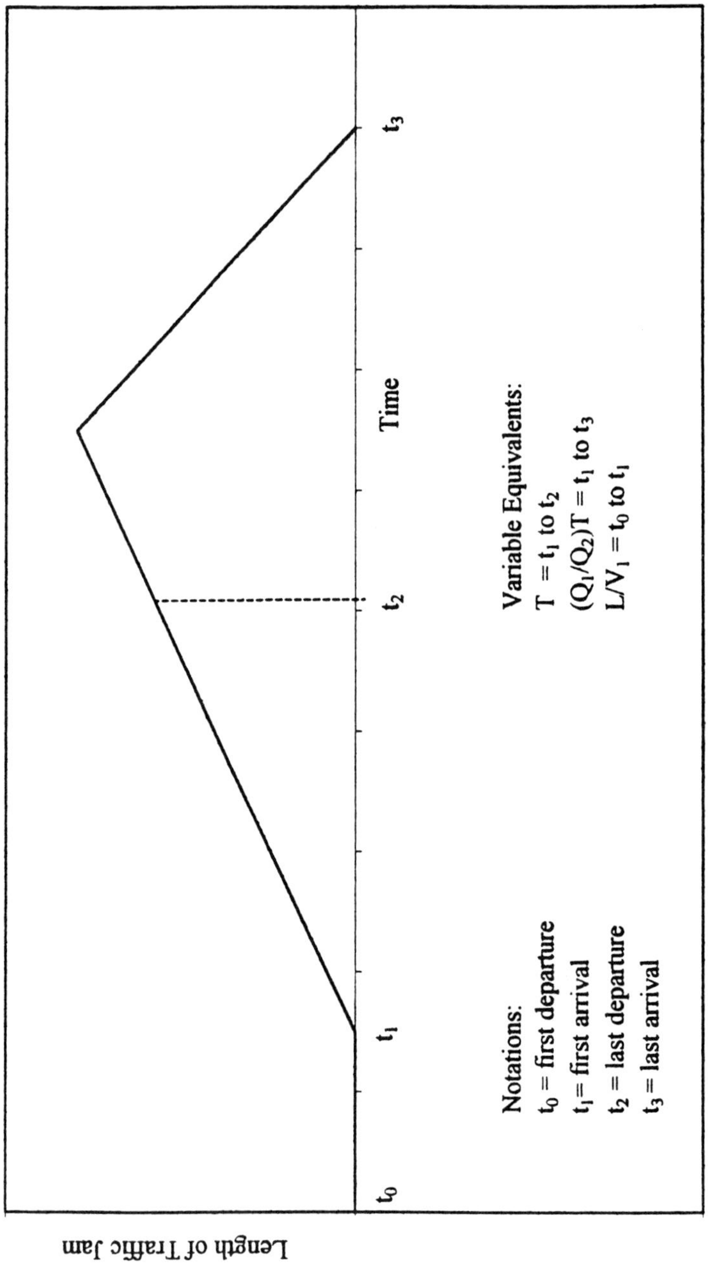

Figure 17.2 Uses, Utility, and Cost of Time

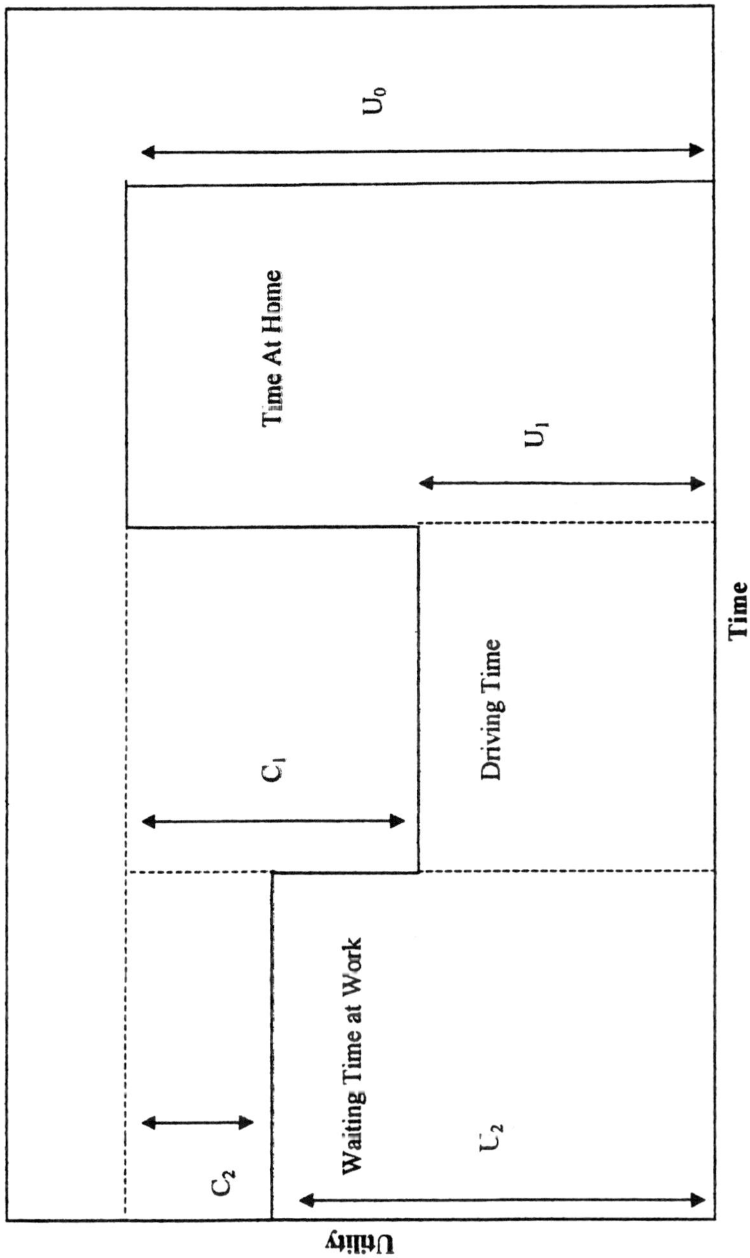

quantified in dollar terms. (Costs are also assumed to be quantified in money terms). The individual takes the trip if his benefit equals or exceeds his cost.

Assume the potential road users are arranged in order with number 1 assigned to the individual with the highest trip benefit, 2 assigned to the next highest, etc. The following conceptual plot is created. On the horizontal axis are the integers denoting the road users. The vertical axis is calibrated in dollar terms. The graph plots each benefit against each numbered individual user. The model assumes that these points can be connected in order with a twice differentiable curve:

$$P\ [\$/\text{vehicle}] = P(X), \quad dP/dX = P' < 0. \tag{14}$$

This curve is referred to as the inverse demand curve for trips. The area of controversy seems to be whether this is a demand for "density" or a demand for "flow". It should be evident that it is neither a demand for N nor a demand for Q as they are defined in this model. X can be considered a "flow" in the *economic* sense of the rate of trip consumption per period of analysis. Since this is a single period model, this is not reflected in the units of measure. If all the vehicles were assumed to use the road at the same time (as in some models, but not this model), and each vehicle were to take one trip, then the trip consumption would be numerically equal to the "density" measured as vehicles per distance of a trip. In such a model, the denominator of the density measure can be suppressed (taken as equal to one), as is done for the time period of analysis, in a one period model. Problems arise only when an inverse demand schedule such as that constructed here for X is inappropriately treated as being for either N or Q or for that matter V. Demands are always "flows" in the economic sense but economic flows can include "densities" in appropriate cases.

Note also that in this model, the individual user's benefit depends only on whether or not the trip is taken and not on *when* during the commuting period, it is taken. There are no separate demands for trips originating at different times. Trip scheduling affects only the cost of the trip not its benefit.

It is also useful at this point to define certain elasticities for later use. We define

$$\varepsilon = -(dP/dX)(X/P) > 0. \tag{16}$$

This is the elasticity of price with respect to quantity and in a single good model is the reciprocal of the price elasticity of demand. We also define

$$\theta = (dAC/dX)(X/AC) > 0. \tag{17}$$

This is the elasticity of average cost with respect to total trips taken.

F. DETERMINATION OF THE OPTIMAL AND SECOND-BEST Q

The formulation of the second-best case is considered first. The average cost function has two terms which are functions of the time of arrival at the queue (measured from the queue's inception), i.e. terms which vary with departure time:

1. $C_1\{(1 - v)(Q_1 - Q_2)/Q_2\}t$; and

2. $- C_2(Q_1/Q_2)t$.

The average cost is equal over departure times if these two terms sum to zero, i.e. if the flow Q_1 adjusts to equalize average costs over the commuting period. This occurs for :

$$Q_1 = \beta Q_2 \quad \text{where } \beta = C_1(1\text{-}v)/\{C_1(1 - v) - C_2\} \quad (> 1). \tag{18}$$

The coefficient β is instructive. First note that if $C_2 = 0$ (waiting time at work and time at home produce equal utilities), $Q_1 = Q_2$ which will later be shown to be the first-best optimal value. In other words, it is only the existence of the disutility of waiting which prevents the flow from automatically adjusting to the bottleneck in an optimal manner. This makes sense - if it did not matter whether road users arrived at work early they would to tend spread their travel out evenly. Note the term (1 - v) approaches zero as the speed inside the jam approaches the speed outside the jam. If the two were equal, there would be no penalty cost associated with the formation of the queue.

Finally, consider what happens when C_2 approaches $C_1(1 - v)$ As the waiting cost becomes "excessive", the penalty cost of travel time spent in the queue is no longer able to offset it, and the flow on the "open" portion of the road is pushed up to exceed the capacity Q_0 creating another type of hypercongestion (and another and different model). Given that (18) holds, the total variable cost function for the second-best case is simply:

$$TVC_2 = \int_0^T Q_1\, AC_2\, dt = C_1\,(L/V_1)Q_1T + C_2Q_1^2\,T^2/Q_2\,. \tag{19}$$

It is useful to make a change of variables for later analysis. Substituting from equation (19):

$$TVC_2 = C_1(L/V_1)X + C_2X^2/Q_2 \tag{20}$$

To determine the first-best value of Q_1 , first calculate the total cost and change variables as in equation (20) above.

$$\int_0^T Q_1 \, AC \, dt =$$

$$C_1(L/V_1)Q_1T + C_1(1 - v)Q_1(Q_1 - Q_2)T^2/2Q_2 + C_2(Q_1^2/Q_2)T^2/2. \tag{21}$$

Substituting from (19) gives:

$$TVC = C_1(L/V_1)X + C_1(1 - v)X^2/2Q_2 - C_1(1 - v)X^2/2Q_1 + C_2X^2/2Q_2 \tag{22}$$

Accordingly,

$$\partial TVC/\partial Q_1 = C_1(L/V_1)X + C_2X^2/2Q_2 \tag{23}$$

equals zero for $Q_1 = Q_2$ since then $(1\text{-}v) = 0$. In other words, the larger Q_1 is, the larger the cost.

It follows that the first-best value for Q_1 is given by:

$$Q_1^* = Q_2\,. \tag{24}$$

With Q_1 optimized the total "variable" cost is:

$$TVC_1 = C_1(1 - v)X + C_2X^2/2Q_2\,. \tag{25}$$

Attaining the optimal value of Q_1 would require a time-varying toll exactly equal to the cost of waiting time avoided by a commuter due to a later departure time.

G. OPTIMAL FIRST-BEST BOTTLENECK CAPACITY (Q_2)

The standard formulation of the social benefit function is follows:

$$W = \int_0^X P(x)dx \;- TVC_1 \;- C_3Q_2\,. \tag{26}$$

The formulation of capacity cost as C_3Q_2 is simply expedient. Any increasing function may be appropriate. The unit of measure for C_3 is [$ hours/vehicle] i.e. dollars per unit of flow. See (25) for TVC_1. The first order conditions are:

$$\partial W/\partial X = P - C_1(L/V_1) - C_2X/Q_2 = 0 \tag{27}$$

and

$$\partial W/\partial Q_2 = C_2X^2/2Q_2^{\,2} - C_3 = 0. \qquad (28)$$

Equation (27) determines optimal price:

$$P^* = C_1(L/V_1) + C_2(X^*/Q_2^*) \qquad (= \text{marginal cost}). \qquad (29)$$

Equation (28) determines the optimal trip-to-capacity ratio:

$$X^*/Q_2^* = [2\ (C_3/C_2)]^{1/2} \qquad (30)$$

H. SECOND-BEST BOTTLENECK CAPACITY

In this case, the maximization problem is subject to the constraint that price equal average variable cost, (with of course the second-best equilibrium value for Q_1).

Maximize

$$W = \int_0^X P(x)dx - TVC_2 - C_3Q_2 - \lambda(P - C_1)(1 - v) - C_2X/Q_2). \qquad (31)$$

See equation (20) for TVC_2. The first order conditions for this problem are:

$$\partial W/\partial X = P - C_1(1 - v) - 2C_2X/Q_2 - \lambda\ (P' - C_2/Q_2) = 0 \qquad (32)$$

and

$$\partial W/\partial Q_2 = C_2X^2/Q_2^{\,2} - C_3 - \lambda(C_2X/Q_2^{\,2}) = 0. \qquad (33)$$

From (32) and using the constraint that price equals average cost:

$$\lambda = (C_2X/Q_2)/(-P' + C_2/Q_2). \qquad (34)$$

From (33)

$$C_3Q_2^{\,2} = C_2(X^2 - \lambda X). \qquad (35)$$

Substituting for λ from (34) gives:

$$C_3Q_2^{\,2} = C_2X^2\{1 - C_2/(-P'Q_2 + C_2)\}. \qquad (36)$$

Then noting that

$$1 - C_2/(-P'Q_2 + C_2) = -P'/(-P' + C_2/Q_2) \tag{37}$$

and multiplying numerator and denominator on the right hand side in (37) by X and dividing both by P gives:

$$(-P'X/P)/\{(-P'X/P) + (C_2X/Q_2P)\} = \varepsilon/(\varepsilon + \theta). \tag{38}$$

Assuming that ε is not zero (infinitely elastic demand), (36) simplifies to

$$X^{**}/Q_2^{**} = [(1 + \theta/\varepsilon)(C_3/C_2)]^{1/2}. \tag{39}$$

This derivation utilizes the fact that P = AC for all second best solutions. This is the key result. The second-best price is:

$$P^{**} = C_1(L/V_1) + C_2(X^{**}/Q_2^{**}). \tag{40}$$

I. COMPARISON OF OPTIMAL AND SECOND-BEST CAPACITIES

Note from Equations (29) and (40) that the first-best and second-best prices are the same function of the trip-to-bottleneck-capacity ratio, (X/Q_2). The marginal cost for the first-best regime is of the same form as the average cost for the second-best regime. Thus all comparisons depend on the relative size of this ratio, which in turn depends upon whether price elasticity ε is greater or smaller than the average cost elasticity θ at the optimal point:

$$(1 + \theta/\varepsilon) > ? < 2$$

The cost elasticity is necessarily < 1 but it is increasing as trips (X) increase; i.e.,

$$\theta = (C_2X/Q_2)/\{C_1(L/V_1) + C_2X/Q_2\} < 1. \tag{41}$$

The chain of reasoning concerning the relative capacities is as follows:

	Elastic Demand	Inelastic Demand
1.	$\varepsilon < \theta$	$\varepsilon > \theta$
2.	$X^{**}/Q_2^{**} > X^*/Q_2^*$	$X^{**}/Q_2^{**} < X^*/Q_2^*$
3.	$P^{**} > P^*$	$P^{**} < P^*$
4.	$X^{**} < X^*$	$X^{**} > X^*$
5.	$Q_2^{**} < Q_2^*$	$Q_2^{**} > Q_2^*$

Steps 2 and 3 follow directly from the first-order conditions. Step 4 follows from the nature of the demand curve. Step 5 is implied by step 2 and step 4.

Investments in alleviating bottlenecks are certainly not the only type of road investment, but their importance should not be overlooked. It makes little sense to increase road capacity of leading segments which are constrained by a downstream bottleneck. But the second-best bottleneck capacity is greater than the optimal bottleneck capacity (for inelastic demand).

References

Arnott, R., A. de Palma, and R. Lindsey, 1990a, Economics of a bottleneck, Journal of Urban Economics 27 , 111-130.

Arnott, R., A. de Palma, and R. Lindsey, 1990b, Departure time and route choice for the morning commute, Transportation Research 24B, 209-228.

Arnott, R., A. de Palma, and R. Lindsey, 1993a, A structural model of peak-period congestion: A traffic bottleneck with elastic demand, American Economic Review 83, 161-179.

Arnott, R., A. de Palma, and R. Lindsey, 1993b, Properties of dynamic traffic equilibrium involving bottlenecks, including a paradox and metering, Transportation Science 27, 148-160.

Arnott, J., A. de Palma, and R. Lindsey, 1998, Recent developments in the bottleneck model, in K. Button and E. Verhoef, eds. Road Pricing, Traffic Congestion, and the Environment, Cheltenham, England: Edward Elgar,

Arnott, R. and M. Kraus 1995, Financing capacity in the bottleneck model, Journal of Urban Economics 38, 272-290.

Else, P., 1981 A reformulation of the theory of optimal congestion taxes, Journal of Transport Economics and Policy XV, 217-232.

Evans, A., 1992, Road congestion : The diagrammatic analysis, Journal of Political Economy 100, 211-217.

Mun, S., 1994, Traffic jams and the congestion toll, Transportation Research 28B, 365-375.

Small, K., 1992, Urban Transportation Economics, Chur, Switzerland: Harwood Academic Publishers.

SUMMARY AND CONCLUSIONS

This final chapter presents a brief summary and set of conclusions that we have reached for each topic in the book. We also point out some areas for further research, especially empirical research.

In Part I of the book we conclude that the "fundamental diagram of traffic" is a reasonably accurate depiction of the behavior of traffic on congested limited-access highways in urban areas. The fundamental diagram of traffffic shows that traffic volume rises and then falls as traffic density increases. Furthermore, we conclude that the point of maximum traffic volume (of about 2000 vehicles per lane per hour) coincides with a traffic density that is often reached, or exceeded, in normal rush-hour traffic and coincides with an average speed of 20 to 25 mph. These are the "stylized" facts upon which we base our analysis. We base our conclusion on the previous econometric literature, on a simple engineering model of traffic flow, and on our own econometric study.

Our conclusion is directly at odds with the views of some other prominent researchers such as Chu and Small (1996), Newell (1988), Small (1992), and Verhoff (1999), who contend that only bottlenecks cause situations in which volume falls as density rises. The most recent presentation of their opposite view is that of Verhoff (1999, 365), which states that

> A practical consequence (of Verhoff's analysis) is that whenever 'hypercongested' speeds are observed in reality, it is unlikely that the cause is to be found in 'flow congestion' on the road itself. Instead, the true reason for such speeds may often be a downstream bottleneck. Therefore, optimal pricing rules should then not primarily be based on the road's characteristics, but rather on the bottleneck's capacity. A theoretical consequence is that the standard backward-bending supply curve is flawed. Instead, it was argued that when replacing the endogenous output variable of 'traffic flow' by the arrival rate of new cars at the entrance of the road - two variables that should equal each other in stationary states only, but that do not presuppose this stationary state like the traditional output variable 'flow' does - a non-backward-bending supply curve can be found, which coincides with the standard supply curve only for its lower segment, but rises vertically at the road's maximum capacity.

The implication of this statement is that the backward-bending supply curve will not be observed unless there is a bottleneck downstream. The empirical work that we have presented made use of data that were carefully chosen to avoid a downstream bottleneck. We therefore challenge these other researchers to produce empirical studies that confirm their view, that thusfar is based entirely on theoretical argument. We believe that the bottleneck model is a valuable contribution to our understanding of urban traffic congestion, and that a more complete explanation of traffic congestion includes both models.

In Part II of the book we show that commuters make rational choices between urban tollways and freeways based on time and money cost. We show that commuters are quite sensitive to differences in time and money cost in their choice of routes for the journey to work. Our basic finding is that reductions in commuting time are worth at least 50% of the after-tax wage rate (for commuters in suburban Chicago in 1972). We also hypothesize that the most accurate estimates of the value of reductions in auto commuting time are to be found in studies that are based on the choice of route (rather than choice of mode). Most studies of the value of time make use of data on choice of mode (e.g., bus versus private auto). This issue is a topic for further research as well.

Part III, the section of the book devoted to congestion pricing in the short run, contains lengthy and fairly technical theoretical arguments and simulation results. However, the basic message of all of this work is pretty simple. It is probable that significant portions of an urban highway and road system cannot be subjected to congestion tolls. For example, many people reside on arterial streets and highways that carry a good deal of rush-hour traffic. It is not likely that any politician will ever suggest that people should pay a toll to drive on their own streets. In our view congestion tolls are not likely to be imposed on more than the limited access portion of the urban highway and road system.

Mohring (1999) recognizes this constraint on policy and, in a recent set of simulation studies for the Minneapolis-St. Paul metropolitan area, examines its implications for optimal second-best congestion tolls for the limited-access highways. The basic finding is that the optimal rush-hour tolls are 25% of the difference between the marginal cost and average cost on a highway link. In other words, in this case the optimal second-best toll is 25% of the optimal first-best toll on limited-access highways. Mohring's finding is consistent with the results obtained in Part III - with one exception.

Mohring assumes that congestion tolls can be imposed on the entire system of limited-access highways, a system that connects all portions of the Minneapolis-St. Paul metropolitan area. In this situation the other highways and arterial streets can be considered primarily to be substitutes for the limited-access highways because it appears that commuters do not have to travel very great distances after they leave the limited-access highway. However, as we discuss in Chapter 10, important cases exist in which many other highways and arterial streets are complementary to the tollway. This appears to be the case with the SR-91 tollway facility in sourthern California. The tolled lanes of the SR-91 substitute for the untolled lanes of the same facility, but most of the commuters must drive well beyond the terminus of the SR-91 facility to reach their places of employment. If a congested freeway is complementary to a tollway, then the toll on the tollway should be higher than it otherwise would be. The toll on the tollway is, in effect, also a toll imposed for the use of the congested complementary freeway. It is therefore not clear whether the optimal second-best toll on a tollway such as SR-91 should be greater than or less than the difference between marginal cost and average cost on the tollway itself. Optimal tolls for tollways that are embedded in an urban highway system in this way are subjects for further research.

Part IV, the final section of the book, is a series of theoretical studies of road capacity and pricing in the long run. We first examine the optimal capacity of a single facility in isolation. Conditions are derived for the efficient facility to be larger in the absence of a congestion toll (compared to efficient size of the facility in the presence of the optimal congestion toll). Such second-best capacity is the larger if demand is inelastic and if the elasticity of substitution of drivers' time for road capital is small.

We next turn to the question of optimal capacities for substitute highways, only one of which can be subject to congestion tolls. If the two highways are perfect substitues, then only the tollway should be built (to its first-best capacity). We derive capacity rules for the case in which the two highways are less-than-perfect substitutes. These rules depend upon the cross elasticity of demand of the free highway for the tollway and upon the relative capacity costs of the two highways.

The remaining chapters examine:

- optimal road capacity with hypercongestion and no tolls,
- optimal road capacity if demand is considered to be a demand for traffic density,
- optimal road capacity with uncertain demand, and
- optimal bottleneck capacity.

We find that, in the absence of congestion tolls and in the presence of high costs of road capital, a second-best optimum might involve hypercongestion. Our general conclusions regarding optimal capacities do not change if demand is considered to be a demand for traffic density rather than traffic flow. However, optimal road capacity is larger if demand is uncertain because the costs of erroneous demand predictions are not symmetric. The cost of a low demand prediction is bad traffic congestion, which is worse than the cost of a high demand prediction. Our last chapter in this section is our contribution to the bottleneck literature in which we examine the optimal size of the bottleneck given that bottleneck capacity is costly. Each of these models can lead to further research as applied to particular situations.

It is fair to say that the policy implications in the book that are of the most immediate applicability in the U. S. are those that pertain to congestion pricing in the short run. It would seem that major highway building projects are unlikely in the major urban areas in the U. S. However, the models of optimal capacity in the long run may well be of some immediate use in other countries. For example, in recent years the city of Shanghai has constructed an entire modern limited-access highway system, most of which is elevated above the congested city street system. The models in Part IV of this book possibly could have informed the planning of this system. Planners of urban highway systems such as the one in Shanghai may find value in these parts of our work.

References

Chu, X. and K. Small, 1996, Hypercongestion, Paper prepared for the 1997 AREUEA meeting in New Orleans.

Mohring, H., 1999, Congestion, in J. Gomez, W. Tye, and C. Winston, eds., Essays in Transportation Economics and Policy: A Handbook in Honor of John R. Meyer, Washington, D. C.: The Brookings Institution.

Newell, G., 1988, Traffic flow and the morning commute, Transportation Science 22, 47-58.

Small, K., 1992, Urban Transportation Economics, Chur, Switzerland: Harwood Academic Publishers.

Verhoef, E., 1999, TIme, speeds, flows and densities in static models of road traffic congestion and congestion pricing, Regional Science and Urban Economics 29, 341-369.

AUTHOR INDEX

SUBJECT INDEX

Transportation Research, Economics and Policy

1. I. Salomon, P. Bovy and J-P. Orfeuil (eds.): *A Billion Trips a Day.* Tradition and Transition in European Travel Patterns. 1993 ISBN 0-7923-2297-5
2. P. Nijkamp and E. Blaas: *Impact Assessment and Evaluation in Transportation Planning.* 1994 ISBN 0-7923-2648-2
3. B. Johansson and L.-G. Mattson (eds.): *Road Pricing: Theory, Empirical Assessment, and Policy.* 1995 ISBN 0-7923-3134-6
4. Y. Hayashi and J. Roy: *Transport, Land-Use and the Environment.* 1996 ISBN 0-7923-3728-X
5. T.F. Golob, R. Kitamura and L. Long: *Panels for Transportation Planning.* Methods and Applications. 1997. ISBN 0-7923-9966-8
6. T.H. Oum and C. Yu: *Winning Airlines: Productivity and Cost Competitiveness of the World's Major Airlines* ISBN 0-7923-8010-X
7. I. Savage: *The Economics of Railroad Safety* ISBN 0-7923-8219-6
8. I. L. Pitt and J. R. Norsworthy *Economics of the U. S. Commercial Airline Industry:* Productivity, Technology and Deregulation ISBN 0-7923-8505-5
9. J. F. McDonald, E. L. d'ouville and L. N. Liu *Economics of Urban Highway Congestion and Pricing* ISBN 0-7923-8631-0

Kluwer Academic Publishers — Boston / Dordrecht / London